Just-in-Time Real Estate

How Trends in Logistics Are Driving Industrial Development

Primary Contributing Authors

Margery al Chalabi
Luis A. Belmonte
Jon B. DeVries
Anne B. Frej
Peter V. Hall
John D. Kasarda
Ann Moline
Laurel Rafferty

Urban Land Institute

ULI–the Urban Land Institute

About ULI–the Urban Land Institute is a nonprofit education and research institute that is supported by its members. Its mission is to provide responsible leadership in the use of land in order to enhance the total environment.

ULI sponsors education programs and forums to encourage an open international exchange of ideas and sharing of experiences; initiates research that anticipates emerging land use trends and issues and proposes creative solutions based on that research; provides advisory services; and publishes a wide variety of materials to disseminate information on land use and development.

Established in 1936, the Institute today has more than 20,000 members and associates from nearly 70 countries representing the entire spectrum of the land use and development disciplines. Professionals represented include developers, builders, property owners, investors, architects, public officials, planners, real estate brokers, appraisers, attorneys, engineers, financiers, academics, students, and librarians. ULI relies heavily on the experience of its members. It is through member involvement and information resources that ULI has been able to set standards of excellence in development practice. The Institute has long been recognized as one of America's most respected and widely quoted sources of objective information on urban planning, growth, and development.

Richard M. Rosan
President

Recommended bibliographic listing:
ULI–the Urban Land Institute. *Just-in-Time Real Estate: How Trends in Logistics Are Driving Industrial Development.* Washington, D.C.: ULI–the Urban Land Institute, 2004.

ULI Catalog Number: J02
International Standard Book Number: 0-87420-904-8
Library of Congress Control Number: 2003111464

Copyright 2004 by ULI–the Urban Land Institute
1025 Thomas Jefferson Street, N.W.
Suite 500 West
Washington, D.C. 20007-5201

ULI Project Staff

Rachelle L. Levitt
Executive Vice President, Policy and Practice
Publisher

Gayle Berens
Vice President, Real Estate Development Practice

Anne B. Frej
Director, Office and Industrial Development
Project Director

Leslie Holst
Senior Associate

Nancy H. Stewart
Director, Book Program

Duke Johns
Manuscript Editor

Betsy VanBuskirk
Art Director

Helene Y. Redmond/HYR Graphics
Book Design/Layout

Byron Holly
Senior Graphic Designer
Cover Design

Diann Stanley-Austin
Director, Publishing Operations

Authors and Reviewers

Primary Contributing Authors

Margery al Chalabi is the president of ACG: The al Chalabi Group, Ltd., a firm specializing in transportation and economic development and the impacts of one upon the other.

Luis A. Belmonte is executive vice president and director of development at AMB Property Corporation, a San Francisco–based global owner and operator of industrial real estate. He is a member of ULI–the Urban Land Institute and a former president of the San Francisco chapter of the National Association of Industrial and Office Parks (NAIOP).

Jon B. DeVries is director of strategic development planning at URS Corporation and director of the Chicago School of Real Estate at Roosevelt University in Chicago.

Anne B. Frej is director of office and industrial development at ULI–the Urban Land Institute.

Peter V. Hall is professor in the Department of Geography, Faculty of Environmental Studies, University of Waterloo, in Waterloo, Ontario.

John D. Kasarda is director and Kenan distinguished professor of management at the Frank Hawkins Kenan Institute of Private Enterprise, Kenan-Flagler Business School, at the University of North Carolina in Chapel Hill. He is a fellow and trustee of ULI–the Urban Land Institute.

Ann Moline is a business writer specializing in international economic development. She writes frequently about logistics and corporate real estate for a variety of publications.

Laurel Rafferty is a practicing urban planner and principal of Portscape, a consulting firm in Lexington, Massachusetts, with a special focus on city-port-waterfront relationships.

Other Contributors

Jeff Ashcroft
President
Strategic Logistics Partners
Newmarket, Ontario
Canada

Chris Barnett
Journalist
San Francisco, California

Joseph H. Boardman
Commissioner
New York State Department of Transportation
Albany, New York

Timothy B. Butler
Senior Analyst
URS Corporation
Chicago, Illinois

Russ Haywood
Subject Group Leader
Faculty of Development and Society
Sheffield Hallam University
Sheffield, England

Markus Hesse
Department of Geography
Free University of Berlin
Berlin, Germany

James Keebler
Assistant Professor
G.R. Herberger College of Business
Department of Marketing and Business Law
St. Cloud State University
St. Cloud, Minnesota

John T. (Tom) Mentzer
Bruce Chair of Excellence in Business
Department of Marketing, Logistics, and
Transportation
University of Tennessee
Knoxville, Tennessee

John T. Meyer
Senior Vice President and Director
Airport Facility Group
AMB Property Corporation
San Francisco, California

Adam Ploetz
Planning Consultant
State University of New York at Buffalo
Buffalo, New York

John Skowronski
Senior Manager
Deloitte & Touche Credits and Incentives Team
Parsippany, New Jersey

David C. Twist
Vice President and Director of Research
AMB Property Corporation
San Francisco, California

Reviewers

Alan F.J. Artibise
Dean and Professor
College of Urban and Public Affairs
University of New Orleans
New Orleans, Louisiana

Skip Case
Chief Executive Officer
Case Industrial Partners, Inc.
Columbia, Maryland

Rene M. Circ
Research Analyst
First Industrial Realty Trust, Inc.
Chicago, Illinois

Martin Dresner
Associate Professor of Logistics and Transportation
Robert H. Smith School of Business
University of Maryland
College Park, Maryland

Scott Elliff
President
Capital Consulting and Management
Alexandria, Virginia

Noel Greis
Director
Center for Logistics and Digital Strategy
Kenan Institute of Private Enterprise
Kenan-Flagler Business School
University of North Carolina
Chapel Hill, North Carolina

Gary H. London
President
The London Group Realty Advisors, Inc.
San Diego, California

Irving F. Lyons III
Vice Chairman and Chief Investment Officer
ProLogis
Fremont, California

Thomas McNamara
Office of the Secretary
U.S. Department of Transportation
Washington, D.C.

ACKNOWLEDGMENTS

Many professionals from diverse backgrounds related to real estate, logistics, supply chain management, distribution, and transportation contributed to this book. Each had an individual perspective on a topic that is relatively new: the impact of changes in logistics on industrial real estate.

Special recognition goes to the chapter authors who gave generously of their knowledge and provided constructive advice for the reader. Their patience as this book went though the writing, rewriting, editing, and production phases is appreciated. In addition, warm thanks goes to those who offered guidance in the early stages of book conception—Jack Kasarda, Markus Hesse, Scott Elliff, Rene Circ, and Chris Barnett.

Gratitude also goes to members of the review team, who took time from their busy schedules to read draft manuscripts and offer insightful comments that ultimately made this book clearer and more practical.

Many others contributed feature boxes, photos, graphics, and data. Some of those who assisted in these ways include Mike Daly at First Industrial Realty Trust, Inc.; John Meyer, David Twist, Lauren Barr, and Paula Dwyer at AMB Property Corporation; David Navarro at ProLogis; Neil Medley at Fortna; Charles Canale at Colliers Bennett and Kahnweiler; Dave Pelletier at Hillwood; Suzanne Connell at Aviation Facilities Company; David Tirman at East West Partners; and Bruce Field at Solectron.

Assistance in writing and reviewing case studies was provided by John Hummer at the North Jersey Trans-portation Planning Authority, Peter Beaulieu at the Puget Sound Regional Council, Michael Cummings at the Washington State Department of Transportation, and James C. Hankla at the Alameda Corridor Transportation Authority.

At ULI, Rachelle Levitt gave direction and encouragement throughout the production process. Gayle Berens provided valuable input on conceptual and editorial issues. Leslie Holst assisted in countless ways, from photo selection to research. Joan Campbell and Rick Davis responded to numerous requests for information and provided up-to-date information on the state of the industrial market. Former interns Adam Ploetz, Mel Myers, Erinn Dowling, and Jennifer Good produced case studies and answered research questions. The excellent editorial team directed by Nancy Stewart included Duke Johns, who ensured that the text was clearly written, and Helene Redmond, who put all the pieces together to create a final design.

The world in which logistics, supply chain management, and industrial real estate are currently converging is changing rapidly. I hope that this book can provide an introduction to its many facets and serve as a useful guide for those interested in learning more about it.

Anne B. Frej
Project Director

CONTENTS

Chapter 1

INTRODUCTION

Anne B. Frej

Trade, distribution, and industrial real estate have always been linked. Every step of the supply chain process—the system of moving goods from producer to end user—requires places to make, store, and distribute products. The factories, warehouses, and distribution centers that support global supply chains are an important segment of commercial real estate. In the United States alone, industrial real estate encompasses to over 12 billion square feet (1.1 billion square meters) of space, making it the largest sector of the nation's real estate both in area and value.

Transportation systems serving the supply chain process have modernized and changed considerably since the 1800s, when railroads dominated goods distribution. The advent of the air age in the 1950s made shipping by air cargo possible. But it was not until the 1980s when distribution began to really pick up speed. "Just-in-time," a new approach to manufacturing and on-time delivery that started in the automobile industry, led to a fundamental shift in the supply chain process. Rather than storing goods in a warehouse until they are shipped in quantity to users, this system requires goods to arrive in precise quantities at the exact time they are needed. The introduction of express deliveries at the same time and the growing popularity of e-commerce and Internet shopping in the late 1990s have led to even higher expectations about delivery speed from businesses and consumers. Storage has given way to velocity as the emphasis has shifted from static inventory to the movement of goods. To meet the challenges associated with the need for speed, the supply chain has become a highly complex process dependent on sophisticated technologies and logistics.

As in real estate, timing is critical in successful supply chain management. Any delay—a shipment missing a flight, a truck breakdown, a ship delayed by bad weather—has a domino effect. A wholesaler may not have inventory to meet its customer orders, which prompt it to seek a new supplier. Out-of-stock items represent lost sales for both the manufacturer and retailer. And an inefficient distribution center with an inadequate number of truck bays, a congested truck staging area, a distant location from an airport, and traffic-choked highways all chew up precious time to market.

The real estate supporting the supply chain process has had to adapt to these transportation and logistics changes. The concept of building a square box and then filling it with specialized machinery and equipment is no longer adequate. Today's successful industrial buildings are built from the inside out, with the user's requirements first and foremost in the design process.

The role of the real estate provider is changing as well, and the concept of adding value must be understood by those considering entry into the marketplace associated with logistics and the supply chain process.

As businesses continue their quest for ever-more-efficient supply chains, the notion of seamlessness—no lag time or delay in any step along the way from supply to distribution—will dominate their planning. Seamlessness requires absolute coordination and full integration between and among all the stakeholders that play a role in a company's supply chain.

Increasingly, companies are looking toward their outsourcers, including real estate providers and advisers, to help them as their supply chains become more global and complex. And as companies outsource more aspects of the chain that are not part of their core competency—such as construction and management of distribution facilities—the challenges will involve how to effectively coordinate so that the smooth, seamless flow of goods is achieved.

The creation of global supply chain networks requires more than short-term, transaction-oriented relationships. Companies now seek partners who can add value to the entire enterprise by effecting savings, enhancing earnings, and getting goods to market in better, faster, and cheaper ways.

To become a partner in the supply chain process, astute real estate professionals must:

- appreciate the size of the logistics market—an industry valued at over US$3.4 trillion worldwide—and speak its language;
- learn how to build relationships with clients by being a knowledgeable partner who can add measurable benefits;
- realize that technology is embedded in every aspect of distribution and is changing constantly;
- stay abreast of the changing building requirements that will result as more companies reconfigure and streamline their supply chains;
- understand the factors that influence a company's distribution strategy and location decisions;
- constantly monitor the impact of globalization on import and export flows, materials sourcing, product assembly, and logistical services such as sorting, repackaging, and subdistribution; and
- remember that every company's supply chain is different.

Why Pay More?

Although airfreight is fast and reliable, it is also expensive. Long-haul airfreight rates per kilogram are typically seven to ten times higher than comparable ocean rates. To forecast future airfreight demand, it is critical to understand why shippers (the end users) are willing to pay such large premiums for air transport.

Different types of shippers use airfreight for different reasons. However, all air shippers have one thing in common: they do not focus on minimizing transportation costs but instead concentrate on minimizing total distribution costs (TDC) and maximizing economic value added (EVA).

Total distribution costs include all the costs incurred in the process of packing, storing, and distributing a product to the end customer. Transportation charges are the largest, but not the only, component of TDC. Product packaging, warehousing, and inventory shrinkage are also significant expenses.

Economic value added reflects the benefits of a well-functioning distribution system—and, conversely, the costs of not having the right goods in the right place at the right time. For example, stock shortages can result in lost sales and production line shutdowns, with economic consequences that far outweigh total distribution costs.

For both TDC and EVA reasons, airfreight is most attractive to producers of high-value and perishable goods. High-value goods include obvious examples such as semiconductors and precision instruments.

Source: Air Cargo World, May 2003. Copyright license 3.5565.583394–50555.

Book Approach and Summary of Chapters

Just-in-Time Real Estate offers a guide to recent trends in distribution and the implications for industrial real estate. Its focus is on the types of facilities potentially provided by a commercial developer, either on a speculative or build-to-suit basis. The book presents background on the distinctive opportunities and challenges of developing on or near airports, rail intermodal centers, and seaports. Finally, it presents examples of how the public and private sectors are working together to address distribution-related land use and environmental issues.

Chapter 2, "Understanding Logistics and the Supply Chain Process," provides an overview of the supply chain process—what it is and how it works. The transportation modes used to move freight are described, and important issues such as technology, e-commerce, globalization, and security are addressed.

Chapter 3, "The Intersection of Logistics and Real Estate," charts the evolving relationship between logistics, distribution, and real estate. From the deregulation of the rail and trucking industries to the advent

of the air age and the emergence of e-commerce, significant milestones have affected the size, shape, location, and demand for industrial real estate. The chapter focuses on the trends for faster and more efficient distribution that are creating demand for new types of buildings where goods are rapidly processed rather than merely stored. To illustrate the realities of building for velocity, case studies of air cargo developments at the Washington Dulles International Airport and Dallas/Fort Worth International Airport are provided.

Chapter 4, "Implications for Building Demand, Design, and Location," details the changes that have taken place in the demand, design, and location of facilities associated with the supply chain process. It identifies and describes each of the categories of industrial real estate that support the supply chain process. Special attention is paid to the design and location characteristics of the new type of high-throughput buildings located both at on-tarmac and off-airport locations. Location trends and security considerations are also addressed, and a new tool for forecasting industrial space demand is presented.

Chapter 5, "Airports: Short- and Long-Term Trends," provides two perspectives on the real estate opportunities on and around airports. Margery al Chalabi argues that large airport hubs such as Chicago O'Hare International Airport have lost their potential share of cargo traffic owing to growing congestion and the lack of land for cargo facility expansion. Small- to medium-sized hubs, as well as all-cargo airports, have been the winners. John Kasarda describes a dynamic new form of urban development known as the "aerotropolis." These airport-focused urban concentrations, such as Amsterdam Airport Schiphol in the Netherlands, combine multiple transportation modes and many of the same employment, retail, and entertainment functions found in city centers.

Chapter 6, "Rail Intermodalism and New Industrial Location Dynamics," offers an overview of new location trends for major rail intermodal facilities: new intermodal freight facilities being developed by U.S. railroad companies in key gateway cities; the redevelopment of urban brownfield sites for new intermodal facilities; and the consolidation of scattered freight facilities into large-scale intermodal yards in suburban areas.

Chapter 7, "Development Opportunities around Seaports," describes the role of port authorities and the different types of cargo ports as background to an analysis of opportunities and constraints for industrial development along waterfront areas. Examples of successful port-city planning models around the world highlight the conditions that facilitate compatible co-

Dan Granville

Today's distributors are faced with supplying an evolving market of smarter and more demanding customers. Distributors are constantly presented with new challenges and are frequently asked to do more with less. To achieve profitable growth, they must look deep within their operations to ensure that productivity, customer service, and costs are optimized.

Shipping thousands of orders per day, each with diversified order characteristics, from an inventory with tens of thousands of SKUs (Stock Keeping Units) to customers with varying order criteria: this is a common scenario in today's distribution centers. Add selling through multiple channels, covering more geography, meeting increased customer compliance rules, offering more value-added services, and responding to the consistent pressure to reduce costs, and you have an even more realistic picture of what distribution managers grapple with each day.

Developing improvements that deliver results is no easy accomplishment. It requires clearly defined goals, an effective strategy, and an ongoing measurement plan.

The Goals

Every potential action to optimize distribution operations must be measured—before it is implemented—against how it will increase a company's profitability. There are two ways for distributors to increase profit: by increasing sales revenue and/or decreasing the cost of goods sold.

To increase sales revenue, distributors can:

- provide revenue-generating value-added services;
- provide a competitive edge through improved order cycle and customer delivery times; and
- reduce lost sales through increased order accuracy.

Distributors can decrease the cost of goods sold in several ways that are often more obvious. They can:

- reduce facilities costs;
- reduce distribution labor costs;
- optimize distribution capital equipment costs;
- eliminate costs associated with order inaccuracy;
- reduce work-in-process inventory; and
- minimize customer compliance chargebacks.

Many other goals should be added to the above lists, and each needs to be broken down further, based upon each distributor's particular operations.

The Strategy

In the world of distribution, strategies to increase profitability are often based upon rules of thumb, assumptions, and rough estimates. Savvy distribution companies use specific operational data and a comprehensive evaluation of alternatives to develop a corporate strategy. A solid approach starts with a thorough understanding of existing business conditions and an accurate baseline of current operations. Information that is valuable in assessing existing operations includes order data, velocity data, inventory data, and performance-related data. The improvement process should also factor in information such as space and storage use by functional area, material and information flow within the facility, direct labor staffing by functional area, and operations task descriptions.

A distribution center's operations can be evaluated from five perspectives: inventory, processes, storage media, facility layout, and technology.

Inventory. Today's customers are demanding just-in-time delivery, resulting in smaller and more frequent orders, and this trend can be seen throughout the entire supply chain. Everyone wants to reduce their inventories, as long as they are able to fully meet order demand and customer service goals. But without good client and supplier communication and collaboration, forecasting demand and achieving optimal inventory levels is nearly impossible. So the first priority should be to put processes in place for effective client and supplier communication regarding demand planning.

The next job is to ensure that inventory reflects this forecast; this is where historical statistics can aid the process of optimizing inventory. Software tools make it possible

The development of efficient facilities is one way to reduce costs for distributors.

Courtesy Fortna

Distributors are under greater pressure today to streamline their processes.

Courtesy Fortna

to capture inventory velocity down to the SKU level and to match actual shipments to predictions. This information can enhance both forecasting and merchandising. Statistics can also identify profit contribution by SKU and by client for decisions regarding what products to sell, what to sell out of inventory, and what to declare obsolete.

Processes. Distribution processes, functions, and methodologies should be based on order characteristics. Best practices encompass every function within a distribution center, including:

- receiving;
- inbound quality control;
- put-away;
- replenishment;
- order picking;
- outbound quality control;
- packing;
- order consolidation;
- sorting;
- manifest preparation; and
- shipping.

To optimize the entire distribution operation, each step of the process must be evaluated individually, and must financially justify any investment to improve it.

Storage Media. Storage media decisions are based on cubic velocity, and all the processes employed within a distribution center directly affect each other. Poorly applied equipment, for example, can result in inefficient picking, and ineffective picking processes can result in inflated storage equipment requirements. Today's software tools provide the ability to select the right storage equipment down to the SKU level, based on size, weight, and order characteristics.

Facility Layout. Once best practices and storage media are determined, the layout of the facility should aim to achieve optimum space use and reduced costs through efficient material flow. Design and planning software tools can project anticipated square footage needs. Growth estimates, including both SKU counts and order volumes, can be applied to current levels to factor in future facility, staffing, capital, and related requirements.

Technology. A distributor should not start with technology as an improvement project, but rather finish with it to optimize performance. There is no shortage of technology options for today's distribution center. Systems can be automation-related, such as conveyors; software-related, such as warehouse management systems (WMS); or a combination, such as radio frequency communication devices.

When correctly applied and supported, technology can deliver significant results, but sometimes the benefits are oversold. So the second rule for any technology-related improvement project is to model it into operations prior to any significant outlays. Any investment in technology should pay for itself within an acceptable period of time, and should be based on concrete savings that have a high probability of being achieved. Soft savings factors should be eliminated from a return-on-investment analysis and evaluated after calculating return.

The Results

The only way to prove a return on investment is to measure results, and that requires a well-developed process. Some indexes that are relatively easy to calculate include space requirements, labor savings, and increased profit from value-added services revenue. Other factors are more difficult to measure and are best captured through automated data collection devices that can present software-generated reports on statistics such as increased productivity rates, costs per line/unit, increased order accuracy, increased inventory accuracy, and increased inventory returns.

A results measurement plan should be developed in advance of investment and implementation of improvements. Breaking measurements down to the smallest level and measuring all critical areas of a distribution center will help ensure an optimized operation that continues to deliver results.

Dan Granville is vice president of sales for Fortna, a single-source provider of software, professional services, and equipment for companies involved in the design and implementation of logistics and distribution systems.

existence between industrial and nonindustrial waterfront uses. Descriptions of real estate opportunities at the ports of Seattle, Tacoma, Oakland, and Portland, Oregon, are presented.

Chapter 8, "Freight Transportation Challenges and Solutions," reviews the impacts on communities from increasing freight traffic and the development of distribution facilities. Case studies illustrate the range of current practices and solutions being undertaken by local, regional, and state authorities to address the issues of road congestion, pollution, demand for development sites, and other issues related to growing demands on freight delivery systems and the supply chain. Significantly, these and other public sector projects have not only provided benefits to communities

but have also created new opportunities for the private sector. The case studies include the Alameda Rail Corridor, a major rail cargo expressway linking the ports of Long Beach and Los Angeles to transcontinental rail yard lines near downtown Los Angeles; the Puget Sound Region Freight Action Strategy, a system of freight access improvements in the Everett-Seattle-Tacoma metropolitan area; North Jersey Brownfield Economic Redevelopment, a broad-based planning effort to encourage freight businesses to locate in brownfield sites near the region's port and airport; and the Daventry International Rail Freight Terminal, an intermodal freight terminal and distribution hub southeast of Birmingham, England.

Chapter 2

UNDERSTANDING LOGISTICS
AND THE SUPPLY CHAIN PROCESS

Ann Moline

The supply chain is a business's beginning-to-end process of satisfying the customer's need—"from thought to finish," as the marketing slogan of one professional services firm goes. The process includes virtually every aspect of a company's operations: manufacturing, logistics, distribution, finance, marketing, planning and forecasting, and customer service.[1] Supply chains can be as diverse as the products and customers they serve, and no two are exactly alike, although they share many common characteristics.

Background and Definitions

Logistics, a specialty within the supply chain process, is defined by the Council on Logistics Management as "that part of the supply chain process that plans, implements, and controls the efficient, effective forward and reverse flow and storage of goods, services, and related information between the point of origin and the point of consumption in order to meet customers' requirements." Simplified, it can be understood as the management of inventory, whether moving or stored.

Logistics is involved in every step along the supply chain, from the sourcing of raw materials to their delivery on the manufacturing plant floor; from the pickup of finished goods at the plant to their timely delivery to the customer. Ensuring that the right goods are at the right place at the right time in the right quantity involves a complex planning matrix that includes

forecasting, procurement, production planning and scheduling, inventory control, warehousing, transportation, customer service and related information systems.[2]

In the past, most companies handled all aspects of the supply chain in house, often relying on separate fiefdoms that had relatively little interaction. Logistics functions were considered second-tier activities, not tied into the strategic operations of the business. Today, however, as in the military, where "every battle that was ever lost, every battle that was ever won, was because of logistics," companies today understand both the strategic and operational importance of logistics-related decisions.[3]

This sea change began in the 1980s, as new approaches to manufacturing, rapidly evolving technology, and the introduction of timed-delivery services converged to transform the ways companies think about their businesses. Originating in the automobile industry and swiftly adopted by other industries, "just-in-time" manufacturing calls for goods to arrive in precise quantities at the time they are needed rather than being stored in a warehouse. Thus, inventory carrying costs shrink, efficiency increases, and customer orders are filled with great speed. This fundamental shift has changed the way goods are manufactured and shipped, with the goal of reducing inventories to cut costs, increase efficiency, and fill orders ever more rapidly. With this shift, the logistics function has been

Warehousing is an integral component of the supply chain and logistics process.

elevated from an afterthought in an organization's planning to a key aspect of strategic planning—an integral part of the supply chain. In fact, logistics today involves the development of strategies for optimal approaches to getting a company's goods to the desired destinations in an optimal time frame at the lowest cost.

The need for speed has demanded greater integration within companies, meaning that departments that previously did not work together now must combine forces so that their supply chain functions smoothly. Technology, including company-wide systems software that enables a complete view of all company operations at the touch of a keystroke—as well as real-time tracking of all processes—helps with alignment and coordination of activities. These changes have also affected the way companies think about inventory management, moving the focus from the storage of inventory to movement of inventory—an increasingly complex process involving multiple inputs from a global web of vendors and deliveries to customers located throughout the world. The responsibility for coordinating the components of the supply chain process, often with the underpinning of technology, is considered supply chain management.

The logistics equation thus comprises two separate but interrelated activities: transportation/distribution and warehousing. Transportation managers must make decisions on optimal freight modes, factoring the company's cost/efficiency matrix in scheduling pickups and deliveries. Warehouse management functions include location strategy for distribution centers, inventory management and control, facilities management, and loading dock strategies—achieving optimal design

for loading docks and coordinating delivery schedules and carrier loading for maximum efficiency. Each task involves careful planning. For example, a logical goal such as packing a truck so that the last load on is first load off can become a monumental organizational feat when thousands of products must be picked up from multiple distribution points and delivered to multiple locations on a given day.

The ongoing quest for less expensive, more efficient methods of managing and transporting inventory has driven improvements in logistics productivity. Since 1981, logistics costs as a percentage of gross domestic product (GDP) have dropped from 16.2 percent to 9.5 percent in 2001. Macroeconomic factors such as 30-year-low interest rates and regulatory reforms such as the 1980 deregulation of the trucking industry have contributed as well.[4] Technology has also helped increase logis-tics productivity.

Increasingly, companies are outsourcing the logistics function to third-party logistics providers, or "3PLs." Such companies—Ryder, Exel, Penske, for example—aim to get their clients' goods where they need to go while sparing their clients the associated organizational, administrative, and technical headaches. Complex distribution challenges, including time-sensitive deadlines for supplying materials for complicated manufacturing processes and delivery to global customers, have led many companies to discover that the operation of distribution hubs falls too far outside their core competency.

While many 3PLs began life as freight transporters, they now provide everything from various transportation options to inventory management and warehousing services to distribution. Their other services include e-commerce and supply chain management services, as well as customs brokerage, freight forwarding, consulting, information technology, trade facilitation, and international transportation solutions. Some 3PLs have moved into the business of finance as an extension of their core mission. In 2002, UPS purchased a financing arm, now known as UPS Capital, to help customers finance construction, purchase equipment, or invest in additional inventory. The company also acquired Fritz, a major freight forwarder, to offer these services as well.

In addition to the trend toward offering bundled services, the 3PL industry is undergoing consolidation through mergers and acquisitions, as the big players look to expand their reach by buying the assets of

Access Logistics
ADP Logistics
Airborne Logistics
AIT Worldwide Logistics
Alliance Shippers
Americold Logistics
A.N. Deringer
APL Logistics
Arnold Logistics
Aspen Alliance Group
Averitt

BAX Global
BDP International
Bekins Worldwide Solutions
Bender Group

Cardinal Logistics
Caterpillar Logistics
CCW Group
Cendian
C.H. Robinson
Cogistics
Computrex Logistics
Concentrek
Continental Traffic Service
Con-Way Logistics
Corporate Traffic
Crowley Logistics
CRST Logistics
CT Logistics

Danzas AEI
DDD Company
Distribution Solutions International
Ditan
DSC Logistics

EGL Eagle Global Logistics
Elite International
England Logistics
Exel

FedEx Supply Chain Services
FMI International
Fresh Warehousing
F.X. Coughlin

Genco Distribution System
GeoLogistics

Hub Group

InSite Logistics

Jacobson Companies

Kane Is Able
Kenco Logistic Services
Kuehne & Nagel

Land-Link
Landstar Logistics
Logistics Insights

Maersk Logistics
MegaSys
Menlo Worldwide
Merchandise Warehouse

New Breed
NFI Industries
northAmerican Logistics
NT Logistics
NYK Logistics (Americas)

ODC Integrated Logistics
ODW Logistics
Olson Logistics
OMNI Logistics
Ozburn-Hessey Logistics

Pacer Global Logistics
Panalpina Worldwide
Patterson Warehouses

PBB Global Logistics
Pegasus Logistics Group
Penske Logistics
Plant Site Logistics
Power Group

Redwood Systems
RMX Global Logistics
Ruan Logistics
Ryder

Saddle Creek
Salem Logistics
Schneider Logistics
ServiceCraft
Standard Corporation

TBB Global Logistics
Tibbett & Britten Group
TNT Logistics North America
Total Logistic Control
Transfreight
Transmanagement
Transplace
TSi Logistics
Tucker Company

Unicity Integrated Logistics
Union Pacific Distribution Services
UPS Supply Chain Solutions
USCO Logistics
USF Logistics

Wagner Industries
Weber Distribution

Source: Inbound Logistics,
www.inboundlogistics.com.

smaller regional companies or of firms offering complementary business lines. So-called "lead logistics providers" (LLPs), also known as "4PLs," offering total oversight, accountability and control of all 3PLs employed by a company, have further altered the landscape. Major automotive companies such as Ford and GM have jumped on this trend, and experts suggest that other Fortune 100 companies will soon follow suit.[5] It has been suggested that LLPs are emerging as the "supply chain masters" for their customers. They offer companies a wide range of outsourcing services through a single point of contact, providing broad geographic coverage and sophisticated technology while relying on a network of smaller LLP subcontractors to deliver services.

Since the mid-1990s, growth in third-party contract logistics has exceeded growth in the general U.S. economy. In 2002, turnover increased by 6.9 percent, net revenues increased by 7 percent, and net income increased by 1.3 percent. Results for individual companies varied widely; the most profitable 3PLs in 2002 continued to be transportation managers. The value-added warehousing segment grew and improved net income margins in 2001 and 2002.[6]

Transportation

Transportation accounts for 62 percent of logistics costs.[7] Yet even as companies look to drive down logistics costs, they are transporting more goods than ever. The U.S. Department of Transportation estimates that domestic volumes will nearly double by 2020, while international volumes will more than double. USDOT pegs the current value of transported goods at $9 trillion in the fourth quarter of 2002. By 2020, cargo value will increase to almost $30 trillion.

Freight is transported by air, rail, water, ground, or a combination of these. The choice of which mode

to use is determined by tradeoffs between speed and cost. Ground transportation accounts for the majority of freight tonnage, and this mode will continue to dominate. However, airfreight traffic has grown by more than 60 percent between 1990 and 2000, while truck freight increased 20 percent between 1993 and 1997.[8] The rising importance of airfreight is driven by increased demand for higher levels of service, particularly in the transporting of higher-value, time-sensitive goods.[9]

According to the Federal Highway Administration's Office of Freight Management and Operations, the picture will remain largely the same in future years. It is estimated that by 2020, trucks will carry 80 percent of domestic goods, rail will carry 13 percent, air will carry 1 percent, and water will carry 6 percent. In terms of value, the projections for the United States in 2020 show that the value of goods carried by air will increase to 9 percent, trucks will be responsible for 84 percent, rail will be responsible for 5 percent, and water 2 percent. Significantly, the value of goods shipped via air by all businesses internationally in 2020 is estimated to reach about 16 percent.

Trucking

Trucks move more of the nation's freight, whether measured by value, tons, or ton-miles, than any other mode, accounting for 50 percent of total U.S. logistics costs.[10] In the transportation industry, trucking claims about 80 percent of total market share. Indeed, Americans spent over $313 billion on goods and services that were transported on the nation's highways in 2001 alone; hence the slogan, "if you bought it, a truck brought it."

Trucking companies carry freight and charge for it by the full truckload—the most economical way to send cargo—or at less-than-truckload (LTL). The growing popularity of catalog purchasing and direct buying over the Internet has contributed to an upswing in LTL traffic as well as parcel delivery traffic—individual packages delivered direct to the customer's doorstep. LTL services often require expedited delivery timetables; same-day or overnight delivery is not uncommon.

Trucking companies typically offer a range of services including long-haul service, characterized by long-distance coverage such as coast-to-coast; short-haul, characterized by regional, inner-city, and intrastate deliveries; flatbed service for construction mate-

Figure 2.1 Emerging U.S. Intermodal Rail Corridors

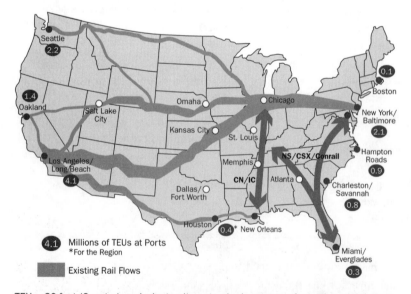

TEU = 20-foot (6-meter) equivalent unit, a standard measure of container throughput.

Source: American Association of State Highway and Transportation Officials, Washington, D.C. From *Transportation: Invest in America, Freight-Rail Bottom Line Report,* copyright 2003. Used by permission.

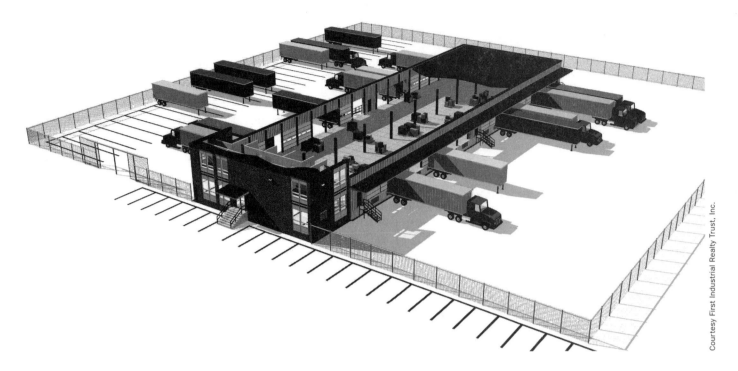

rials; and refrigerated service for perishable deliveries. Large trucking firms operate their own freight terminals, strategically located for customer proximity, in locations throughout the nation. Big-name players such as Omaha-based Werner Enterprises also offer a variety of value-added services such as additional truckload capacity planning, freight management programs, shipment mode selection/cost analysis, load planning and route optimization, facility site selection and pool point analysis, and customized reporting.

Pressure on trucking companies has mounted, owing to increased competition from within the industry and from other modes, as well as other factors such as congested highways and delays at border crossings with Canada and Mexico. In the past two years alone, 60,000 owner/operator businesses folded.[11] During 2001, trucking costs increased 2.7 percent, while tonnage shipped declined between 5 and 10 percent. The industry faces another challenge as new Environmental Protection Agency (EPA) guidelines on diesel fuel emissions go into effect. EPA estimates that compliance costs will approach $2 billion.

There have been encouraging signs for the trucking business recently, though. An increasing emphasis on trucking to move expedited goods has put this industry in greater competition with the air cargo industry. Some see this as a temporary result of a sluggish economy, while others foresee a long-term trend in time-definite service away from overnight express service to two- or three-day service.

Rail Industry

Prior to the deregulation of the rail industry in the 1980s, trucks offered some of the most cost-effective ways to ship long-distance freight. Since the passage of the Staggers Act of 1980, rail companies have been able to offer competitive pricing, making rail another cost-effective option for long-distance transport of goods. This legislation resulted in a 60 percent reduction of rates in inflation-adjusted terms between 1981 and 2001, saving shippers and their customers more than $10 billion per year.[12] Consequently, rail traffic has increased, showing nearly 50 percent growth between 1980 and 1997. Some leveling off occurred in the late 1990s, but some rail industry experts now predict a return to growth, although trucks will re-

Truck terminals are used to forward rather than store goods, so the number of dock doors is important.

The Isle d'Abeau industrial park is adjacent to the Lyon (France) International Airport and has excellent rail and highway connections.

Figure 2.2 **Rail Shipping Rates**

Competition among railroads and with trucking has reduced rail rates, benefiting shippers, consumers, and the economy

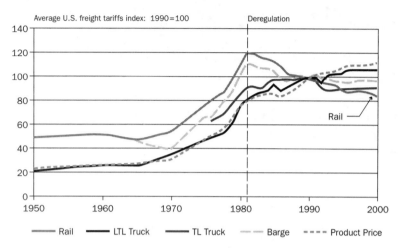

Average U.S. freight tariffs index: 1990=100

— Rail   — LTL Truck   — TL Truck   — — Barge   - - - - Product Price

Source: American Association of State Highway and Transportation Officials, Washington, D.C. From *Transportation: Invest in America, Freight-Rail Bottom Line Report,* copyright 2003. Used by permission.

main more competitive on short hauls. Rail freight productivity today, however, is challenged by congestion and capacity choke points along national corridors, at intermodal terminals, and at urban rail interchanges.[13]

The nation's rail carriers include Class I railroads, or those with operating revenue in excess of $266.7 million, and an assortment of smaller regional and local line-haul carriers. Another type of railroad, known as switching and terminal (S&T), offers pickup and delivery services for connecting line-haul carriers. A total of 561 railroads were in operation in 2001,

Major North American Freight Railroads

BNSF	Burlington Northern and Santa Fe Railway
CN	Canadian National Railway
CP	Canadian Pacific Railway
CSX	CSX Transportation
FXE	Ferrocarril Mexicano (a subsidiary of Grupo Ferroviario Mexicano)
KCS	Kansas City Southern Railway
NS	Norfolk Southern
TFM	(a subsidiary of Grupo Transportación Ferroviaria Mexicana)
UP	Union Pacific Railroad

Source: Association of American Railroads, www.aar.org.

with Class I rail carriers accounting for 68 percent of rail freight.[14]

Today, the majority of goods shipped by rail are lower-value commodities such as coal, which accounts for 41 percent of tonnage and one-quarter of Class 1 revenues.[15] However, change may be on the horizon. Future rail growth could benefit from the dramatic rise in intermodal transport—the movement of trailers and containers by rail, ocean carrier, and truck. Rail is already the primary transportation mode for moving containers and trailers across countries or continents to reach international destinations. In the past 20 years, rail intermodal traffic has tripled, and estimates suggest that this growth will continue, eventually taking over as the top source of revenue for the rail industry.[16] Increased reliance on double-stack trains could influence the design and construction of new rail terminals.

As rail transport growth continues, terminal space will reach or exceed capacity, and the search will be on for new terminal locations. This could be a challenge for the industry, owing to limited land availability in or near major cities. Railroads are seeking to redevelop existing yards for intermodal use. For example, in October 2002, the Burlington Northern and Santa Fe Railway (BNSF) opened BNSF Logistics Park to complement the CenterPoint Intermodal Center 40 miles (64 kilometers) southwest of Chicago, the rail capital of the nation. The park serves major automotive companies such as Suzuki, Honda, Ford, Nissan, and Subaru and will integrate direct rail, truck, intermodal, and transload services with distribution and warehousing.[17] (See the CenterPoint case study, chapter 6.)

In other cases, railroads are developing greenfield locations where land may be cheaper and more available. This pattern could lead to the establishment of new freight hubs, much as the selection of Memphis for Federal Express's main operations put that city on the map as a major transportation hub. Aside from Chicago, other U.S. rail centers include St. Louis, Kansas City, New York, Baltimore, Hampton Roads (Virginia), Atlanta, Savannah, Dallas, Jacksonville, Miami, Gulfport (Mississippi), New Orleans, Houston, Los Angeles/Long Beach, Oakland, and Seattle/Tacoma.

Airfreight

The air mode continues to grow in importance, in part owing to increased demand for individual package deliveries, and in part driven by increased demand

Figure 2.3 The World's Busiest Cargo Airports, 2002

Rank	Airport	Total Cargo	Percent Change Since 2001
1	Memphis (MEM)	3,390,800	28.8
2	Hong Kong (HKG)	2,504,584	19.3
3	Tokyo (NRT)	2,001,822	19.1
4	Los Angeles (LAX)	1,779,855	0.3
5	Anchorage (ANC)*	1,771,595	(5.5)
6	Seoul (ICN)	1,705,880	43.2
7	Singapore (SIN)	1,660,404	8.5
8	Frankfurt (FRA)	1,631,322	1.1
9	Paris (CDG)	1,626,400	2.2
10	Miami (MIA)	1,624,242	(0.9)
11	New York (JFK)	1,589,648	6.3
12	Louisville (SDF)	1,524,181	3.8
13	Chicago (ORD)	1,473,980	13.4
14	Taipei (TPE)	1,380,748	16.0
15	London (LHR)	1,310,615	3.7
16	Amsterdam (AMS)	1,288,626	4.4
17	Bangkok (BKK)	956,790	13.7
18	Indianapolis (IND)	901,917	(18.9)
19	Newark (EWR)	850,050	(5.0)
20	Osaka (KIX)	805,430	(7.5)

ACI Traffic Data: World airports ranking by total cargo; 2002 airports participating in the ACI monthly traffic statistics collection.
Total Cargo: loaded + unloaded freight + mail in metric tonnes.
*Anchorage includes transit freight.
Source: Airports Council International, www.airports.org.

for airfreight services for high-value products. This aspect of the airline industry remains its sole bright spot while commercial airlines struggle to cut costs and remain solvent. Although global air cargo transport declined after September 11, 2001, experts suggest that this decline was a temporary glitch for an industry predicted to grow in the next 20 years.

Cargo facilities construction at airports often incorporates intermodal capabilities, as well as buildings for light manufacturing to finish goods. For example, a joint venture between the Taiwanese government and Taiwan Sugar Corporation includes cargo warehousing and a manufacturing facility at Kaohsiung International Airport. Part of the project includes enhancements to the nearby port that will support the seamless transport of goods. (For more on development at airfreight hubs, please see chapter 5.)

Airfreight is attractive for high-value goods, perishables, and overnight or emergency shipments, as well as electronic equipment, apparel, shoes, printed material, and chemicals. The advantage of time gained outweighs the cost—estimated at three times more than ocean carrier—for such goods, which can be delivered in days rather than in weeks.[18]

Freight forwarders—middlemen that help companies ship their cargo—are looking with interest at the emergence of cargo-only airports, which are trying to find a foothold as air traffic congestion increases at the major passenger/cargo hubs and available warehousing space shrinks. The Southern California Logistics Airport, for example, at the former George Air Force Base in Victorville, has its own air route, separate from the paths of Los Angeles International and other Southern California airports. It has been designated a foreign-trade zone, which reduces tariffs on international shipments.

Ocean Shipping

The first shipping containers appeared on the freight scene in 1956, but it was not until the 1970s that containers revolutionized the shipping industry.[19] Containers—massive metal cylinders or boxes that can handle huge loads of cargo—are on- and off-loaded from ships using mechanized equipment, reducing loading times and making more efficient use of space on the ships. This technology has reduced the labor costs required to manually on- and off-load. Container manufacturing and servicing have emerged as a new subindustry, and the massive equipment needed to manipulate containers at ports has generated multimillion-dollar contracts for heavy equipment manufacturers.[20]

Containerships, which vary in size depending upon port limitations and water depth among other factors, carry general cargo packaged in steel containers that range from 20-foot (6-meter) boxes to receptacles more than 40 feet (12 meters) long. The international measure for container cargo is the 20-foot (6-meter) -long container or the 20-foot-equivalent unit (TEU).

After ships dock at deepwater ports, large cranes load and remove containers, a system known as lift-on, lift-off (lo/lo). Alternatively, cargo is rolled on and rolled off (ro/ro). The containers are transferred to trucks or to container rail for transport to the next destination. Ships also carry noncontainerized bulk

and break bulk cargo. Transshipment occurs when containers are lifted off one ship and loaded onto another ship for the next leg in the cargo journey.

Like the other modes, the container industry has consolidated, with almost 60 percent of TEUs controlled by the top 20 shipping lines. Four of the largest carriers—Maersk-Sealand, Evergreen, P&O Nedlloyd, and Med Shipping—controlled 25 percent

of the world's shipping container capacity in 2002.[21] These carriers also own, develop, and operate private terminals, often located near major deepwater ports to support their warehousing and intermodal hub facilities. For example, in Virginia Maersk-Sealand is building a private terminal near Norfolk International Port, also close to the gateways of Portsmouth and Newport News.

Another large carrier, Japanese-owned Hanjin Shipping Company, recently marked the opening of a massive new container terminal at the Port of Long Beach. The $576 million facility sits on 375 acres (152 hectares) equivalent to the size of 280 football fields. Known as Pier T, the terminal features a 29-lane truck gate, 140,000 square feet (13,006 square meters) of terminal buildings, and an on-dock rail yard with more than 83,000 feet (25,298 meters) of rail linked to the newly opened Alameda Corridor.

Aiming to carry more TEUs at one time, carriers continue to demand ever larger containerships. Since 1990, demand for ships that can carry more than 6,000 TEUs has grown, even though such ships are too wide and too tall to fit through the Panama Canal, the international standard for shipping size. Known as "post-Panamax," such ships continue to evolve. The newest generation of post-Panamax ships, unveiled in January 2003 by Samsung Heavy Industries, includes capacity for up to 18,000 TEUs. Few ports are

Figure 2.4 **Top World Container Gateway Ports**

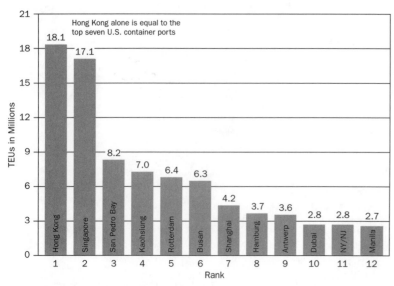

Source: Transystems Corporation.

equipped to handle such massive vessels, which require customized docking facilities and huge loading cranes. In the United States, only Tacoma, Norfolk, and Los Angeles/Long Beach have the capacity for the largest post-Panamax ships.

Estimates from the Port of Long Beach suggest that as cargo traffic quadruples in the next 20 years, and as ship size increases as well, the ports of Long Beach and Los Angeles will require development of 3,624 new acres (1,446 hectares) of container terminals.

Until recently, transportation by barges and smaller ships navigating inland waterways has not been a significant factor in freight shipping, according to the Federal Highway Administration, which estimates the compound growth rate between 1990 and 1998 at zero percent. For certain commodities such as grain, however, barges have remained an important mode of transportation. In addition, innovations such as an emerging container-on-barge sector for inland intermodal port transport, and new intermodal capabilities at inland ports such as Kansas City and Pittsburgh, have heightened interest in cargo sent by barge. The Port Authority of New York and New Jersey recently created the Port Inland Distribution Network to move container cargo by barge or rail between their marine terminals and other cities in the Northeast. The network is designed to compete for highway intermodal business and to speed the flow of goods to market.[22]

Internationally, the privatization of ports has led to a wave of private investment that has boosted profit and improved efficiency. Some of the largest owners of port real estate have invested throughout the world to extend their reach and to offer global services to carriers. For example, Hong Kong–based Hutchinson Ports has holdings in Panama, Freeport (Bahamas), Myanmar, Great Britain, and China.[23] Much of this activity has occurred in South America, where rail privatization, too, has improved the efficiency of freight railroads.[24] Southern Asia and Mediterranean nations have also experienced an uptick in port investment following privatization.

Intermodal Transport

The complexity of today's supply chain requires a combination of transportation modes to achieve the desired efficiencies. For example, raw silk fibers produced on a silkworm farm in China may be sent to a textile plant in the Far East for weaving into cloth. The fabric then may travel to a *maquiladora* (assembly-for-export factory) on the Mexican border for cutting and sewing into jackets that are sent into the United States for finishing and distribution to customers.

Intermodal transport involves the transfer of cargo between vehicles of different modes. Cargo can be carried by trailer or by container. Intermodal transport enables shippers to take advantage of the cost/service benefits of each mode, driving down costs while enhancing efficiency and competitiveness.[25]

Parcel, Postal, and Courier Services

Parcel, postal, and courier shipments, in terms of weight, remain a relatively insignificant part of the total freight picture. When compared by value, however, shipments by this mode represented nearly 11 percent of the total $8 trillion value of shipments even as early as 1997. The phenomenal growth in the value of shipments in this category largely reflects online sales with deliveries by the U.S. Postal Service or by logistics companies such as UPS or FedEx.[26]

Internationally, small package services are growing. Courier services in particular are attractive, owing to the relative ease with which packages can clear customs—shipments are declared as baggage. As nations in emerging markets develop stronger consumer bases hungry for popular brand-name goods that can be ordered online, the need for expedited small package international delivery services will increase. In some promising markets, however, establishing a foothold in the logistics industry—particularly in competition with nationally owned and operated airlines and with nationalized postal authorities—has been a challenge.[27]

This situation appears to be changing, however. China, for example, recently liberalized its policies toward foreign ownership in the logistics industry in general, clearing the way for foreign direct investment in a variety of logistics sectors. As of 2004, 3PLs are able to operate freely as wholly owned foreign enterprises in China. This change will open the door further to foreign operators in all sectors of the logistics industry, from manufacturers to freight consolidators through to warehouse operators.

Currently, the industry is dominated by the major players. In the United States, FedEx controls 42 percent of the domestic air express market and 12 percent of the domestic ground market. UPS's share of domestic air express is 34 percent, and it controls 70 percent of the domestic ground market.[28]

Federal Express Corporation was founded by Frederick W. Smith. In 1965, as a Yale undergraduate, Smith wrote a term paper about the passenger route systems used by most airfreight shippers, which he viewed as economically inadequate. He stated that what was needed was a system designed specifically for airfreight's accommodation of time-sensitive shipments such as medicines, computer parts, and electronics.

In August 1971, after a stint in the military, Smith bought controlling interest in Arkansas Aviation Sales, located in Little Rock. While operating his new firm, he experienced tremendous difficulties in getting packages and other airfreight delivered within a day or two. This problem motivated him to undertake the necessary research for resolving the inefficient distribution system. Thus, the idea for Federal Express was conceived.

The company officially began operations on April 17, 1973, with the launch of 14 small aircraft from Memphis International Airport. On that night, Federal Express delivered 186 packages to 25 U.S. cities—from Rochester, New York, to Miami.

The company was named Federal Express because Smith was working at the time on obtaining a contract with the Federal Reserve Bank. Although the proposal was denied, he believed the name was a particularly good one for attracting public attention and maintaining name recognition.

Memphis was selected as the headquarters since it was the geographical center of the original target market for small packages. In addition, the city's fine weather meant that Memphis International Airport rarely closed because of inclement conditions. The airport was also willing to make the necessary improvements for the operation and had additional hangar space readily available.

Although the company did not show a profit until July 1975, it soon became the premier carrier of high-priority goods in the marketplace and has been the standard-setter for the industry it established. The company's growth gained rapidly following air cargo deregulation in 1977, which allowed Federal Express to use larger aircraft such as Boeing 727s and McDonnell-Douglas DC-10s. In recent years, it has acquired McDonnell-Douglas MD-11s and Airbus A-300s and A-310s.

Today, FedEx Express handles about 3.3 million packages and documents every night. FedEx aircraft, which compose the world's largest all-cargo fleet, have a combined lift capacity of more than 26.5 million pounds (12 million kilograms) daily. In a 24-hour period, FedEx planes travel nearly one-half million miles (800,000 kilometers). FedEx couriers log 2.5 million miles (4 million kilometers) a day, the equivalent of 100 trips around the Earth.

Source: Excerpted from FedEx Web site, www.fedex.com

Courtesy FedEx

Handling over 3.3 million packages requires the largest all-cargo fleet in the industry. The FedEx Express fleet, seen here at the company's main hub in Memphis, Tennessee, includes more than 650 aircraft.

Warehouse Distribution Strategies

Cost has played an important role in the elevation of the logistics functions to the strategy level. Since the 1980s, expenses on logistics-related functions have declined to less than 8 percent of sales revenues in some industries. However, in other industries, logistics costs amount to as much as 40 percent of gross revenues.[29] For the end user, these costs account for approximately 6 percent of the retail cash price. U.S. companies spent nearly $1 trillion on logistics in 2001, and of this, 34 percent was associated with inventory carrying costs.[30] Smaller companies, with less leverage, will spend more on these functions.[31]

Increasingly, companies are focusing on transportation and distribution strategies to make the most efficient use of resources, since management and control of the accumulated supply chain logistics costs are essential to their competitiveness.[32] Companies have learned that these interrelated factors cannot be viewed in a void. Because logistics functions support manufacturing functions, each firm's approach to transportation and distribution will depend upon its approach to manufacturing and fulfillment. Where a company locates its distribution centers, for example, depends on where it is sourcing raw materials and components, as well as where its customers are located. If the company is sourcing products overseas and receiving containerized cargo by ship, then it will likely have a distribution center in proximity to the port.

In recent years, companies have used a number of strategies to keep costs down and to respond to changing manufacturing trends. As just-in-time, lean manufacturing and fulfillment become the status quo, the challenge becomes the efficient management of the flow of raw materials and distribution of finished goods without costly inventory buildup. The goals are to move the product closer to the customer and to reduce the time between completion of goods and arrival on the customer's doorstep. In some cases, this push to be proximate to customers results in the "cluster" phenomenon—a buildup in certain regions of companies engaged in complementary and sometimes competitive businesses within the same industry. A classic example of cluster is Seventh Avenue in the heart of New York City's garment district, where one can watch workers steering racks of clothing up the street, dodging cars, buses, taxis, and pedestrians, on

Figure 2.5 **Logistics Costs as a Percentage of Sales**

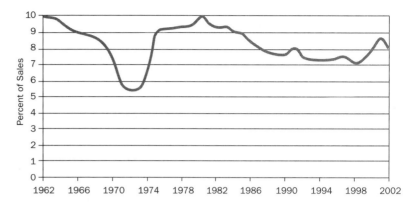

Source: Establish Inc./Herbert W. Davis and Company.

Figure 2.6 **Logistics Cost and Company Size**

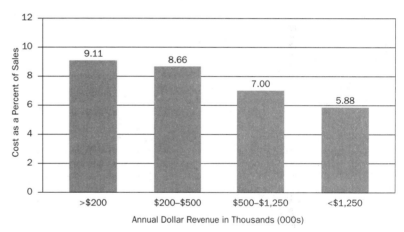

Source: Establish Inc./Herbert W. Davis and Company.

the way from finishing shops to wholesalers, where they are prepared for distribution to retailers.

Suppliers to the automotive industry have long understood the advantages of clustering. Detroit became "Motor City" because of the buildup of suppliers to support the "Big Three" American automotive manufacturers operating plants there. In the 1990s, the Southeast—in particular Tennessee, Alabama, Georgia, South Carolina, West Virginia, and Mississippi—began to supplant Detroit as a growth center for automotive manufacturing, as foreign car companies in particular took advantage of low land costs and a quality labor force to create "Motown South." A secondary boom of first- and second-tier suppliers followed.

Other distribution strategies include:

- Hub-and-spoke: Industries frequently use this model, in which major hub centers serve scattered geographic locations. These centers in turn serve small regional distribution sites.

- Regional: This strategy, in which warehouses are located in the regions the company serves, gives companies proximity to customers as customers become more far-flung. A regional warehouse strategy also helps companies save on transportation costs, a primary driver of this strategy. For example, Henkel Consumer Adhesives, German-based manufacturer of "Duck" brand duct tape, employs distribution centers located so that shipments reach customers in two days or less. When demand for duct tape spiked in early 2003 following heightened alert status and calls for emergency preparedness announced by the U.S. Department of Homeland Security, Henkel increased its production capacity by 40 percent and instituted seven-day production cycles. The company's regional distribution strategy, combined with integrated supply chain management software that monitored real-time inventory levels, ensured that it was able to replenish inventory at stores rapidly, keeping pace with demand.[33]
- Supplier parks: Also known as co-location sites, these industrial parks, populated by a number of suppliers, are sited close to the main manufacturing operations they support. First popularized in Europe by automotive manufacturers, the supplier park concept is just now taking hold in the United States. General Motors is building a massive complex outside Chicago that features such a park. Inside, complementary suppliers manufacture components, sending them to the next supplier along the carefully designed route to add another piece to the assembled component, which is then transported by a light-rail system to the plant floor at exactly the point where assembly takes place (see more in chapter 3).
- Centralized distribution: This approach consolidates goods from numerous manufacturing sites to a central location for shipment to customers. American Honda Motor, for example, centralized its distribution in Chicago as part of a massive logistics park project. For Honda, access from all sources in the Pacific Northwest, Pacific Southwest, East, and South was vital for its distribution needs. This setup enables Honda's manufacturing facilities in Ontario, Ohio, and Alabama to send vehicles through the logistics park to "state-of-the-art stra-

tegically located railheads for distribution to its dealer network."[34]

Some real estate companies specialize in building new facilities to suit the distribution needs of their clients. For example, ProLogis owns and manages distribution centers in North America, Europe, and Asia for an A-list of corporations. The company has built a global network of distribution facilities that enables its clients to streamline critical supply chain operations. For Coors, the brewing company, ProLogis developed several state-of-the-art industrial facilities in Colorado tailored to meet the company's multiple supply chain demands. This segment of operations continues strong growth; in 2001, 3PLs reported a 13.3 percent increase in their warehouse/distribution operations.[35]

Inventory Management

Understanding the flow of goods throughout the life cycle of a company's product is key to developing a strong distribution strategy. Inventories must be present in some form at every point along the cycle. They ensure a smooth transition from raw materials to goods-in-process to finished product, without interruptions owing to shortages. However, inventories can cost companies millions if not managed properly. Finding the right balance between optimal levels so no shortages occur and so companies do not carry too much is the critical challenge.

While management of inventory levels at the raw materials and work-in-process stages depends upon the company's approach to manufacturing and the most efficient handling of inventory, finished-goods inventory levels are influenced by additional factors, including the increasing power of buyers both in retail and in manufacturing. "The shift in power from manufacturers to megaretailers such as Wal-Mart and Costco Wholesale requires manufacturers to maintain adequate levels of finished goods inventory to ensure reliable service and consistent availability for an expanding range of products," reports Robert Delaney, CEO of Cass Information Systems in his "State of Logistics Report" for 2002. "So, higher finished-goods inventory may reflect sound brand management and market strategy." In addition, because the buyer has the power, the buyer may control where the vendor locates inventory.

ProLogis: A Global Services Provider

ProLogis is a leading global provider of integrated distribution facilities and services, with more than 1,700 facilities owned, managed, and under development in over 90 markets throughout North America, Europe, and Asia. The company's arsenal includes state-of-the-art bulk distribution facilities, light industrial facilities, and master-planned full-service industrial parks.

ProLogis aims to be more than a facilities provider by offering a range of services to create optimal distribution solutions. In an industry composed of warehouses and supply chains, ProLogis was among the first distribution facilities providers to frame its business in terms of relationships in-

ProLogis Services

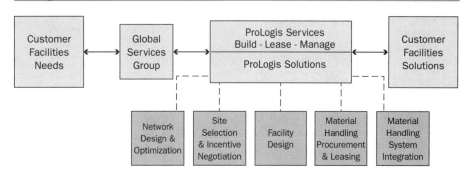

stead of bricks and mortar. Widely recognized as a pioneer of the customer-driven approach, the company has evolved from providing distribution services and facilities on a site-by-site basis to forging partnerships with customers to build the industry's first distribution facility network.

In addition to leasing inventory facilities, ProLogis builds custom facilities through its Corporate Distribution Facilities Development Group. The company also provides consulting services to manufacturers and distributors with worldwide operations, helping to configure or streamline customers' supply-chain procedures. ProLogis's business location services assist customers in strategic site evaluation, incentives negotiation, and conducting due diligence.

ProLogis was founded in 1993 as Security Capital Industrial Trust. In July 1998 the company changed its name to ProLogis Trust to more accurately reflect its growing global business. The company operates as a real estate investment trust (REIT) and is listed on the New York Stock Exchange.

Source: www.ProLogis.com.

Courtesy ProLogis

ProLogis has built a global network of distribution facilities that are tailored to meet the specific supply chain demands of its clients. Shown here is Rialto Distribution Center, Southern California.

Clearly, part of the challenge includes location decisions. For more on the location aspect of warehousing and distribution management, see chapter 3.

Companies want proximity to their customers so that their transportation costs and order fulfillment times will be reduced. As just-in-time manufacturing has become standard practice, the importance of the distribution center—along with location decisions—has grown. In the case of a supplier to a large manufacturer, the supplier's customer will not want to build up

a large inventory (because it is expensive, it takes up room, and it could be outdated before it is used up), but wants components and raw materials in an expedited time frame. Determining the optimal levels of order quantities and reorder points and setting safety stock levels at each stocking point are critical, since they have a direct impact on customer service and satisfaction.[36] In this typical situation, the supplier might choose to locate a distribution center—which may or may not be a part of a production facility—within a

Courtesy AMB Property Corporation

day's distance to the customer. And the distribution center will probably contain an inventory carefully tailored to the needs of this large manufacturing customer.

3PLs have moved into this aspect of logistics outsourcing as well. Companies such as Abbott Laboratories, Compaq, Ford, Nabisco, Wal-Mart, Unilever, and Whirlpool rely on 3PLs to manage inventory functions as well as distribution.[37] In turn, the 3PLs may rely on other outsourcers with particular expertise in distribution center management.

Reverse Logistics

Reverse logistics is the newest member of the logistics family. The Reverse Logistics Council defines it as the process of moving goods from their typical final destination to another point, for the purpose of capturing value otherwise unavailable or for the proper disposal of the products.

According to the Reverse Logistics Council, reverse logistics activities include:

- processing returned merchandise for reasons such as damage, seasonal restock, salvage, recall, or excess inventory;
- recycling packaging materials and reusing containers;
- reconditioning, remanufacturing, and refurbishing products;
- obsolete equipment disposition;
- hazardous material programs; and
- asset recovery.

Proper disposal of assets and management of returns is a growing issue for American companies, which spend more than $35 billion a year on reverse logistics. Consumers are returning packages at an increasing rate—with consumer-direct returns volumes forecast at 182,000 units for 2003.[38]

Technology

The explosion in technological innovation underpins manufacturers' abilities to optimize the supply chain. Beginning with production—such as robotic and computerized innovations on the shop floor—the application of technology has spread throughout the supply chain.

Inventory tracking software and electronic data interchange (EDI) started the trend. Using such tools resulted in more efficient inventory handling and better balance between demand and production—essentially taking the guesswork out of the planning.[39]

Integrating Internet-based technologies has catapulted supply chain management into a seamless process that moves without interruption and excess cost. Web-enabled technologies have also altered the ways logistics professionals seek to squeeze costs out of the distribution equation. Aggregation of purchases, inventories, orders, and shipments and slower cycle times to achieve logistics economies are giving way to customized orders, transactions in units of one or a few, and fulfillment completion within hours, not weeks. Meeting higher customer expectations has required a shift away from full-truckload to LTL freight, as well as a dramatic increase in the amount of freight moved by parcel delivery companies.[40]

When companies harness this technology in the right way, the cost efficiencies—as well as customer service levels—can skyrocket. For example, a Wal-Mart–Proctor & Gamble alliance allows instant reordering, meaning that inventory levels are substantially reduced and rapid fulfillment becomes the norm.[41]

By contrast, recent evidence has shown that failure to harness this power to a company's advantage could bring about the downfall of Wal-Mart's once high-flying competitor, Kmart.

Inventory management technology has become sophisticated to the point that individual products can be tracked throughout their life cycle. For example, advances in bar code tracking have enabled identification of individual products from the minute they arrive at a warehouse through the stocking and purchase process and on through delivery. Other inventory management technologies include automated

storage, systems to analyze and sequence orders for maximum efficiency, systems to control major resources and inventory items and to analyze inventory performance, as well as retrieval and overall warehouse management systems.[42]

When time is crucial, such advancements can be particularly helpful for online or catalog businesses such as apparel company Lands' End. Lands' End warehouses are linked directly to its Web site so that order tracking and inventory management are seamless.[43]

Indeed, technology is embedded in every aspect of logistics functions:

- transportation software to determine optimal modes and delivery routes;
- transportation trading platforms such as Colinx, a joint venture involving a number of companies to provide Web-based services and integrated logistics for premium-brand industrial manufacturers;
- site selection software;

Kmart's Supply Chain Struggles

In January 2002, at a time when discount stores such as Kohl's, Target, and Wal-Mart were recording strong sales, Kmart Corporation—the granddaddy of them all—declared bankruptcy. Several factors contributed to its downfall, but one of the biggest was that Kmart did not compete on price, a failure some attribute to its inability to master supply chain technology and, consequently, benefit from supply chain efficiencies.

As Wal-Mart moved away from a promotions-driven business model that relied on special sales to bring customers into stores to one that focuses on everyday low prices, Kmart stuck with the former approach, which resulted in sharp spikes and drops in demand for products, analysts say. Sale merchandise often was out of stock when customers got to the store. It is difficult to get supply chain management software to work in that model without a lot of customization, and Kmart never built a supply chain planning and execution system to

effectively manage demand, according to Eric Beder, an equity analyst at Ladenburg Thalmann who tracks Kmart. Over the years, some at Kmart saw the need for better software to manage demand, but Beder says top executives never executed the vision.

Meanwhile, Wal-Mart built an e-business system to communicate sales and inventory data from every store to thousands of suppliers and buyers, and deployed a private trading hub to consolidate its purchasing globally and bring suppliers online to bid on contracts—all part of a plan to lower costs and pass on savings. Promotions cause no delivery problems for Wal-Mart because of its tight links with suppliers.

The contrast between the retailers' supply-chain systems has been evident in stores, says Gartner analyst Gale Daikoku, who worked in the retail industry. Wal-Mart has almost no supply storage areas because its vendor-managed inventory system makes suppliers responsible for delivering

product when Wal-Mart needs it, she says. At Kmart stores, she observes, it was not unusual for a supplier's sales representative, wanting to discover why something was not selling at a certain branch, to find shelves empty but inventory piled up in stockrooms.

Despite Kmart's plan to restructure itself—making it easier to fix its supply chain by selling off as many as 250 unprofitable stores—it may be too late to take even small steps forward in the competitive arena, Beder believes. The bankruptcy judge will not let Kmart buy more software to deal with its problems while creditors are clamoring to be paid, and meanwhile Target and Wal-Mart will not be sitting idle. "They're saying, 'This is more opportunity for us; let's go for it,'" says Beder.

Source: Excerpted from "Now in Bankruptcy, Kmart Struggled with Supply Chain." Used with permission. CMP Media LLC, INFORMATION-WEEK, January 28, 2002.

- virtual manufacturing, in which a design change is authorized at one location and electronically sent directly to the plant floor in another location while a warehouse near the plant site sends necessary parts;
- inventory management;
- 24/7 real-time transportation oversight;
- warehouse design and loading dock efficiencies;
- truckload management; and
- planning and forecasting.

The movement toward globalization, with emerging markets, cheaper supply sources, and new trading partners, is compelling enterprises of all sizes to build alliances and online e-business systems that efficiently deliver products to customers while providing a worldwide view of operations. Companies employ Internet-enabled strategies to track orders and react to changes in real time, handling and transporting materials as they move across the supply chain from originating suppliers to end customers. For example, the Port Authority of New York and New Jersey developed its Freight Information Real-time System for Transport (FIRST) as a real-time, Web-enabled platform accessible by all participants in the platform. The system provides updates on cargo availability, individual container status, ship and train schedules, highway traffic conditions, and live camera feeds.[44]

The goal is to link all the forecasting, planning, sales, procurement, production, delivery, freight payment, and revenue collection processes into one seamless electronic flow of information across borders, time zones, and differing languages, creating a global view of the supply chain. Webcasts, publish/subscribe techniques, and online trading platforms enable all interested parties to respond to breaking situations, including changes in customer demand, order revisions and cancellations, adjustments in quantity or locations for deliveries in progress, customs clearance problems, and on-time delivery or installation issues. An integrated, virtual solution can diagnose when a critical piece of equipment is about to fail and can flag when a hub is short of replacement or repair parts while locating the source of the problem.[45]

Supply chain management software integrates all these aspects so that the company can have a total view of operations, as well as all of the elements that are key to each function. For example, Henkel Consumer Adhesives, the duct-tape company, discovered that sophisticated software, integrated in house to incorporate all functions, has enhanced the company's ability to plan and forecast, helping it to understand how the business was growing and where the growth was located. In the past, the company's planners had tried to answer all such questions, but the task was monumentally time-consuming without an overarching solution designed for strategic analysis. Among the first impacts of the software, the company estimates that it will save close to $500,000 per year on shipping costs by rerouting freight to more efficient routes.[46]

Globalization

The fundamental shift to just-in-time manufacturing has revolutionized the way companies think about their supply chains. Of equal importance has been the globalization of the manufacturing process enabled by technology, enhanced by free-trade agreements, and driven by the quest for cost efficiencies and proximity to markets.

Globalization of manufacturing has resulted in an increased focus on logistics and led to real estate development in locations with strategic importance for the supply chain. For example, the North American Free Trade Agreement (NAFTA) opened the borders between the United States, Mexico, and Canada. Beginning in the mid-1990s, companies began shifting manufacturing operations to Mexican border towns at great savings. Today, locations close to major border crossings at El Paso, Tijuana, and Laredo, among others, are valued as distribution hubs.

More recently, shifts in manufacturing to Asia—China, Korea, and Singapore most notably—have changed the way cargo flows. Inbound cargo to the United States flows through West Coast ports and Anchorage, Alaska, one of the fastest-growing logistics centers in the nation. Alternatively, goods originating in Asia are shipped to the east coast of Africa, where they are off-loaded and sent overland to a port on the Mediterranean. Containerized cargo is then reloaded onto ships bound for East Coast U.S. ports and eventually transferred to rail intermodal for distribution inside the country.[47]

Globally, three major events have influenced—and will continue to influence—the way goods flow. The earliest of the three was NAFTA, which created a North American free-trade corridor, amounting to more than $500 billion in annual trade, and dotted the Mexican border with *maquiladoras* and the Canadian border with auto-assembly plants. Now companies are pushing further inside Mexico and establishing distribution centers to ready themselves for expansion into Latin America. While Latin American fortunes have fluctuated in recent years—the Argentine financial crisis of 2001–2002 being the most recent problem—experts suggest that this vast continent will soon become a rapidly growing consumer market, particularly following passage of the pending Free Trade Agreement of the Americas (FTAA), which should ease cross-border tariffs and duties. Argentina, Brazil, and Chile are considered prime areas for future distribution activity, in part because the privatization of the railroads in these nations has encouraged the development of a newly efficient rail freight industry. Chile in particular could be poised to become a logistics hub in the future, with freight shipped via rail from Brazil and Argentina, as well as from the interior of Chile, to the coast for export to the Far East.[48]

The European Union (EU) is a 15-country duty-free zone with standardized tariffs, regulations, and incentives. EU membership includes many western European nations, although Switzerland is a notable exception. Ten more countries, mostly former Soviet satellites in central and eastern Europe, are slated to gain accession to this massive trading zone over the next four years. The impact will be felt as globalized manufacturing operations expand even further, and as the economies of newly capitalist nations improve, thus offering a wider marketplace for companies to sell their goods. The result: an increased focus on logistics, which are becoming ever more complicated. "Given the geographic spread of the effective European market, a single distribution model is increasingly challenged," says Mark Hughes, senior European consultant with Ernst & Young's global real estate practice. "The model pre-2000 was strongly a single center based in Benelux countries. Now we see multiple centers, and configuration will be based on product (nature, scale, perishability), customer location, and service requirements and suppliers. So we see Nordic, Mediterranean, central Europe, plus Baltic centers established."

In western Europe, several nations—primarily in the south—have experienced an increase in interest from companies seeking to slash costs from their supply chain. Spain, for example, is emerging as a hot

spot for automotive manufacturing and for co-located supplier parks with sophisticated infrastructure such as internal rail lines, enabling component parts to arrive at the exact spot on the manufacturing floor where assembly will take place. Spain's Cataluña tops the list of European locations for logistics facilities with 32, according to Ernst & Young's "European Investment Monitor 2003." Other key European logistics centers include Madrid; Antwerp, Belgium; the Alsace-Lorraine and Normandy regions of France; and London, Staffordshire, and the western Midlands in the United Kingdom.

Logistics efficiencies have been hampered in the EU by a lack of coordination among national rail lines, as well as congested highways and restrictions on trucking activity.[49] Now companies are looking east to nations such as Poland, the Czech Republic, Hungary, Slovakia, and Russia.[50] ProLogis, for example, has established extensive warehousing operations in Poland for a number of large U.S. firms aiming to take advantage of lower-cost labor and real estate. Much of the logistics activity in central and eastern Europe is centered in capital cities such as Budapest and Warsaw, although St. Petersburg is experiencing significant logistics activity, as is Moscow.[51]

While U.S. companies have been eyeing China since the 1980s—and a number of pioneers such as

Globalization of manufacturing and distribution has created opportunities for industrial real estate development in strategic locations around the world. Shown here is the Coventry Distribution Center in Coventry, England.

Motorola have been doing business in this nation of over 1 billion since the mid-1990s—admission into the World Trade Organization in November 2002 means that the pace of reform will speed up, as will the opportunities. Particularly in the logistics sector, which had previously been closed to foreign-owned competitors, the policy reforms will stimulate increased competition among the various international players in the logistics industry. Manufacturing activity has exploded along the coast in cities such as Shanghai, where the Chinese government established incentivized foreign-trade zones to encourage foreign companies to manufacture for export. The program has worked. China now produces 50 percent of the world's cameras, 30 percent of televisions, and 25 percent of washing machines. Indeed, China accounts for more than one-quarter of the world's manufacturing output.[52]

All this output requires a logistics infrastructure to get goods where they need to go. Add to the mix that the Chinese government has begun to allow foreign-owned companies to manufacture for the domestic population, and the logistics challenges and opportunities become evident. Maersk Logistics is among the first wholly owned foreign enterprises to receive permission to operate in China. And FedEx now offers regular service to and from various points in China.

The Impact of E-commerce

Electronic commerce has significantly changed the way companies go to market. The impact of the Internet on the supply chain cannot be overstated, given its contributions to improved planning, improved asset management, shorter cycle times, tailored product positioning, and customer service. The emergence of virtual storefronts such as Amazon.com has greatly stimulated growth in parcel package and courier delivery services. And the trend continues unabated. Retail sales via the Internet in the third quarter of 2002 (not including holiday data) grew 34 percent over the same period one year earlier.

Business "futurists" in the mid- to late 1990s predicted the downfall of the retailer as we know it, suggesting that Americans would shift en masse to online ordering. Such a massive change did not pan out, although most mainstream retailers today have added a new sales channel to their mix, allowing customers to shop either online or in the store.

The shift to e-commerce business models did not come without some supply chain horror stories. In the fall of 1999, Toys"R"Us went online with an extensive interactive Web site that would enable customers to do their Christmas toy shopping from their own computers. The value proposition, the company told its customers, sidestepped long lines and empty shelves and gave 11th-hour procrastinators new hope that they could still find the perfect gift for their children. Toys"R"Us heavily touted its new service, and millions confidently pointed and clicked their way to Christmas list completion. Except . . . the packages never arrived. The company's supply chain was not flexible enough to allow for successful fulfillment of so many orders. The fiasco created some rocky times for company executives. Aside from the embarrassment and its tarnished image, Toys"R"Us faced Federal Trade Commission fines for late delivery, as well as a class-action lawsuit over Christmas gifts that were not delivered or that arrived late.

The lesson for companies evaluating the addition of an electronic buying channel: plan an effective distribution and fulfillment strategy that will provide an infrastructure to support the immediacy of customer demand. Toys"R"Us solved its fulfillment problem by partnering with an expert in online fulfillment and delivery—Amazon.com. During the 2000 Christmas season, following its alliance with Amazon, use of the Toys"R"Us Web site increased by over 200 percent, and Amazon announced that 99 percent of the retailer's shipments had arrived in time for Christmas. But Toys"R"Us also moved to correct fulfillment problems on its own by opening two new distribution centers and hiring seasoned professionals in inventory management, distribution, and order fulfillment.[53]

Security and Contingency Planning

In the immediate aftermath of the September 11, 2001, attacks on the World Trade Center and the Pentagon, all traffic in U.S. airspace halted. The nation's borders were locked down. Trucks lined up for miles at the Canadian border, waiting for permission to enter. Some U.S. factories, desperate for components and raw materials that were marooned on the trucks, were forced to shut down production. In the months immediately following the attacks, businesses reevaluated their transportation and distribution strategies. Should they move their warehouses to the United States?

New fast cargo ships such as FastShip are being developed that have the potential to compete with airfreight for the transport of time-sensitive goods.

Should they source key parts domestically? Such questions were part of the panic and uncertainty of the time. There was a great deal of talk about a wide-scale readjustment away from just-in-time (JIT) principles. But mostly, it was just talk. Since then, the pressure to make massive changes has eased. Many companies, however, have reevaluated the safety and security of their supply chains as part of their business continuity strategy. There is not a wholesale repudiation of JIT, but some companies are also implementing "just-in-case," adding backup inventory in other locations. For freight and transportation companies, the post-9/11 changes have meant significant expenditures on new security measures such as locking cockpit doors in airplanes, as well as changes in procedures to reflect the heightened attention to security.

Events other than terrorist attacks or war can impede the smooth flow of even the best-planned supply chain. When a train carrying chemicals derailed and burst into flames inside Baltimore's Howard Street tunnel in July 2001, freight traffic along the East Coast was disrupted for four days while the fire burned, creating a nasty domino effect and sending logistics managers scurrying to reroute deliveries. A massive West Coast longshoremen's strike in fall 2002 brought all port activity to a complete standstill in some of the nation's busiest deepwater ports—including Long Beach and San Francisco—and costing companies millions. The economic shock waves from the dispute spilled across the nation—the 29 West Coast ports handle more than $300 billion in trade annually. According to an account of the strike in the *Long Beach Press Telegram*, "As huge cargo ships sat at anchor, part-starved auto assembly lines shut down, perishable farm cargo rotted and irate truckers idled

in miles-long lines."[54] Vigilant companies had had prior warning of the strike, however, and some shifted to airfreight during this time, resulting in fewer interruptions to their supply chains.

To be sure, these types of events occurred prior to September 11, 2001. Forward-thinking companies had already begun to establish backup data centers in remote locations to ensure the security of their knowledge base. The difference in the post-9/11 world is that companies are focusing more on this important means of protecting business continuity. They are doing better contingency planning, aided by real-time routing technology to help ease the pain of such events.

Future Visions

The logistics industry will continue to evolve as processes become ever more streamlined, customer demands change, and technology innovations further alter the landscape.

One trend to watch is so-called "FastShip" technology, being developed in Philadelphia. Once operational, these cargo ships will cross oceans in record times, operating at half the cost of standard airfreight. FastShip, Inc, developer of the technology, estimates that the new ships will reduce the Asia-Europe sea voyage time for a typical containership from eight weeks to two weeks, and the transatlantic trip time from eight to 3.5 days. Once the concept moves from prototype to reality, FastShips could begin to cut into the airfreight market share for transporting high-value, time-sensitive goods.[55]

Tube freight technology—also known as capsule pipelines—delivers freight through underground pneumatic tubes, which resemble the tubes used at bank drive-in windows, built on a much larger scale. The concept, being developed by a number of private companies as well as by a government/business consortium, offers an automated system for moving general commodity freight through underground concrete pipelines, connecting metropolitan centers nationwide. Capsules carry the cargo, which is pumped through the pipeline using electric energy. Proponents of tube freight say the technology has the potential to displace a majority of long-haul trucks from the nation's roads and highways. The system will be fully automated by computer, so delivery times will be predictable, unaffected by surface traffic, accidents, or weather.[56]

A variation of the pneumatic capsule is the hydraulic capsule pipeline, in which cargo capsules are carried by a flow of water. When the speed of the flow reaches a certain point, the capsule becomes waterborne. This technology is being tested, particularly for coal transport. Coal is crushed and compacted into a capsule shape that is then fed into a pipeline containing water. Upon arrival, the coal "log" is broken up, and water is removed. The first commercial installation of coal log pipelines could come within the next few years, according to researchers.[57]

Slightly farther into the future lies the use of nanotechnology in manufacturing processes. Nanotechnnology refers to the manipulation of individual atoms to build tiny machines on the scale of a nanometer, or one-billionth of a meter. Nanotechnology is anticipated to make most products lighter, stronger, cleaner, less expensive, and more precise. While the first tentative steps toward harnessing this technology have occurred, practical applications are estimated to be years away. If the technology does advance, the impact on the logistics industry might be seen on the manufacturing floor—with molecular assemblers performing tasks at lightning speed, reducing just-in-time manufacturing to levels of efficiency that are unheard of today. The ability of molecular-sized machines to assemble replicas of themselves could revolutionize the concept of the manufacturing floor and eliminate the need to maintain inventory at any level. Molecular-based computer storage is a possibility as well, resulting in computers able to retain massive amounts of data.[58]

With the Internet constituting an integral part of operations and ever-evolving technology underpinning every aspect of the supply chain, companies are facing new challenges. In the 21st century, firms will have to strike the right balance between innovation and workability within their own corporate cultures. Some companies that rushed headlong into expensive enterprise-wide supply chain management solutions are now finding that they may have purchased too big or too unwieldy a solution. Some retrenchment may occur as these firms determine optimal ways to make the technology work for them.

While some business experts have suggested that virtual systems may replace entirely the human component, in fact the key to riding the next wave of change will be integrating the virtual with the real to improve efficiency, decrease costs, increase productivity and customer service, and shorten response times. One thing is certain: companies will continue to seek ways to enhance their supply chain efficiencies and streamline their own operations to achieve maximum productivity. Of course, one firm's efficiency could be another firm's bottleneck, so companies will have to examine the question of how to design a supply chain to promote their business's efficiency. A new round of outsourcing could occur as firms are better able to identify core strengths, meaning even more growth for logistics providers.

Looking ahead, more companies will use optimized, customized supply chains as a competitive differentiator as they aim to maximize their core strengths. How does a company implement a system that will help plan production based on consumer demand? Why would direct distribution work for some companies but not for others? How can a firm in head-to-head competition—say Ford with General Motors—use supply chain management to get an edge? How will a particular location strategy affect a streamlined supply chain? Companies will continue to seek answers to such questions as they move toward increasingly efficient supply chains.

Notes

1. Gary S. Weiss and Rene Circ, "Industrial Real Estate—Today's Supply Chain," *Professional Report,* Winter 2002, p. 23.

2. John T. Mentzer and James S. Keebler, "Current Trends in Logistics and Distribution," unpublished paper, 2001, p. 2.

3. Lt. Gen. William G. "Gus" Pagonis, quoted in Manuel Roig-Franzia, "In a Dance against Time, a Division Packs for War," *Washington Post,* February 19, 2003, p. A22.

4. "Logistics and Supply Chain Predictions for the Transportation Industry in 2003," www.eyefortransport.com (January 30, 2003).

5. Benjamin H. Gordon, "The Changing Face of 3rd Party Logistics," *Supply Chain Management Review,* March 12, 2003, p. 4.

6. "U.S. 3PL Market Grew 7% in FY 2002," www.eyefortransport.com (April 2, 2002).

7. "Logistics and Supply Chain Predictions."

8. Bureau of Transportation Statistics, *National Transportation Statistics,* tables 1-44 and 1-53, www.bts.gov/publications/national_transportation_statistics/2002 (May 29, 2003).

9. Bruce Lambert, "Freight Analysis Framework" *Freight News* (Federal Highway Administration), October 2002, p. 1.

10. Mentzer and Keebler, p. 8.

11. Robert Delaney, "State of the Logistics Industry 2002," Cass Information, www.cassinfo.com (April 14, 2003), p. 6.

12. Association of American Railroads, "Impact of the Staggers Rail Act of 1980," p. 2, www.aar.org/getFile.asp?File_id=151 (March 18, 2003).

13. American Association of State Highway and Transportation Officials, "Freight Rail Bottom-Line Report Summary," August 2002, PowerPoint presentation, slide 36.

14. Association of American Railroads, "Class I Railroad Statistics," www.aar.org (March 18, 2003).

15. American Association of State Highway and Transportation Officials, "Freight Rail Bottom-Line Report Summary," slide 16.

16. Dan Emerson, "Transportation Equipment Rolls On Despite World Economic Woes," *Plants Sites and Parks,* p. 5, www.bizsites.com/2003/jan/article.asp?id=225 (March 25, 2003).

17. Michelle Porter, "Webxtras: BNSF Logistics Park Opens outside Chicago," *Plants Sites and Parks,* www.bizsites.com/webxtras/bnsf/html (April 10, 2003).

18. Gerhardt Muller, *Intermodal Freight Transportation,* 4th ed. (Washington, D.C.: Eno Transportation Foundation, Inc., and Intermodal Association of North America, 1999), p. 111.

19. Martin Dresner, Robert H. Smith School of Business, University of Maryland, College Park, note to author, May 10, 2003.

20. Muller, *Intermodal Freight Transportation,* p. 25.

21. John Vickerman, "Marine Terminal Design and Container Handling Systems," www.transystems.com/presentations/2003/Pres_02_03 (March 26, 2003).

22. "The Week," *Traffic World,* April 7, 2003, p. 9.

23. Muller, *Intermodal Freight Transportation,* pp. 350–351.

24. Ann Moline, "Track Record—Railroad Privatization," *Impact,* Winter 2000, p. 20.

25. Muller, *Intermodal Freight Transportation,* p. 3.

26. Mentzer and Keebler, p. 14.

27. Muller, *Intermodal Freight Transportation,* p. 362.

28. Angela Greiling Keane, "DHL Buys Airborne Ground," *Traffic World,* March 31, 2003, p. 8.

29. Institute of Management Accountants, www.imanet.org (April 28, 2003).

30. "Logistics and Supply Chain Predictions for the Transportation Industry in 2003," www.eyefortransport.com (January 30, 2003).

31. Establish Inc./Herbert W. Davis and Company, "Logistics Cost and Service 2002," Council on Logistics Management presentation, www.establishinc.com/index.html (April 30, 2003).

32. Mentzer and Keebler, p. 4.

33. Merrill Douglas, "Sticking with the Strategy," *Inbound Logistics,* December 2002, and www.duckproducts.com (March 7, 2003).

34. Michelle Porter, "BNSF Logistics Park Opens outside Chicago."

35. Robert Delaney, "State of Logistics Report 2001," p. 2, Cass Information, www.cassinfo.com (March 13, 2003).

36. Ram Ganeshan and Terry P. Harrison, "An Introduction to Supply Chain Management," unpublished paper, p. 3.

37. Weiss and Circ, "Industrial Real Estate," p. 24.

38. Flextronics, www.flextronics.com/ValueAdded/ReverseLogistics/reverseLogistics.asp (April 28, 2003).

39. Weiss and Circ, "Industrial Real Estate," p. 24.

40. Mentzer and Keebler, p. 17.

41. Weiss and Circ, p. 24.

42. Mayfield Education Centre, www.mayfield.edu.au/pdf/stores.pdf (April 30, 2003).

43. "Building a Smarter Warehouse," *Plants Sites and Parks,* April 2001, p. 54.

44. Vickerman, "Marine Terminal Design."

45. Mentzer and Keebler, p. 25.

46. Douglas, "Sticking with the Strategy."

47. Vickerman, "Marine Terminal Design."

48. Moline, "Track Record—Railroad Privatization."

49. Muller, *Intermodal Freight Transportation,* p. 372.

50. Ann Moline, "Global Review: EU Accession Looms Large," *Plants Sites and Parks 2003 International Resource Guide,* January 2003, p. 2.

51. Ernst and Young, "European Investment Monitor 2003," www.ey.com/eim (April 4, 2003).

52. Sir Stephen Brown, "The China Conundrum" (address delivered to Mid-Yorkshire Chamber of Commerce and Industry, February 21, 2003), www.tradepartners.gov.uk/files/sb_speech_feb03.doc.

53. Jon Weisman, "Toysrus.com Rebounds after 1999 Stumble," *Ecommerce Times,* January 5, 2001.

54. Mark Edward Nero, "New Era Begins at Ports," *Long Beach Press Telegram,* January 22, 2003.

55. Vickerman, "Marine Terminal Design."

56. Jeff Ashcroft, "The Impact of Transportation Innovations and Mega-Projects," unpublished paper, p. 11.

57. Capsule Pipelines, "Definitions," www.capsu.org/what/technology.html (April 29, 2003).

58. Jeff Ashcroft, "Scanning the Horizon—Future Technologies in Logistics," unpublished paper.

Chapter 3

THE INTERSECTION OF LOGISTICS AND REAL ESTATE

Luis A. Belmonte

The logistics industry and the industrial property sector of the U.S. commercial real estate industry have been distant in-laws for too long and to their own detriment. They resemble relatives who only connect at infrequent family gatherings and rarely keep in touch afterward. These two powerful economic forces have historically met only when a manufacturer or distributor needed a warehouse or distribution facility. The distance has often been exacerbated by the traditional real estate professional's mission: build a box, lease it, keep it or sell it, then move on to the next opportunity.

In the past, both industries have been transaction-driven rather than alliance builders. Commercial real estate developers have focused on the user's specifications; most did not venture beyond the requirements contained in a request for proposal. Or property owners, eager to lease a vacant building to creditworthy companies, assumed that existing designs and configurations could be adapted to their new tenants' requirements. Rarely would the real estate provider focus on issues such as effective space use, cargo throughput, cycle time, total cost of carry (including financing merchandise in transit), cargo theft, or whether a 75-foot (23-meter) 16-wheeler could easily maneuver in the truck court. With the exception of a handful of large real estate investment trusts that focus on the distribution requirements of major corporations, most industrial property owner/developers

have simply been happy to turn over the keys and collect the rent.

On the other hand, the transportation provider—truck line, railroad, ocean line, airline, freight forwarder, or customs broker—has historically looked to a shipper only for a steady flow of freight, a contract rate at a good yield, and a profit. Transport vendors traditionally have not been concerned with a building's configuration. Most have not given much attention to ways to improve the efficiency and productivity of a facility—unless it were being built expressly for them.

As a result, until the mid-1980s, there were few ongoing, long-term alliances or relationships among industrial real estate owners and developers, commercial property brokers, the various transportation carriers, and the shippers they serve. Each operated independently. Only the two most powerful forces in distribution and transportation—third-party logistics providers and municipally owned major airports—have taken a leadership role in working closely with real estate developers to create facilities that meet the design, operational, and financial criteria of all parties involved.

This situation is not surprising, considering that industrial property developers, wanting to insulate themselves against industry downturns, traditionally have not specialized in distribution facilities. In an effort to spread their risk and capitalize on growth in

More real estate developers today are finding opportunities in the specialized requirements of the logistics industry. Shown here: the UPS Worldwide Logistics warehouse and distribution center in the Park West International Industrial Park in northern Kentucky.

© Gary Knight and Associates/Courtesy IDI Associates

other industries, industrial developers have tended to build a spectrum of products—a manufacturing facility, a distribution center, a fabrication/assembly facility—and to redevelop existing structures or to reposition existing buildings for specialized tenants.

In the past, the freight transportation sector had no economic incentive to look beyond its primary missions: selling vehicle space and keeping its assets productive. Its plate was piled high. Air, ground, rail, and ocean transport providers had endless challenges managing their labor, fuel, maintenance, safety, and operating costs, and coping with regulatory constraints, capital flow, economic fluctuations, and governmental actions in the United States and worldwide. In tough times, a real estate developer could retrench and wait on the sidelines more easily than asset-intensive transportation companies, which needed to keep their capacity moving and their technology current.

The customers—usually manufacturers or distributors—did not really expect or value a close relationship with real estate or logistics vendors beyond basic job performance. All too often, these customers sought out the lowest-cost provider to deliver reliable products on time with no surprises. Generally—and there were exceptions—relationships took a backseat to short-term considerations: *Get it out the door to the consignee. Get it billed and paid.* This was the modus operandi in manufacturing and distribution for decades, and developers either responded and delivered or lost the account.

The Evolution of Logistics, Distribution, and Property

Several important milestones in the evolution of warehousing and freight distribution have affected real estate professionals over the past 30 years. Understanding the historical context and the growing importance of domestic and global physical distribution will help property owners, investors, developers, lenders, and brokers spot and capitalize on the current and future trends discussed in this chapter.

Railroads and Warehouses

In the late 1800s, with little competition and transcontinental dominance over the movement of goods, the railroads kept shippers, wholesalers, distributors, and consignees in a viselike grip. Customers were squeezed with rates arbitrarily established by whim, favor, or punishment—and little else. Railroad companies also muscled landowners to develop warehouses adjacent to main rail lines, connecting them to rail sidings and spurs for loading and unloading. Warehousing, a byproduct of the transportation process, became a key component of the rate-making formula for railroads and their prime customers.

Railroads gave loyal shippers moving large volumes of goods a through-transportation rate. This arrangement usually allowed them to offload and store their goods for up to a year in railroad-controlled warehouses along the route. Breakdowns of rates and tariffs were never disclosed, putting smaller shippers at a competitive disadvantage. But larger volume shippers and consignees could control their inventory and develop flexible distribution plans based on demand and other market variables. The system was a win-win for railroad companies and major shippers. Landowners and warehouse builders willing to play ball with the railroads were rewarded as well.

What today would be considered efficient vertical integration of services and door-to-door pricing was fiercely opposed by smaller manufacturers, farmers, and other shippers. The Interstate Commerce Act was passed in 1887 as the first consumerist legislation in the United States. The act created a federal commission that regulated the railroads and forced them to publish prices and tariffs for all transportation services they offered.

The American Warehouse Association, formed in 1891, successfully lobbied Congress for federal legislation blocking the railroads from offering free warehousing to their biggest customers and discriminating against smaller-volume shippers who had to pay. The Hepburn Act passed in 1906, and the warehousing link in the supply chain began to grow, dominated by family owners and operators of smaller warehouses. These so-called third-party providers were competitive in their pricing. Many would evolve to become marketers of a full spectrum of outsourced transportation services.

Seven decades of tightly controlled rail transportation led to a bipartisan effort by Congress to deregulate the railroad industry, an action that would change the face of warehousing and dramatically alter the flow and speed of transported goods. The campaign for deregulating the national transport system included airlines and motor carriers as well as railroads. Deregulation started during the Carter Administration, carried through to the Reagan Administration, and extended into the Clinton Administration.

Between the mid-1970s and the mid-1990s, a series of new laws dismantled the Interstate Commerce Commission (ICC) and other government agencies. Federally approved rail and air freight rates disappeared, and free market pricing emerged. Many shippers moved to more flexible, price-competitive road transportation, and the percentage of total cargo moving by rail dropped dramatically. Today, railroads chiefly haul chemicals and other liquid cargoes, grains and bulk products, containers, and automobiles.

Railroad deregulation in 1980 also had a profound impact on warehouse owners and commercial real estate developers. Warehouses no longer had to be built adjacent to a rail siding. The continuing rising tide of outbound cargo was moving by truck and being stored in warehouses with proximity to major thoroughfares and highway systems. International shipments were moving intermodally, and third-party warehousing quickly became both an art and a science: the art of selecting a site that could maximize access and avoid traffic delays, and the science of planning and designing operational and logistical efficiencies for the building. By the mid-1990s, these skills were twin priorities for tenants, owners, operators, transport providers, and ultimately consignees.

Trucking: The Workhorses Hit the Highway

Some say the trucking industry was born in 1895, when piano manufacturer William Steinway bought U.S. production rights to Europe's Daimler gasoline motor vehicle and made two 3.5-horsepower versions for "commercial purposes." Steinway instantly eclipsed the electric battery-powered delivery wagon introduced that same year. His invention coincided with the debut, also in 1895, of a "road vehicle" with a small, open truck bed developed by Rochester lawyer George B. Selden, who had been granted the first patent on the basic features for a gasoline automobile in 1879.

Early trucking was used for door-to-door retail delivery and included rolling contraptions such as a self-propelled, six-horsepower steam wagon for hauling furniture that went into service in 1896. For the first 40 years, the trucking industry morphed from

As trucking has usurped rail in the movement of goods, the prime criterion for warehouse location has switched from access to rail lines to proximity to highways. Design changes have also occurred to accommodate truck loading and parking.

Courtesy IDI Associates

mechanically powered buggies and buckboards to big rigs. Trucking companies were freewheeling and fast growing, commandeering smaller shipments that moved by rail but mainly forging the early links of a primitive supply chain. Long before roads became highways, truckers gave manufacturers the freedom to locate factories near labor pools and, later, warehouses near customers and markets instead of always being tethered to a railhead. Free-market pricing, a booming industrial revolution, and zero barriers to entry fueled the infant industry. All a new trucker needed was a rig and gasoline.

When trucking companies started hauling across state borders, red flags unfurled. The federal government had been regulating prices and competition since Congress created the Interstate Commerce Commission in 1887 to oversee the railroad industry. Unregulated truckers were seen as renegades and pirates, and state regulators and the railroads lobbied fiercely to get the mushrooming motor carrier industry under ICC control as well.

Their success came in the heart of the Great Depression: Congress passed the Motor Carrier Act of 1935, requiring new truckers to seek a "certificate of public convenience and necessity" from the ICC—which granted very few certificates. Truckers operating before the act was passed had to document prior proof of operation. The new law also required motor carriers to file all rates or tariffs with the ICC 30 days before they became effective. Competitors could inspect new tariffs and protest them. From 1940 to 1980, the trucking industry stagnated; certificates for new or expanded service were almost impossible to secure from the ICC, which maintained a stranglehold on competition.

Deregulation of the surface freight transportation industry began in 1962 with the Kennedy Administration and ended in 1995 during the Clinton Administration. The ICC's abolition has returned trucking to free-market status, with the federal government focusing almost solely on truck safety and security. Today, 586,000 interstate trucking companies are registered with the U.S. Department of Transportation.

The face of warehousing and the movement of goods changed in 1980 with the passing of the Motor Carrier Act. Before that date, most major warehouses had railroad sidings or were built on spurs, because rail was the primary mode of delivery and distribution

for high-volume components and finished goods. "It was unthinkable to construct a warehouse without a rail siding before the 1970s," says Ken Ackerman, a Columbus, Ohio, management adviser on warehousing and supply chain management. As trucking expanded, companies like Sears would build a 4-million-square-foot (371,612-square-meter) distribution center on the west side of Columbus, Ohio, and Ford Motor would construct a 3-million-square-foot (278,709-square-meter) parts center near Detroit —with no railroad sidings.

With a nationwide network of truck transportation, companies could reduce the number of warehouses used for distribution. The Ross Division of Abbott Laboratories once relied on 100 warehouses to distribute its canned Similac baby formula, thus assuring retailers it had adequate stocks of fresh products; today it has nine large distribution centers throughout the United States.

Design considerations for warehouse and distribution facilities have since been driven by the explosion in truck transportation and goods moving over the road. For example, more yard space is being devoted to parking trailers as more distribution centers and 3PL operators adopt a "drop and hook" policy. Instead of backing into a truck bay for loading or unloading, truckers are dropping either empty or filled trailers within a secured area; the tenant/operator then hooks it up to a tractor and moves it to a dock door. "Drop and hook" lets the shipper, 3PL, or customer optimize scheduling of its labor, freight handling equipment, and facilities. Yard management system software also helps coordinate freight loading, off-loading, and handling today. (Facility design is discussed in detail in chapter 4.)

The Air Cargo Age and Emergence of Speed

Another important milestone was reached in the early 1950s: the dawn of the air cargo age, when the thousands of war-built DC-3s and C-47s were decommissioned by the military. The airline industry as we know it today was born, and with it came the ability to carry expedited freight in cargo aircraft. This trend was accelerated in the early 1960s by the introduction of the commercial jet engine, with its ability to cover great distances and connect continents in relatively short periods. The global air cargo market was created, and with it the synergy between warehousing, logistics, transportation providers, and commercial real estate developers first became apparent. By the early 1970s, the mutually beneficial relationship was unmistakably clear. As consumers demanded ever more products from the global marketplace, shippers of high-value, time-sensitive cargo were buying space in the bellies of narrow-bodied Boeing 707s and Douglas DC-8s. They were willing to pay rates considerably higher than ocean shipping and ground transportation to access the latest fashions from Europe, state-of-the-art electronics from Asia, or flowers from South America. This "first-class" shipping enabled companies to increase the shelf lives of their products and avoid transportation delays caused by the congested ports and inadequate road infrastructures often found in developing countries. It also allowed them to tighten security measures on high-value goods.

Another economic driver was fueling the shift toward airfreight. Shippers of high-value goods could not afford to maintain inventories of airworthy products at warehouses adjacent to manufacturing, production, or assembly facilities. This was not because the real estate costs were prohibitive, but because the invisible and indirect costs of flooring, storing, and financing goods—goods that needed to be on the consignee's receiving dock, at a distribution center, on a shelf, or in a showcase—were far greater.

This trend could be seen in the gradual shift from industrial space devoted to manufacturing and storage to space designed for distribution. As of 2001, estimates of the total industrial space pie of 12 billion square feet (1.1 million square meters) in the top 55

U.S. markets allocated 29.6 percent for manufacturing and factory facilities and 70.3 percent for distribution facilities. This ratio compares with 31 percent and 69 percent, respectively, just five years earlier. In 1989, some 33 percent of the industrial space was occupied by manufacturing/factory facilities, and 67 percent was devoted to distribution facilities.[1] These distribution centers are generally located near major transportation hubs—highway arterials, seaports, rail yards, and airports. However, the decline of factory warehousing and the growing importance of distribution centers are especially pronounced for airworthy products, where cost-effective "speed to market" is now the most important issue for every link in the supply chain from manufacturer to end user.

Today, time is an even more sensitive and expensive commodity for manufacturers/shippers and their customers/consignees. Indeed, one U.S. company changed the entire face of cargo transportation by selling the importance and benefits of time. In the early 1980s, a then-upstart Federal Express urged shippers to use its services "when it absolutely, positively has to be there overnight." It guaranteed a delivery time or your money back.

"Absolutely, positively," hammered home through catchy, nonstop television and radio commercials and newspaper and magazine advertising, was originally aimed at document shippers. It sold urgency, time-sensitivity, and a no-excuses message to American businesses for a premium price. It demonstrated the value of getting shipments to customers just in time—

The growth in airfreight for the distribution of high-value goods has created demand for air cargo facilities on or near airports in major hub cities.

Third-Party Logistics Providers Are Prime Targets for the Property Professional— But Know Their Language

They are not household names, rarely advertise for business, and work largely behind the scenes as important service suppliers and business partners to U.S. and multinational corporations. But the 150 major third-party logistics providers (3PLs) listed in Armstrong's "Who's Who in Logistics" (www.3plogistics.com) and the 1,000 smaller 3PLs that did not make the list can be attractive prospects for commercial real estate developers, investors, real estate investment trusts, or brokers specializing in the industrial property sector.

However, deep knowledge of 3PLs' capabilities and value proposition is critical. A real estate professional should assess prospects according to criteria including creditworthiness, expansion potential, and financial heft. And 3PLs work with real estate companies "based on their deep knowledge of our business," maintains Larry Georgen, sales manager of Chicago-based AIT Worldwide Logistics. "Our real estate requirements have grown exponentially because more and more companies are outsourcing logistics."[1]

Real estate providers with "specialized skill sets in logistics" will find the welcome mat out, says John Spychalski, professor of supply chain management at Pennsyl-vania State University. "Real estate specialists who can advise on sectors and sub-markets that offer the greatest earnings potential for the 3PL will find opportunities in logistics. They must understand the durability of demand for the logistics activity conducted in the facility. They should know the current and potential flow patterns of inbound and outbound cargo and the existing and new transportation methods. Plus, they must be thoroughly grounded in the political and taxation risks and labor supply issues in that submarket."[2]

A logistics trend that could directly benefit a real estate provider is 3PL involvement in light assembly, which traditionally occurs in the shipper's manufacturing facility. Some companies are outsourcing the final stages of production to a logistics provider that arranges transportation and distribution.

To thoroughly grasp the importance of today's 3PLs and the potential they hold as buyers or influencers of various property services, a real estate professional need only look at the broad menu of different logistics services and support activities they deliver. Here's a list of what 3PLs do for their clients and what the buzz-words mean:

- *Integrated logistics:* Shipping goods intermodally or via two transport modes such as truck to air or ocean to rail.
- *Just-in-time (JIT) inventory management:* Ordering or shipping enough raw materials or finished goods as needed with zero surplus for storage.
- *Inbound logistics:* Transporting and receiving raw materials and partially finished or finished goods for inventory, manufacturing, or redistribution.
- *Payment audit processing:* Paying, managing, and auditing all transportation costs for a client.
- *Subassembly or light manufacturing:* Assembling components to finish a product before shipping and final distribution.
- *Transportation management:* Choosing and booking different cargo transportation vendors such as rail, truck, ocean, and air.
- *Location services:* Site inspection, selection, configuration, and real estate liaison.
- *Cargo security:* Advise, manage, and strengthen security at terminals and in transit. Arrange armed convoys in high-risk areas.
- *Order fulfillment:* Processing and shipping customer orders.

when they had to have them—and not just when it was convenient for the shipper or the transportation provider. Suddenly, the infant so-called air express industry, also known as "integrators," put a stopwatch to the supply chain and guaranteed next-morning delivery to justify the price.

3PL Growth

As FedEx rivals jumped in—UPS, DHL, Emery, Airborne, Purolator, the U.S. Postal Service, and fleets of lesser-known express air carriers—three trends began that continue to benefit the astute real estate developer. First, freight forwarders and other transportation companies added expertise and repositioned themselves as third-party logistics providers, known as 3PLs.

Actually, these hybrids date back to the 1930s, when Sears, Roebuck & Company, then the nation's biggest retailer, signed a contract with a third-party firm to handle its logistics. It was not until 1980, however, when transportation was deregulated, that the practice of outsourcing to 3PLs gained widespread acceptance. Freedom from governmental price approval gave both transportation vendors and logistical service providers great flexibility and incentives to be creative. At that time, Leaseway Transportation Corporation was the nation's biggest provider of contract logistics, and Sears was still pioneering. A Leaseway subsidiary, Signal Delivery Services, Inc., was generating $250 million a year in revenues by providing trucking, home delivery, cross-docking, and warehouse services for Whirlpool

- *Packaging and labeling:* Preparing products for shipment.
- *Pick-and-pack:* Custom fulfillment of orders composed of more than one component.
- *Subdistribution:* Allocating specific quantities to different locations or customers.
- *Import and export customs brokerage clearances:* Coordinating documentation and clearing shipments through U.S. Customs and the U.S. Department of Agriculture. Meeting various security requirements.
- *Reverse logistics:* Handling transportation for returned merchandise.
- *Small package air cargo:* Coordinating courier and express shipments.
- *Airfreight:* Negotiating spot, contract rates, and allocations and consolidations for loose, palletized, and containerized cargo including outsized freight. Selecting carriers, tracking and tracing, pickup, and delivery/recovery.
- *Motor freight:* Selecting, rate negotiating, and booking all forms and modes of ground transportation based on distances and deadlines.
- *Ocean:* Rate negotiating, booking.
- *Railroad:* Pricing and booking railcars and piggybacking systems; arranging bulk, liquid, and dry commodities movements.
- *Freight forwarding:* Planning, booking, and coordinating shipper-to-consignee moves using one or more transportation vendors and modes. (Example: a through-shipment from Minneapolis to Nairobi.)
- *Vendor management:* Selecting and coordinating with all of a client's transportation, warehousing, and logistics vendors.
- *Loss control:* Working with insurance companies, adjusters, brokers, security consultants, and law enforcement officials on loss recovery.

These logistics services and more are offered in various combinations by different 3PLs in multiuser warehouses and distribution centers or in the customer's own facility using the provider's own labor and expertise. Larry Georgen of AIT Worldwide says that 3PLs value the real estate professional "with demonstrated expertise in freight. Someone who can look at an existing building in, say, St. Louis and determine whether it is suitable for a cross-dock operation or a pick-and-pack operation and whether it meets the necessary logistics criteria that make it a candidate for us or our customers."[3]

AIT's clients include multinationals like Nestlé, Kellogg Company, and Kraft Foods. These giants might occupy a full building owned by the 3PL as part of their logistics handling contract, rather than leasing or owning a facility that would commit their capital and possibly put it at risk. Other large, leading-edge 3PLs like Menlo Logistics and Exel also serve Fortune 100 companies, but they tend to have existing relationships with real estate providers. Still, there remains a vast pool of smaller but expanding, cost-conscious, efficiency-driven manufacturers and distributors who could be connecting with second-tier, emerging 3PLs.

The real estate developer or broker who has a clear focus on the potential property needs of these shippers and logistics concerns—and who has the expertise to meet them—will have the upper hand over competitors.

Notes

1. Interview with Larry Georgen, AIT Worldwide Logistics, July 9, 2002.

2. Interview with John Spychalski, Pennsylvania State University, May 15, 2002.

3. Interview with Larry Georgen.

Corporation, which manufactured 75 percent of the appliances Sears sold under its Kenmore brand name. Signal delivered Kenmore products to Sears retail stores and hauled inbound parts and components to Whirlpool's five U.S. plants to be manufactured into more appliances.

With deregulation came intense competition among hundreds of 3PLs eager to sign up corporate manufacturing and distribution customers. Industrial real estate developers hit a bonanza as 3PLs invested in facilities and other hard assets to create the capacity needed to physically handle the outsourced logistical requirements of the companies they were courting. In 1991, a watershed event occurred when Sears signed Menlo Logistics as its 3PL contractor; two years later,

Whirlpool gave its account to Ryder Logistics. By then, fierce pricing competition and an ever increasing 3PL portfolio of logistical services—traditionally performed in house by shippers—created a mini–gold rush for customers hungry to outsource such activities as packing, labeling, subdistribution, handling returned merchandise, and more.

By outsourcing these distribution functions, companies were able to reduce their own operating and overhead costs and obtain outside professional assistance in managing their own supply chain. At the same time, third-party logistics providers were assured of a continual cash flow from a client under contract. They thus had more responsibility and clout with which to negotiate better rates and delivery schedules from airlines, trucking companies, and ocean shippers. Those 3PLs with global reach also added substantial value as their clients expanded internationally. These collaborations, coupled with ongoing advances in new information technologies, have produced efficiencies and competitive advantages that companies previously could not generate on their own.

For real estate professionals well versed in logistics and supply chain management, 3PLs can be a solid new business prospect. Their property needs range from new construction—headquarters facilities customized to provide a spectrum of services and regional/branch facilities—to transforming and tailoring existing buildings and leasing new or additional space to accommodate growth. Some 3PLs are building or leasing facilities to serve a single large client. Just as the 3PL cements its relationship with its manufacturer/shipper customer by handling more of the logistical services, a developer that knows the specialized needs of a 3PL or even a direct shipper can build a similar relationship by providing a variety of real estate services.

America's premier manufacturers outsource some or all of their logistics to 3PLs. There are plenty of development, leasing, and redevelopment opportunities for real estate professionals who are able to think long-term. Some 75 percent of major U.S. manufacturing companies surveyed in 2001 by the accounting firm Ernst & Young LLP reported that they either use or intend to work with contract logistics providers. Eighty-six percent of those that have outsourced to 3PLs said they were satisfied.

Expedited Air Service

The success of FedEx and the air express industry holds even greater potential for the industrial property specialist. Beginning in the late 1980s, all airlines and, by the mid-1990s, truck lines began selling expedited services, again at a premium.

Airlines ranging from passenger carriers with belly capacity and freighter aircraft such as Lufthansa or Korean Airlines to all-cargo airlines like BAX Global or Cargolux, are now selling premium, express, time-sensitive, and airfreight services. Like FedEx, they also include a money-back guarantee. At the same time, the express operators such as FedEx, UPS, and DHL are buying larger freighter aircraft, adding international routes, and aggressively targeting the so-called heavyweight freight market—shipments of 100 pounds (45 kilograms) or more. These are

shipments that traditionally were carried in the belly compartments of passenger airlines or on long-range 747 freighter aircraft.

The importance to real estate developers? These express airlines that traditionally had one giant on-airport sorting center—usually in their hub city—now have sizable cargo receiving and handling centers or even secondary sorting centers in major U.S. and foreign cities. Normally, they are major tenants in new or existing facilities, but occasionally they occupy 100 percent of an on-tarmac facility. Again, they are multinational operators with multiple property needs and opportunities.

Express Trucking

A trend that gained prominence in the late 1990s, and is rapidly growing today, is express or expedited trucking of regional less-than-truckload (LTL) shipments with next- and second-day delivery. This transport mode sells speed at premium rates and is aimed at the shipper or consignee using a just-in-time (JIT) or fast-cycle time (FCT) inventory model to replenish parts or stock. In 1998, FedEx quietly moved into expedited trucking when it acquired Caliber Systems, an Akron, Ohio, transportation holding company that owned RPS (formerly Roadway Package Systems), and rebranded it as FedEx Ground. Caliber owned Roberts Express, which became FedEx Custom Critical. Viking Freight, a San Jose, California–based regional LTL truck line, was later rebranded as FedEx Freight.

To understand the importance and profit potential of the expedited trucking market to the logistics industry, the visionary commercial real estate developer needs only to consider FedEx's 2001 acquisition of the 17,000-employee American Freightways, also rebranded as FedEx Freight. This Memphis-based transportation Goliath now offers shippers and consignees a portfolio of time-definite expedited air and ground services domestically and globally.

There are approximately 100 LTL motor carriers in the U.S. offering expedited trucking service, according to Pete Robinson, senior director of corporate communications, Jevic Transportation Inc.[2] Expedited trucking is being embraced by supply chain managers because it reduces costs without sacrificing time on shipments—moving up to 1,000 miles (1,609 kilometers) overnight or even second day. By using two drivers—one drives, one sleeps—and operating virtually nonstop, shippers can cover one-third of the nation in approximately the same time it takes to move a shipment by air, door-to-door, and at a cost savings of 30 to 50 percent. Road transportation experts estimate there are "hundreds" of national and regional LTL express truckers—including five to ten smaller operators in every metropolitan area—who specialize in high-speed service on popular routes. Express trucking can cut freight costs in half: next-day air service is about $1 a pound or half kilogram, while goods can move by expedited trucking at about 40 to 50 cents a pound or half kilogram.

The impact of expedited trucking on the real estate professional can be measured in several ways. Manufacturers will likely consolidate smaller warehousing facilities into large regional distribution centers—for example, in Salt Lake City; Columbus, Ohio; and Washington, D.C./northern Virginia—and service customers in those regions with overnight or express trucking. The facilities will be cross-dock configured so goods arriving from the manufacturer can be immediately unloaded, sorted, and then loaded again onto trucks destined for customer warehousing or retailer shelves.

Depending on the characteristics of the manufactured goods and channels, existing buildings could be converted into smaller regional subdistribution facilities. Other opportunities that expedited trucking generates for real estate professionals include reconfiguring existing buildings into truck terminals, repositioning them into other buildings, and, of course, selling or re-leasing them to smaller companies.

The impact of express trucking on new construction will likely be reflected in the architectural and exterior structural design, interior layout, construction materials, and location of warehouses and distribution centers. Developers might agree to expand the number of truck docks offered. Or an infill location with proximity to highways and transportation hubs could be preferable to a remote locale. In managing the supply chain strategy, options and solutions are seemingly endless.

Real estate developers should not make the mistake that a regional trucking company would need only "sheds" and smaller terminals. Jevic Transportation, Inc., has ten facilities nationwide, including a 100,000-square-foot (9,290-square-meter) building with 100-plus loading doors and truck bays adjacent to its headquarters. The other nine are approximately the same size but are not cookie-cutter replicas of the

Philadelphia building. Exterior design and interior configuration decisions are driven by local factors, traffic patterns, and regulatory constraints, as well as freight flows and proximity to other transport modes.

When asked what he expects from a real estate professional, a senior LTL trucking company executive did not mince words. "We look for someone who understands the region, zoning, freight transportation flows, and the history of the area. For someone who asks the right questions, like 'How many (loading) doors do you need?' not 'How many square feet are you looking for?' For someone who asks 'How many levels of racking do you need? Will trailers be parked overnight? Do you think a 130-foot (40-meter) -long truck court will be large enough?'"

E-commerce

"Clicks, not bricks" was the marketing mantra that fueled the dot-com mania of the late 1990s, promising to revolutionize retailing and presenting a bright scenario for industrial property developers, owners, and brokers. Log on to the Internet, browse, point, click to order, key in a credit card number, and virtually anything—from a book to a bicycle to five bags of groceries—would be delivered to your doorstep in 24 to 72 hours.

Business-to-business (B2B) marketing, where sales of supplies, solvents, and software were expedited by online ordering and air or motor carrier ful-

The facilities needs of express trucking companies go beyond standard warehouses and typically require greater attention to loading facilities as well as the interior layout.

fillment, was suddenly dwarfed by a land rush to direct-to-consumer selling. Seemingly overnight, new e-commerce retailers sprang up on the Internet, while established marketers and catalog companies added dot-com channels. Newly minted entrepreneurs with bright ideas and eye-catching domain names were being funded by venture capitalists or IPOs and were in business selling everything imaginable—particularly time-sensitive, high-value merchandise. The press heralded the visionaries and predicted doom and demise for Old Economy stalwarts. The new Internet-enabled merchants knew speed would be critical to customer satisfaction. It would require shortened supply chains and lightning-fast logistics.

Meanwhile, there was fast-growing demand on industrial real estate providers to create new bricks and mortar. These distribution centers were designed, configured, constructed, and equipped with a single goal in mind: swift, seamless, door-to-door throughput from shipper to customer, whether the consumer was a business or a household. Goods were now bar coded and tracked—often in real time—and at every step of the way. By 1999, most airlines, truck lines, freight forwarders, 3PLs, shippers, and consignees were clocking their own and each other's performance down to the minute. The business model developed by UPS—

knowing exactly how long it takes to deliver a shipment or an entire route and holding drivers accountable to these benchmarks—was adopted or attempted by e-tailers and the supply chain participants feeding this heavily touted distribution channel.

Indeed, retailing through the Internet was delivering convenience and choice to those consumers who had little time to shop or lacked the energy needed to fight traffic and crowds. The logistics and real estate providers delivered the transportation and infrastructure needed and were building more, yet the excesses of e-commerce abruptly imploded around April 2000. A marketing channel appeared to vanish amid market meltdown of overvalued technology stocks, the collapse of money-losing dot-coms, and a retreat by battered venture capitalists. In 12 months, 400 of the estimated 500 Internet "stores" went out of business. The more agile industrial property owners were able to re-lease dedicated distribution and fulfillment centers, and buildings in blueprint stages were shelved or scrapped. At least in the short term, consumer e-commerce became a metaphor for struggle—or outright failure.

Of course, the astute real estate professional should not write off future opportunities from online selling. Online retailing during the 2002 holiday season rose in the United States between 25 and 40 percent, depending on the forecast. That was near the growth rate of the year before and stood in sharp contrast with the broad-based sales weakness of traditional retailers that same year.

Research from New York–based eMarketer, a top source of statistics and trend data on the Internet and adviser to Fortune 1000 companies, put worldwide B2B e-commerce sales at $823.4 billion at the end of 2002. It also predicted that strong growth in Internet-based trading would continue, hitting the $2.4 trillion mark in 2004.[3]

When dealing with companies that sell via the Internet or other electronic means, real estate professionals must invest the time to develop a deeper understanding of their property needs and chart their industrial space requirements. When evaluating potential customers, selectivity is obviously paramount. An example of a dot-com that understands the important synergy between Internet retailing, logistics, and real estate—and moved decisively to capitalize on opportunities few others have spotted—is Overstock.com in Salt Lake City. Founded in 1999, it offers an alternative to retail liquidators, buying the merchandise inventories of other traditional and Web retailers and reselling them at 50 to 70 percent off at www.Overstock.com. Its marketing advantage is quick delivery. "We guarantee to ship the merchandise within 24 hours for a flat $2.95," says Rich Paongo, investor relations director. The backbone of Overstock.com's operation is a 220,000-square-foot (20,439-square-meter) warehouse and distribution center leased from a developer and located 15 minutes from Salt Lake City's airport. Some 7,000 different products—cameras, jewelry, computers, books, and CDs—are stored and shipped via FedEx, UPS, and other expedited carriers.[4]

With revenues up 40 percent in 2002, including heavy sales during the fourth-quarter Christmas season, Overstock.com is continually reevaluating its warehousing and distribution center capacity. In its time-sensitive, high-value, air cargo and expedited trucking environment, logistics and real estate decisions are not afterthoughts but rather essential elements of its planning and marketing strategy. In fact, the company, which had a successful IPO in the dismal May 2002 market, is generating additional revenues by acting as a consignment marketer for other retailers. Overstock.com will list their inventory on its Web site, process the order, and take the credit-card payment, but the participating retailer must make the promise to Overstock's customer of fast delivery.

The impact of the e-commerce evolution on warehousing and distribution has other implications for industrial property providers. There has already been a significant shift from high-rent shopping centers, malls, and department stores to high-volume, stand-alone megawarehouse retailing. This is where ordering and inventory management must maintain a critical balance: enough goods on the selling floor to meet shopper demands but minimal to zero storeroom stock to maximize sales-per-square foot. Internet retailing by traditional bricks-and-mortar merchants requires an even more disciplined inventory ordering to maximize return on assets. It also requires a greater need for speed in shipping and delivery.

The trends are thus toward less "supply chain" real estate required per unit of economic activity, and toward more efficient, less expensive industrial space. There will be a greater demand for expedited pass-through—what AMB Property Corporation calls High-Throughput Distribution (HTD®) centers—in key hub or gateway cities for both business-to-business and business-to-consumer shippers and consignees serving both the domestic and international markets. (An online retailer's customer today can be in Singapore or Savannah.) The demand will also grow for fulfillment centers in locations with low land and labor costs. Ideally, such locations will have favorable local and state zoning and tax environments, with good proximity to hub and gateway cities that have access to fast transportation.

Historically, industrial space was concentrated in manufacturing centers—cities like Akron, Ohio; Pittsburgh; and St. Louis, to name just a few. Today, it is concentrated in distribution markets, primarily six to eight U.S. cities with proximity to at least two and ideally four transportation modes. The leaders are Los Angeles/Long Beach, Chicago, New York/northern New Jersey, San Francisco Bay Area, Dallas/Fort Worth, Atlanta, Miami, and Seattle. Of the 53 major domestic markets typically tracked by institutional investors, the distribution requirements of the top six markets result in a significant density of industrial real estate: 44 percent higher on a per capita basis than the remaining 47 markets tracked. These distribution cities and their surrounding submarkets should clearly be on the property professional's radar.

With Internet retailing still a growing sales channel at the end of the supply chain, with its promise of fast fulfillment and shipping, inventory will never be eliminated as it has with some manufacturers. But it can be moved at a rapid pace.

Online retailing has huge advantages over storefront or even catalog selling, but can online retailers fulfill orders in a reasonable time and at a realistic cost? Amazon.com, the premier and possibly the prototype dot-com retailer, is expanding internationally, but its growth does not depend on giving customers the best discounts on best-sellers or electronics. Convenience is the prime reason book buyers and others shop at Amazon, and that demand for convenience is driven by their expectations of fast delivery.

Convenience and instant gratification both depend on swift order fulfillment. Diego Piacentini, Amazon's senior vice president for worldwide retailing and marketing, admits that the e-commerce company's decision to enter a particular international market is based not just on the size of the country's existing customer base but also on the efficiency of the local supply chain. Amazon tracks a metric that real estate professionals must understand and help their logistics clients to manage: cost of fulfillment as a percentage of sales. Amazon's goal is single-digit efficiency, which it first achieved in the fourth quarter of 2001.[5]

Developers of e-commerce fulfillment and distribution centers for sophisticated online retailers, either in the United States or overseas, must realize that fulfillment efficiency will be defined, measured, analyzed, improved, and controlled—constantly. The building's design, construction, configuration, costs, technology, maintenance, safety, and security all impact efficiency. For instance, Amazon's inventory-record accuracy—having the product in its right location within the facility—can affect annual inventory turns, a key efficiency barometer. Being sensitive to these logistical metrics and helping clients and tenants improve them can help the real estate professional cement a relationship.

Still, the closely watched costs of fulfillment as a percentage of sales may include other logistical considerations such as location and proximity to transportation vendors. Except in the case of a build-to-suit, landlords must make sure that new facility locations are consistent with a variety of supply chain benchmarks and are not so client-centric that they cannot be re-leased. For example, placing a major fulfillment/distribution center in a remote location to save building and land costs could become an albatross for the owner who might later lose the tenant and have to find another one who has the same needs.

Debut of the 4PL or Lead Logistics Provider (LLP)

An emerging trend that has remained largely off the radar screen to those outside the logistics industry is the creation of a new consulting function loosely described as a logistical "supermanager." The thesis, advanced by logistics consultants, is that many manufacturers and distributors have such intricate supply chains, and the information technology functions are so critical and complex, that a separate umbrella company is needed as a strategic and tactical megacoordinator. This entity would orchestrate the diverse activities outsourced to—and provided by—the contracted 3PL, different transportation modes, and specific vendors along with any warehousing or logistical functions that remain in house.

While there is truth to the rationale and growing support for this idea among educators, chief logistics officers, and, surprisingly, some of the biggest 3PLs, there is disagreement over who should be what is called the "lead logistics provider." (Some 3PLs use this term to describe a service they offer along with transportation management and reverse logistics.) Muddying the waters and further fracturing the debate was the shrewd marketing decision by Andersen Consulting, subsequently renamed Accenture, to coin and trademark the term 4PL.

If this trend gains momentum, it could have a positive impact for the industrial property developer and broker. Usually (but not always), logistics consultants assist manufacturers, shippers, and distributors in designing and configuring the supply chain, and then 3PLs implement and execute the plan. Logistics consulting firms often have input and influence over the configuration, number, and types of warehousing and distribution facilities needed. Hence, they can be an important contact for the industrial property developer with an understanding of logistics. On the other hand, consulting firms can also have their agendas, pet products, and services. Developers and landlords should request the opportunity to evaluate a logistics consultant's facility recommendations to determine whether they are realistic from design and construction cost-benefit viewpoints, and to verify that there are no hidden project agendas.

On the other hand, the continuing trend toward outsourcing logistics functions to 3PLs or other providers means that the consulting firms acting as 4PLs may not significantly influence real estate decisions after all. Large, multifactory, multinational manufacturers want to get large asset/liability concentrations off their balance sheets, reduce their labor costs, and, most important, get service expertise that is impossible or impractical for them to obtain in house. Cultivating a relationship with the consultant could well alienate a manufacturer's 3PL provider that does, indeed, influence or make real estate decisions. The 3PL also sells consulting services and helps design the front-end supply chain strategy, thus acting as a 4PL.

The industrial property developer's vendor/partner relationship with the 3PL would therefore seem to be more productive. The 3PL's ongoing core competencies remain more visible to the customer long after the logistics consultant has presented its recommendations and collected its project fee. The global 3PL can also point to a substantial track record of assembling end-to-end solutions for shippers, and thus seems to have a stronger argument for establishing itself as the lead logistics provider. There is no right or wrong way to proceed. The astute real estate professional must evaluate each potential business opportunity individually and determine which entity actually controls and manages the crucial customer-shipper relationship.

This turf war will only heat up in the future, and developers should monitor it. Professor John H. Langley, Dove Distinguished Professor of Logistics at the University of Tennessee, sees three emerging competencies that will eventually determine which entity becomes the logistics supermanager. These three competencies are: managing more than one 3PL; managing knowledge by processing, using, and distributing information; and managing the rapid and continual changes in information technology systems themselves. The complexity of IT will become even more of an issue as e-commerce and the e-economy get a deeper, stronger foothold and become greater forces in shaping the future of logistics. Whether some logistics providers or consultants will fully master these three competencies and vault into the role of lead logistics provider is anyone's guess at this juncture. But one thing is certain: to get in the game and win, real estate professionals must monitor the evolution of this debate.[6]

Advice and Strategies for Capitalizing on Logistics Trends

Manufacturers and marketers are taking new routes to efficiency through smarter supply chain management and instantaneous access to information. They are stripping excess inventory out of their distribution systems and searching for costs savings in every operational area. Technology is a big force in streamlining the supply chain. Industry-specific resource planning programs can scan the global enterprise and accurately forecast inventory needs, purchasing and ordering patterns, and seasonal deviations affecting specific Stock Keeping Units (SKUs), whether in Singapore or Dallas. Obviously, technology can let shippers track the exact whereabouts of a single SKU—anywhere, anytime.

Globalization has relandscaped business, but even with the most complex supply chains, real estate is playing a more important role in the logistics process. The need for speed is influencing the size, shape, location, and demand for industrial buildings; astutely designed facilities can speed the flow of goods by saving steps and critical minutes. The reality, however, is that corporate logistics directors, known in many companies as chief logistics officers (CLOs), typically are not acutely focused on such property requirements as the size of truck courts at a distribution center or even facility rental rates and freeway congestion. They have outsourced these concerns, along with a broad array of transportation and logistics activities, to 3PLs.

In the future, it will be more important than ever for real estate professionals to nurture partnerships with players in the supply chain process if they want to take full advantage of potential development opportunities.

Real Estate Development at Dallas/Fort Worth International Airport

John T. Meyer

The world's airports would appear to be a profit paradise for the real estate developer who wants to cash in on growth in U.S and international air cargo tonnage. But this particular niche market intersection of real estate and logistics can be perilous for novices. There are supply constraints, political realities, and administrative and bureaucratic barriers that are invisible, costly, and frustrating. The economics and restrictions of developing on-airport facilities—often in the form of ground leases from governmental entities —are substantial and little understood, regardless of how experienced a builder/ developer/owner may be in working with municipalities.

Indeed, for the commercial property developer, big airports can be seductive. A row of 747 freighters discharging cargo into sleek new buildings is visually exciting. The choreography of a smooth, well-orchestrated distribution of goods is compelling. Yet the potential pitfalls and the business challenges include everything from traffic snarls on feeder highways to the fierce competition for cargo by the newly energized, expedited trucking industry, and to the consolidation, financial woes, and excess capacity plaguing U.S. and international airlines.

In mid-2003, air cargo rates—the per-kilo prices shippers pay to transport goods on jet freighters and in the bellies of passenger planes—stood at a 22-year low on transpacific and transatlantic trade lanes. This type of economic reality, coupled with the velocity of freight throughput and the frequency of aircraft operations and trucking operations, has a major impact on the financial performance of an on-airport freight distribution facility. There is much more at issue with airport facilities than a similar building designed for surface transport.

Against this backdrop, real estate investors willing to educate themselves about

the complex air transportation industry can still be justifiably bullish on the long-term prospects of on-tarmac air cargo buildings at major U.S. and international airports. The most strategically located airports have good proximity to U.S. metropolitan markets and are within jumbo freighter range of international markets with cost-efficient production and assembly capabilities and growing consumer economies.

The Dallas/Fort Worth International Airport Example

A prime example of strategic location is the Dallas/Fort Worth International Airport (DFW), which occupies an 18,000-acre (7,284-hectare) landmass, roughly the size of the island of Manhattan, halfway between Dallas and Fort Worth, Texas. The combined Dallas/Fort Worth metroplex is the single largest market in the Lone Star State. DFW has dozens of other attributes that make it appealing to airlines, shippers, and real estate developers, not to mention passengers. It is located in the center of the nation. For international exporters and importers, DFW is also a prime gateway to the fast-growing Central and South American economies, with their muscular manufacturing base and growing consumer middle classes. New long-range jets can reach Asia, Europe, and the U.K. with nonstop flights.

DFW ranks third in the United States in total aircraft operations, sixth in the world for passenger flights, and 21st in the world for cargo operations, just behind Newark and just ahead of Atlanta and San Francisco. But its greatest allure for property professionals is that one-half of the airport property is undeveloped, with 160 acres (64.7 hectares) earmarked for future air cargo buildings. DFW's property planning department and staff are exceptionally pro-business and familiar with large cargo complexes. A would-be developer there would not be considered a pioneer; there are pre-

cedents and expertise in place. The airport has more than 2.6 million square feet (241,540 square meters) of cargo facilities total. There are three main on-airport freight areas, among which 11 buildings are spread. A fourth area, to accommodate future growth, is in the planning stage.

The tenant mix in the existing structures illustrates the opportunities for astute property development. American Airlines, DFW's flagship carrier, has a 180,000-square-foot (16,722-square-meter) cargo warehouse plus 20,000 feet (6,096 meters) of offices. But American is a passenger airline, a belly-freight operator, with no jet freighters. Its biggest aircraft are 777s, which have a large cargo hold, but the majority of its flight operations are narrow-body aircraft and mid- to wide-body 767s. Hence, the cargo building at its corporate headquarters hub airport is designed more for sorting, connecting, and transshipping. It is a high-frequency operation for high-value goods and perishables rather than for high volumes of oversized freight.

Delta Air Lines, headquartered in Atlanta and an American Airlines rival for South American trade, has its own 116,000-square-foot (10,766-square-meter) facility at DFW, plus a separate mail-handling building. Like American, it has no pure freighters and is largely a narrow-bodied belly-freight operator out of DFW, with some 767 flights flying domestic routes. Like all passenger airlines with belly operations, Delta ranks cargo as its second, albeit highly important, priority after passengers.

This preponderance of narrow-bodied planes is an influencing factor from a facilities standpoint. Freight that moves in the bellies of narrow-body aircraft is loose, neither palletized nor containerized. Unitized cargo, on the other hand, moves on wide-body jets, defined as having at least two passenger aisles. Hence, the configuration of the aircraft and the volume and type of freight passing through them dictate, to a large extent, the design of an airfreight building.

Airline ownership of an airfreight facility is rare at DFW and other airports. Asset-intensive companies such as airlines do not want to tie up their capital in real estate when those funds could be put to use buying new-generation aircraft. Moreover, buildings could become obsolete as new aircraft and innovative loading and unloading systems emerge. Most carriers prefer to lease air facilities to give themselves more flexibility and adaptability within their network of hubs. This arrangement can be attractive from the owner/developer's standpoint, but there is also a fundamental restriction to developing on airport land: Airports will lease, but not sell, ground underneath the facility, and ground lease terms vary for a number of reasons. At the end of the lease, ownership of the facility reverts to the airport, and the owner relinquishes the asset.

As a result, most of the existing air cargo complexes and all of the future facilities at DFW are on 40-year ground leases. That is the length of time the airport can execute a lease with a developer without going to the Dallas and Fort Worth city councils, which combined have 11 members on the DFW Airport Board of Directors. Developers entering this niche will find that lease terms and municipal government approval procedures vary widely among airports.

Air Cargo Facility Design Trends

At DFW, the trend in developing air cargo facilities is toward larger, high-throughput, high-clear-height, column-free distribution centers, not warehouses. The dynamics of the airport's cargo operations influence building design and freight flow. DFW, with its central U.S. location, is fast becoming an airport of choice for the largest foreign airlines operating 747-400 freighters, the workhorses of the air cargo industry. Lufthansa, Singapore Airlines, Korean Airlines, China Airlines, Evergreen Airlines, EVA Air,

At Dallas/Fort Worth International Airport, the trend is toward high-throughput distribution centers designed for rapid freight flow rather than storage. AMB's International Air Cargo Centre I features more than 205,000 square feet (19,044 square meters) of column-free space and 50 truck doors.

Courtesy AMB Property Corporation

and Caribbean Transport Services, a FedEx subsidiary, operate freighter aircraft capable of carrying up to 225,000 pounds (102,060 kilograms) of freight per flight. Their turnaround time—parking, unloading, loading, and takeoff—greatly depends on efficient building design and the skill of the cargo ground handlers.

DFW is also a large base for what are called "integrators"—FedEx, UPS, Airborne Airfreight, and others. The bulk of their revenues are generated by overnight small packages weighing up to 70 pounds (32 kilograms). Increasingly, integrators are soliciting heavyweight freight for international destinations and competing with the combination passenger-cargo airlines and all cargo carriers. Their cargo buildings must be on-tarmac and designed for high-speed freight handling. UPS, which has a regional hub at DFW, clocks its aircraft and delivery truck loading and unloading operations to the minute. UPS has minimum time standards for every step along the supply chain. Time counts in this type of business, and it is counted.

AMB Property Corporation developed the High-Throughput Distribution (HTD®) business model and introduced it at Dallas/Fort Worth International Airport. The model is being replicated at other U.S. airports such as Bush Intercontinental Airport Houston and Portland (Oregon) International

Airport and is tailored to local airport economics, airline cargo operations, and freight flows. AMB designed, built, and financed an HTD facility—International Air Cargo-Centre I at DFW—that has become an industry standard for the rapid passage of air commerce shipments. The concrete tilt-up building has 205,000 square feet (19,044 square meters) of column-free floor space, a 37-foot (11.2-meter) clear-height ceiling to accommodate elevated transport vehicle (ETV) freight-handling systems, four airside doors, and 50 truck doors. It was immediately leased to Worldwide Flight Services, a ground-handling company that has cargo handling contracts with blue-chip freighter operators such as China Airlines, Lufthansa German Airlines, Korean Air Lines, and Singapore Airlines. A second building, Air CargoCentre II, was built 12 months later and subsequently leased to Integrated Airline Services, a ground-handling company for the United States Postal Service. The USPS occupies the entire second building. Doug Bryan, manager of DFW's real property planning and development, says that air cargo facilities are typically leased to a ground handler rather than to an airline because airlines want to write one monthly check for their total cargo operations including the facility space, ground-handling labor, utilities, maintenance, and other services.[1]

continued on next page

These two on-tarmac, high-speed centers in DFW's West Cargo Area cover 430,000 square feet (39,947 square meters). The long, narrow facilities, longer than two football fields end-to-end, can unload eight 747 freighters and load 94 trucks simultaneously. Jeff Fegan, executive director of DFW International Airport, says that "these new pass-through cargo facilities will help us attract new airlines and allow existing airlines operating at DFW to expand their routes."[2]

The Challenges

Working with an airport management company can be daunting regardless of the city. In general, property developers targeting airport-related real estate will work directly with the airport property or real estate departments. Navigating DFW's internal management and administrative byways is considerably easier than at many other airports. Doug Bryan worked in the private sector for Mobil Oil Land Development before joining the airport staff. He has good advice for his former developer colleagues on the realities and frustrations of working in this marketplace. As he explains it, private developers are used to working with fee-simple land on which they can obtain a mortgage, construct a building, and sell it at the end of the investment period. But with on-airport development, the airport leases the land under the new facility, which reverts to the airport at the end of the ground lease period.

Financially structuring an on-airport air cargo center thus requires a different pro-forma approach and base assumptions than an off-airport fee-simple development or acquisition. At DFW, for instance, the facility has a 40-year life with no residual value at the end of the ground lease, because the building ownership automatically transfers to the airport. The developer-owner must earn all profits during the term of the lease. Build-to-suit developers have different pro formas but scant to zero op-

portunities to build on-airport facilities, since airlines are reluctant to buy buildings and assume long-term ground leases as balance sheet liabilities.

Most private developers are surprised by the entitlement process required to construct a facility on an airport. On-airport projects can take anywhere from one to two years before the approval rights are granted to construct a facility. Often a new project is announced in an RFP, whereby a number of private developers are invited to compete for the right to develop the project. According to Bryan, "No matter how hard the airport staff works, they work for a public entity, which traditionally does not act as fast as private industry. The reason public entities are slow is because they would rather take their time and not make a mistake. We're the landlord, and if we jump on a quick opportunity that doesn't work out, we have to live with a failure for 40 years." He contends that Dallas/Fort Worth airport's management moves faster than most airports, a prime reason why DFW is attracting more domestic and international airlines.

The fact that market data on the industrial property sector do not apply to air cargo facilities also makes the development process riskier. Traditional benchmarks and guidelines on occupancy, vacancy rates, and lease rates are meaningless, Bryan emphasizes. "The entire warehouse market can have a 30 percent vacancy factor, as an illustration, but air cargo facilities may only have a 2 percent vacancy, the latter percentage being just as significant because air cargo facilities have airfield access, which is highly prized. As a private developer, airfield access is not something you can buy. You either have it or you don't, and the difference between on-airfield and off-airport is night and day."

On-Airport Advantages

The importance and marketability of having an airfreight distribution center on-airport

versus off-airport can be measured in many ways. A location at an off-airport site costs a tenant time and money. An airline with an off-airport freight-handling warehouse must have flatbed truck vehicles available for draying pallets and containers, and the trucks must be licensed to operate on public streets. In many cities, highways and thoroughfares with airport access are slowed by congested traffic. In addition, shippers using off-airport facilities for staging cargo have shorter closeouts—the time frame within which an airline will accept freight for a particular flight. An on-airfield carrier can accept freight later because it can be staged or consolidated with other shipments located 20 feet (6 meters) from the aircraft, not five to six miles (8 to 9.6 kilometers) away.

Manufacturers and shippers of time-sensitive, high-value goods with closer proximity to an airport overnight courier also have a competitive edge. "Being eight to 10 miles closer to an airport, the world's largest distributor of aviation parts, which moves 70 percent of its products by UPS, can keep its order desk open 20 minutes longer than its competitors and still have the shipment to their customer the next morning," Bryan notes. "When you have a critical part for, say, an aircraft brake mechanism, nobody is concerned over an $8 or $12 shipping cost. The customer is concerned with getting the part the next day and getting its airplane back in the air."

There are distinct advantages for industrial developer/owners who are able to build and lease successfully on-tarmac at major airports, says Bryan. While capital and knowledge barriers to entry are high, "once you learn how to do an on-airfield facility—how the numbers work, how the physical facility itself works, and, most importantly, how the air cargo sector within aviation works—a developer can make significant money by replicating that formula."[3]

Establishing a Partnership with the Airport Management Team

The goal of a developer/owner seeking a presence in this specialized marketplace is to work toward establishing a partnership with the different airport management teams. But winning their confidence is a challenge. Airports and their property department managers have strict criteria in considering an on-airfield air cargo center development and the developer/owner. They will only entertain proposals from the most reputable and financially sound companies with sterling reputations in prior transactions.

A municipally owned, managed, and operated airport is one of the most visible governmental entities in any city, particularly in large metropolitan markets. It is constantly under the microscope, covered relentlessly by the press, environmentalists, community groups, governmental watchdogs, and various other advocates. As a major revenue source for the city treasury, it can ill afford to enter into a 40-year lease with a developer who might experience financial difficulties. Airports are quite leery of working with owners who, several years after construction, might flip the airfreight facility to a buyer with neither adequate financial depth nor sufficient understanding of the airfreight community. This is the main reason that ground leases all have contractual clauses restricting assignability.

Property developers considering this market should expect rigorous scrutiny. "The airport will do the deepest possible due diligence on any developer-investor," says Bryan, who reports to the director of airport real estate. "The DFW Airport staff has no authority to enter into a ground lease agreement with any outsider. Every lease agreement must be approved by the airport board of directors. Before staff will take anything to the board, they want to make sure they can answer every potential question directors will ask."[4]

Developers are grilled on past successes, failures, major litigation, their ability to finance, and their preleasing status. A lender's due diligence of a developer pales by comparison with the exhaustive analysis, questioning, and documentation required by airport staff. "The developer does not make the presentation to the airport board; the staff does," explains Bryan. "The absolute last thing an airport staff wants is to be embarrassed before the airport board by not being able to answer a director's question."

Airport staff will pay particularly close attention to the facility design and site plan submitted by a potential developer. Unlike some build-to-suit project buyers or managers, who may not have much experience in real estate or logistics, airport property executives such as the DFW team know every aspect of both disciplines. As Bryan puts it, "A developer may have great confidence based on its experience in off-airport projects, but we don't want them to build something that is functionally obsolete. [Even if] a developer comes to us with a great design, solid financing, and a construction plan, if it's not 100 percent functional for their clients and the airlines, we wind up with limited land occupied by a structure that is not generating revenue for the airport. In our business, an airport doesn't ever want to build a ghost town."

There is an even deeper reason that airports are extremely selective in choosing industrial real estate developers who may be strangers to airfreight logistics. Airports generate rental income from ground leases underneath airfreight facilities, but the revenue base is also boosted by landing fees, passenger facility fees, parking and concession income, and other airport-related activities. Hence, an airport's financial objective is to grow its core business by expanding existing airline operations and attracting new carriers that, in turn, will increase passenger and freight volume. As a result, any new proposed air cargo building must meet two goals: it must produce

ground lease rent and also appeal, ideally, to an airline that might want to establish flight operations at that airport.

Most airport real estate departments will not work directly with commercial real estate brokers. DFW's real estate staff will refer calls to the building's owner/leaseholder. Airports also do not usually pay real estate broker commissions, because they do not directly lease facility space.

Bryan says that developers unfamiliar with air logistics often labor under common misconceptions. "Their first mistake is thinking an airport has to work with them, that this public entity was created to help them capitalize on business opportunities, that we are here to serve them. We are here to create amenities on the airport, to move more people and more boxes. We are not here for the benefit of developers."

Their second mistake, he adds, is not having a deep and thorough understanding of the aviation business—passenger or cargo. "Real estate developers look at their business as real estate and that the airport is the location for their real estate. Absolutely wrong mindset. To work successfully in this highly specialized market space, a developer, investor, and property manager must understand every single link in the supply chain. He or she must have complete familiarity with the ever-changing logistics strategies that move high-value and/or time-sensitive, airworthy products from the manufacturer's loading dock to the buyer-consignee's receiving dock."

John T. Meyer is senior vice president and director of AMB Property Corporation's Airport Facility Group.

Notes

1. Interview with Doug Bryan, DFW International Airport Real Property Planning and Development, November 14, 2002.

2. Interview with Jeff Fegan, executive director, DFW International Airport, November 17, 2002.

3. Interview with Doug Bryan.

4. Ibid.

How One Developer Landed a Giant Air Cargo Facility at Washington Dulles International Airport

John T. Meyer

Many may remember 1987 as the year the stock market crashed 500 points on a single day. Charles "Skip" Erhard remembers it as the year the U.S. Congress transferred financial and operational responsibility for Washington Dulles International Airport from the Federal Aviation Administration (FAA) to the newly created Metropolitan Washington Airports Authority (MWAA).

Erhard, manager of airport administration for Washington Dulles International Airport for the past 21 years, previously had only the FAA to please. Suddenly, with the stroke of a presidential pen, he and other area airport managers and employees worked for a 13-person board of directors appointed by the governors of Virginia and Maryland, the mayor of the District of Columbia, and the U.S. President.

Almost immediately, the new board took a hard look at the potential for new air cargo tonnage at Dulles (IAD). IAD is the dominant airport in the Middle Atlantic states and could attract freight that might otherwise move through Chicago's O'Hare, New York's Kennedy, or Atlanta's Hartsfield airports. It is also a strategic gateway to and from the U.K., Europe, and beyond for exporters and importers. At the time, it was the Middle Atlantic hub for United Airlines and a major station for FedEx, which was seeking to leverage its expertise in overnight documents and small parcels and capture more heavyweight freight shipments.

But there was a problem. The new MWAA also looked at Dulles's vintage airfreight facilities, which the federal government had financed and constructed. They were small—60 feet (18.2 meters) deep with 18-foot (5.4-meter) heights—outdated, and not suited to accommodate sorting and stacking freight-handling operations or the large number of containers and pallets carried in a wide-body aircraft. In those days, freight was a stepchild at IAD.

Under the FAA's control, most of the federal money, time, and attention at Washington Dulles airport was poured into the passenger terminals, which served a far more visible and verbal constituency: U.S. and foreign visitors who come to sightsee or do business in the nation's capital. "While the new board wanted to catch up, we didn't have the resources to focus on air cargo at that time. We were focusing on the expansion of the main passenger terminal," recalls Erhard. However, becoming an airport authority no longer under federal jurisdiction opened the door to new financing options—including bonds or third-party financings by developers who could own a building and lease the ground underneath it from the airport. Moreover, Dulles needed a new cargo building to house United Airlines and FedEx's rapidly growing airfreight operations. Both entities had strong ideas on facility size and design, and each wanted maximum control of the development.

In early 1987, Francis ("Frank") X. Chambers retired as a colonel from the U.S. Marine Corps after 32 years of service. He had commanded the 12th Marine Regiment and an artillery battery in combat in Vietnam. He was also a logistics and fiscal officer who had moved men and supplies across the Pacific at the beginning of the Vietnam War. He later became an industrial mobilization expert. Upon retiring from the Marines, he moved to northern Virginia, joined a land developer there named West*Group, and worked on apartment buildings, shopping centers, industrial buildings, and office parks in the Washington, D.C., Virginia, and Maryland metropolitan area, which was then enjoying a real estate boom.

In late 1987, Chambers heard that Washington Dulles was seeking bids for a 150,000-square-foot (13,935-square-meter) air cargo facility to be built on airport property. During his Marine career, he had been assigned to the 3rd Marine

Aircraft Wing and had performed the functional tasks of controller and chief financial officer in other large organizations. He understood the efficiencies and economics of freight flows. He also knew that flight operations and administrative and policy restrictions frequently influenced logistical operations and the size of facilities required to expedite shipments. Commercial airlines and civilian airports, he speculated, could not be all that different. He would come to find out that navigating the maze in the private-public sector is far more challenging and complex.

As part of his bid research, Chambers contacted customs brokers, airfreight forwarders, and airlines with operations at Washington Dulles. He quizzed them on how a new air cargo facility could be most productive and efficient. West*Group factored in this feedback and other findings and proposed a 287,000-square-foot (26,662-square-meter) on-tarmac cargo facility. The building would be 1,120 feet (341 meters) long, 235 feet (71.6 meters) deep, and built in two phases. It would be E-shaped to accommodate two nose-loading 747 freighters. Overall it could accommodate eight wide-body or 11 narrow-body jetliners and freighters on the air side.

West*Group's research revealed a growing emphasis on trucking in conjunction with air cargo movements. So it included a truck staging area as part of the facility and added a large customer and employee parking lot, since the FedEx sort center would require a large workforce. The parking lot would accommodate customers who would bring some shipments directly to a cargo terminal instead of using a forwarder.

Chambers and his colleagues wrestled with many considerations and details. The building had to last at least 50 years, but the developer would only get a 24-year ground lease, and so immediate profit had to be factored into construction, operational, and leasing assumptions and decision making.

The retired Marine officer says his company was viewed with skepticism at the onset. "We recognized there was, at that time, a great deal of parochialism within the aviation industry, including airlines. They seemed to think an on-airport developer had to have airport experience and said that an 'outsider'—shopping center, office, and industrial property developer such as ourselves—couldn't possibly do this building with all the details involved."[1]

To neutralize that attitude early in the bidding process, West*Group contacted Moffatt, Nichol & Bonney, a Portland, Oregon–headquartered architectural and engineering firm with extensive experience designing on-airport facilities. It connected as well with Kunkle Properties, a southern California firm that had built airplane hangars and on-airport cargo buildings. West*Group also brought in a group with airline services marketing experience. The four firms formed a joint airport development team to bid on the Washington Dulles facility. The developer also brought in a fifth team member, a subsidiary of Jones Construction Company of Charlotte, North Carolina, to assist with project financing; the Jones subsidiary had a solid line of credit and would eventually become a 50 percent equity partner.

In 1989, West*Group was notified that it topped the 12 initial bidders and the four finalists to win the bid to develop the first major air cargo facility ever built in Washington, D.C. The bid process had been complex. The request for proposal (RFP) had asked each bidder to submit a marketing and management plan, design and construction supervision procedures, and a personnel diversity plan, as well as a detailed design plan. Completing the RFP in the minute detail requested was difficult because an anchor tenant was continually revising the building specifications to reflect operational plans that were in flux at the time. The carrier's space requirements went from 70,000 square feet (6,503

square meters) to 170,000 (15,793) to 90,000 (8,361) to 40,000 (3,716) and back to 90,000 (8,361). "We learned quickly that we had to be very flexible developing on an airport," Chambers says.[2]

Financing on-airport facilities is difficult at best, but this new cargo facility was further complicated because of a number of economic and world events at the time. Lenders were skeptical. In 1990, the demands of the Gulf War put a damper on commercial cargo. Several airlines, including Eastern Airlines and People's Express, had financially crashed. United had not signed its lease, and the two main tenants were wrangling with the developer and the airport over size and control issues. West*Group planned to finance the 187,000-square-foot (17,372-square-meter) first phase with insured special facility revenue bonds through the development authority of Loudoun County, Virginia's development authority.

To get the bonds insured, the developer needed a financial guarantee. West*Group lacked sufficient capital of its own or financing sources, so it turned to its partner, Jones Construction Company, which was partially owned by Deutsche Bank. But the uncertainties over the Gulf War, the airline industry, and the economy worried the giant German bank, and it passed on the deal. Without the guarantee, no bond insurer would take the risk. West*Group had to go another route.

The developer next consulted with Wheat First Securities of Richmond, Virginia. The investment banking firm, which has since merged, recommended that West*Group retail the Loudoun County special purpose bonds to individuals rather than to institutional investors, with Wheat First leading the underwriting. Unrated state and federal tax-exempt bonds worth $16.8 million for Phase I were issued in September 1992 and were oversubscribed. "We did this with 10 percent of our own equity," says Chambers.

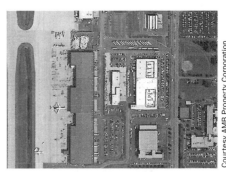

Building a cargo facility on airport property is a complex process that requires knowledge of relevant local and federal regulations, cargo handling systems, and supply chain technologies.

While waiting for the financing to be put in place, Chambers took two fortuitous steps based on what he was "learning on the job" at IAD. He realized that airports preferred to work with third-party developers and investors that had a demonstrated expertise in working with commercial airports or, at least, had a deep specialized knowledge of building on-tarmac cargo facilities. In 1992, Chambers, by then managing director of development and a vice president, suggested West*Group form a separate division to work on logistics buildings exclusively. Chairman Jerry Halpin listened to Chambers's proposal and agreed to form and capitalize a new independent entity called Aviation Facilities Company, Inc., or AFCO. Chambers would become president and CEO. And to generate cash flow and start building its credentials within the global airport community, West*Group took over and completed the rehabilitation and management of a cargo building at Philadelphia International Airport.

Even though the Washington Dulles air cargo bond issue was delayed because United Airlines did not sign its lease until February 1992, the developer began construction on Phase 1 using its own money. Immediately afterward, Air France and Lufthansa signed leases on 20,000 square feet (1,858 square meters), and FedEx decided it wanted more space, so a

continued on next page

100,000-square-foot (9,290-square-meter) second phase was started and a second bond issue worth $5.3 million was floated. (Phase I opened in June 1993 and Phase II in November 1993—six years after the RFP was filed, and four years after the developer won the contract.)

At the outset of the project, the size and scope of the air cargo building at IAD sent a clear message to airlines, shippers, forwarders, and other supply chain participants: the major airport in the Middle Atlantic states was aggressively courting airfreight and would be an energetic competitor for traffic. The timing was perfect. The Dulles area's regional economy was just starting to expand from its traditional federal government, federal contractor, and telecommunications base to include software and information technology, which is heavily dependent on airfreight. IAD would have the capacity and now the facilities.

What Washington Dulles Expects from a Developer

More than a decade after opening its phased 287,000-square-foot (26,662-square-meter) airfreight building, IAD has grown to be the 25th busiest airport in the world. Some 200 flights daily serve 29 international markets as of mid-2003.

The growth in cargo volume at the end of the 1990s further spurred the need for additional on-tarmac freight facilities. This time, though, the Metropolitan Washington Airport Authority designed and developed a 70,000-square-foot (6,503-square-meter) facility (named Building 6) on its own. The 35,000-square-foot (3,251-square-meter) Phase I was leased to Virgin Atlantic and United Airlines, while half of Phase II was leased to Air Cargo, Inc., a cargo ground handler for a consortium of airlines. The other half was purposely kept empty. "Our policy now is to always have space available to offer to new airlines," says Erhard.

Erhard says there are several factors that prospective developers and lenders should

bear in mind when working with the Metropolitan Washington Airport Authority. These may well apply to other commercial airports. At Washington Dulles, as at Dallas/Fort Worth International, developers receive only an unsubordinated land lease. This lease grants them use of the land, any improvements they make, and lease revenue for a period not to exceed 25 years. At that point, ownership of the building, leasehold improvements, and lease assignability revert to MWAA and cannot be extended except at market rates. "This is a jolt for any developer new to this business and to a lender who usually looks at fee title as security and now only has a lease," explains Erhard. "The developer needs to price his product to make his return and the returns for his investors and still retire the debt within the term of the lease."[3]

Erhard says he typically puts RFP notifications in airport publications, including the Washington, D.C.–based Airport Council International's magazine. He also sends notifications directly to a list of a half-dozen developers who have experience developing and building on-airport properties. He again stresses, however, that "it is not a closed or exclusive club."

RFPs are not evaluated simply on the developer's experience and track record, says Erhard. He expects bidders to provide him with current and forecast air cargo market flows and demands from domestic and international viewpoints, a detailed analysis of the airfreight market for the region covered by Dulles, and shipper, forwarder, and carrier options. He also wants a proposed facility design, minimum guarantees, and a percentage of gross receipts forecast over a multiple-year period—20, 30, and 40 years. "Give me business models, financing alternatives, and terms," Erhard tells developers. "At this point, it becomes very obvious if the developers know or don't know what they're doing."

The public bidding process can take up to six months. Erhard breaks down the time

Cargo Building 5, operated by AFCO, features 250,000 square feet (23,225 square meters) of cargo handling space and 440,450 square feet (40,918 square meters) of aircraft apron space.

to monthly blocks: 60 to 90 days from the bidder's receipt of the RFP to prepare a proposal; 30 days for the MWAA to review it; another 30 days to get additional questions answered satisfactorily; and another month to get it to and through the authority's board of directors.

Washington Dulles sees itself as a growth opportunity for all links in the supply chain and expects that shrewd, creative developers can participate. Erhard said in mid-2003 that, although cargo tonnage carried in the bellies of passenger aircraft was still below pre–September 11 levels, all cargo-integrated carriers have seen a strong upsurge in business. In mid-2003, FedEx operated six freighters daily through IAD. Its cargo tonnage had grown 10 percent over the prior year. More freighters are coming, predicts Erhard, enticed by the airport's location, truck and air connections, and landing fees of $2.24 per thousandweight—about half of what New York's Kennedy Airport charges.

Washington Dulles has the space to allow major airfreight forwarders on airport property, a privilege few large airports offer and a great opportunity for developers. Erhard points to Gateway Freight Systems, a large international forwarder with an on-tarmac building at IAD. Gateway was drawn by the increased flight operations and the rise in cargo traffic. An on-tarmac forwarder has an exceptional edge on its competitors, giving shippers later flight closeouts and faster recoveries. Erhard says the airport protects on-tarmac forwarders by denying off-airport forwarders access to the apron. "If you let the off-airport competition come through a hole in the fence, so to speak, you've depreciated the value the developer and the airport have created."

What a Developer Should Expect from Major Airports

Industrial property developers aiming to enter the logistics marketplace will find themselves working in essentially two different worlds: off-property and on-property buildings. The scenarios and strategies for a successful development in these worlds are as different as night and day. Building a cargo distribution center or a marine terminal away from an airport or a seaport is relatively straightforward: You buy the land and build to local zoning codes and ordinances, secure a tenant, write a comparatively short-term, competitively priced lease, and, with fewer barriers to entry, hope that competitors do not encroach on your market. In addition, you want a tenant with the financial viability to meet its lease obligations. While build-to-suits cater more closely to tenant requirements, the developer still has considerable leeway in making decisions.

The hurdles of developing on-airport freight buildings are far higher. Whether on-tarmac buildings are fully leased before or after construction, the airport is always the developer's first priority, given the ground lease nature of the relationship. "A third-party developer of on-tarmac buildings works for the airport first and then for the client, since the building is usually completed before it is totally leased out," maintains Frank Chambers. But not always. Sometimes there is a demand for more space before it's completed.

An on-airport property developer must be constantly aware of current FAA regulations and restrictions and stay abreast of pending proposals and issues. State and community laws, regulations, and ordinances affecting airports are continually changing, and new

legislation or policies can influence airport operations or tenant decision making. Trends in airfreight transportation, the economic health of individual airlines, mergers, acquisitions, cargo handling systems, and breakthroughs in technology affecting the supply chain are just some of the market conditions that must be monitored and factored into bids and pricing.

There are no ironclad guidelines or formulas for negotiating with airport management or identifying and prequalifying potential tenants. "Some airports with a shortage of land for cargo building development will charge a premium for being on-airport," notes Chambers. "That premium can be so high that it precludes even the largest forwarders and brokers from seeking an on-airport location." Commercial airports with vast acreage, such as Rickenbacker International Airport, now an all-cargo airport near Columbus, Ohio, welcome forwarders, express airlines, and other transport providers with much lower rental rates than for an on-tarmac facility at a major airport.

Other airports, such as Los Angeles International, operated by the city of Los Angeles, and Kennedy International, managed by the Port of New York/New Jersey, own and lease land parcels off the airport at rates considerably lower than for an on-tarmac location. This option gives the developer somewhat more flexibility in negotiating for a property. It gives the developer the opportunity to expand the relationship with the airport authority to include both on- and off-airport facility sites.

Indeed, a development company's flexibility can be its greatest asset in seeking an airport's approval to build an on-tarmac cargo building and in creating a relationship. Chambers offers an example: Washington Dulles needed a place for parking passenger planes overnight. The airport had federal airport improvement funds to build an apron but no location, and AFCO had built half of an apron for the first phase of its building but did not need the other half for a while.

Chambers and Erhard worked out a good deal for both parties. MWAA would build the second half of the apron in front of AFCO's building, use it rent-free for two years, and then include it as part of the developer's facility leasehold for the term of its lease. In exchange, AFCO, which agreed to maintain the apron, gave 5,000 square feet (464 square meters) of office space to the airport to house U.S. Customs offices at no cost for 24 years. "That offset the cost of what we would have paid to build the apron," explains Chambers.

The relationship has since strengthened. In 1995, when FedEx told MWAA it quickly needed three more parking positions for its freighters, the airport could not respond rapidly enough. So AFCO stepped in, fast-tracked the construction with a small bond issue, and met the FedEx deadline. It also provided office space for U.S. Department of Agriculture, Customs, and FAA staffers for rental credits. The developer realized that having customs and agricultural inspectors in its building was an important, timesaving benefit for tenants that added even more value to the facility.

Developers on or near an airport must be tremendously diplomatic in dealing with all their different constituencies, says Chambers. Having the support of one or two key people in airport management is not enough to create a successful air cargo building, he cautions. "Developers must realize you cannot get a project completed unless you address everyone's concerns and issues and overcome all their objections."

John T. Meyer is senior vice president and director of AMB Property Corporation's Airport Facility Group.

Notes

   1. Interview with Frank X. Chambers, AFCO, October 6, 2002.
   2. Ibid.
   3. Interview with Charles Erhard, Metropolitan Washington Airports Authority, October 4, 2002.

Real estate providers can build relationships with potential clients—and strengthen ties with existing ones—by quantifying the hard-dollar efficiencies, productivity payoffs, and potential return on investment of intelligently planned distribution and logistics facilities. Shippers today want measurable results. The real estate provider who can document performance improvements has a competitive advantage in cementing ties with shippers, manufacturers, or 3PLs.

For example, Joel Sutherland, senior vice president of Transplace, a Plano, Texas–based nationwide 3PL, fully expects that a real estate developer hoping to sell him a large distribution facility will "be hands on, talk shop, and show me efficiencies." The property professional "should know if I operate one shift, I'll need more [truck] dock doors. If I'm 24/7, I can better balance my inbound and outbound shipments and need fewer dock doors, but I'll want some skylights. He'll ask if I'm using 53-foot-long trucks or 'pups' (28-footers) when he's designing my truck apron. He'll understand transportation costs, my inbound and outbound products, and show me designs to optimize time. Should I be close to an interstate, do I need a rail siding, an inland waterway source?"[7]

Industrial real estate brokers and broker/consultants specializing in the supply chain niche are excellent allies and advisers for property providers wanting to enter the field. The advice of brokers experienced in supply chain real estate, whether they typically represent landlords or tenants, can be invaluable.

For example, CB Richard Ellis, a national commercial real estate brokerage with a specialized practice, is supported by logistics experts who work with industrial property brokers and clients with multimarket facility needs. Real estate advisers need to speak the language of logistics and be able to talk with both the chief logistics officer and the chief financial officer on how a distribution center can help improve the company's core competency. Being successful in supply chain real estate is understanding both sides of the client's house—the operational side and the financial side.

A critical link in the supply chain for global shippers is cargo throughput velocity at on-tarmac airfreight buildings, stresses John Suerth, a managing director in CB Richard Ellis's Chicago office. The shallow, narrow cross-dock design of the typical on-tarmac building—with airplane parking aprons intended to expedite the loading and unloading—solves two problems: aircraft slots are scarce and the on-tarmac rent is expensive. The shipper's cost of "carrying" the freight during transit is a financial expense. Hence, there can be no space for storage, and tenants cannot accommodate backlogged freight, explains Suerth. So an off-airport freight forwarder or 3PL might have a terminal designed with space for temporary storage. These design differences between on- and off-tarmac cargo buildings are important to understand.[8]

Supply chain real estate 101 still starts with location, but traffic congestion and proximity to transportation hubs are prime considerations, driven by the user's logistics requirements and land costs. The usual preference is for infill real estate, which will always have a ready market of buyers. But some seeking network optimization choose to locate a facility at a geographical midpoint of their distribution network.

Real estate professionals are advised to have an exit strategy in place before developing or building a logistics facility. The trend toward ceiling heights of 40 to 42 feet (12.2 to 12.8 meters) or more may be appropriate for some facilities today, where there is movement toward super-regional distribution centers. The higher the ceiling, particularly above 24 feet (7.3 meters), the more expensive and complex the material handling system needs to be to move and temporarily store freight. Five to ten years from now, those facilities may be overbuilt, and selling or re-leasing could be difficult.

Modernizing or upgrading a logistics building in a submarket is a risk for owners unless they are exceptionally experienced. To prepare it for sale or re-lease, it would be wiser to improve its functionality, if possible, by adding extra truck bays and dock doors, a larger truck court, trailer parking, improved lighting, and security. This retrofitting should be accompanied by aesthetic enhancements such as carpeting, painting, and thorough cleaning, and by offering buildouts. By making these changes, the owner is enhancing the asset's functionality and efficiency—the top priorities for logistics-oriented tenants.

CB Richard Ellis maintains that supply chain real estate specialists must take at least a national and intermodal, if not international, view. Seaports, for example, handle different commodities and volumes, which determine the size, type, and function of the logistics facilities near or on port property. The categories are "superload center," "load center," and "break bulk." Superloads are large, high-volume containerized facilities at the world's deepwater megaports. Load centers are often located at large regional ports. Break bulk is for loose freight and can move out of ports large and small.

The ports of Los Angeles and Long Beach serve together as a superload center handling large volumes of high-value cargo—automobiles, computer and technology products, and equipment, usually as containerized cargo. The port of Seattle/Tacoma is the other West Coast superload center. In both cases, most of the freight moves inland to other markets. The new emphasis in logistics buildings is on multi-modal facilities that combine on-dock loading with railcars, proximity to airports, and quick-turnover warehouses. At Hong Kong's frenetic commercial port, where land is scant and steeply priced, multi-modal facilities are reaching ten stories high, according to Insignia/ESG.

On the East Coast, the Port of New York–New Jersey is a superload center, and the logistics facilities there aim to keep the inbound containerized cargoes moving. Norfolk and Miami's ports are load centers, with smaller volumes. Second-tier ports such as Baltimore, Philadelphia, Boston, Savannah, and Charleston handle break bulk freight that is large, of lower value, and less time-sensitive. Hence, the logistics buildings at or near their waterfronts have more warehouse storage capacity and a more traditional design.

Another industrial broker with expertise in logistics agrees that real estate professionals must have a national perspective to be successful in this niche market. Blaine Kelley, vice president in the Atlanta office of CB Richard Ellis, maintains that five industrial real estate markets are important to manufacturers and shippers of time-sensitive, high-value, and high volume freight: Los Angeles, Chicago, Dallas, Atlanta, and New York/northern New Jersey. Any national real estate developer of logistics properties must understand the dynamics of each of these markets. Second-tier key markets that would be candidates for high-volume, high-speed regional distribution centers are Memphis; Miami; Columbus, Ohio; and Reno–Sparks, Nevada. Users in these locations would require flexibility in the terms of the lease that cover expansion, contraction, and subleasing provisions, he says.[9]

According to Kelley, not many experienced developers will agree to a specialized build-to-suit building

Courtesy IDI Associates

with less than a five-year lease commitment from the user—and most prefer ten years, given lenders' resistance to short-term leases. Even if a 3PL with a solid three-year contract from a company such as the Home Depot approached a seasoned developer for a new build-to-suit distribution center with a three-year lease, most developers would have trouble agreeing to those terms. There is a solution: the gap between a developer's need for term and a 3PL's need for flexibility can be bridged by building generic facilities in infill locations.

Kelley has other advice for real estate professionals who are newcomers to supply chain properties: In working with 3PLs, understand that they are typically bidding for a corporation's logistics account and often need flexibility in leasing terms. Realize that a manufacturer's distribution centers are a core element of their business. Any construction delays, infrastructure malfunctions, or other problems can seriously disrupt their supply chain, putting their customers and their own reputations for reliability at risk. Investigate the availability and quality of the local labor markets that a logistics customer will be using. Bear in mind that 3PLs are often bidding against their competitors, and that the lowest bidder usually wins.

Some industrial real estate brokers with a logistics specialty are becoming consultants, working for clients nationwide and hiring local brokers for their submarket knowledge. Skip Case, chief executive officer of Case Industrial Partners, Inc., in Columbia, Maryland, represents corporations looking for supply chain real estate. His perspective from the user/tenant's viewpoint is instructional.[10]

The Airport Exchange Business Park in northern Kentucky was developed by IDI Associates, a full-service industrial development company.

For "today's chief operating officers and logistics professionals," Case says, "real estate is invisible—except, of course, when the facility hinders efficient logistics and transportation." He has fashioned a strong practice in consulting with manufacturers and distributors who need guidance in better development and selection of facilities so that those facilities can become invisible to operations. He advises property developers to begin their design process with the chief logistics officer; that's where he finds the core direction that results in a more efficient facility. "Each corporation has a unique amalgam of material handling, transportation needs, and inventory complexity. The one challenge common to all is increasingly specific service requirements for the retailer or government agency customers."

"Logistics today is about velocity and excellence in serving the manufacturer's customer and meeting their ever-changing demands," explains Case. "Shippers have gone from selling only by the pallet load to selling by the case load to selling individual orders, or 'eaches.' At the same time, Wal-Mart is telling that manufacturer that if it wants to be on the shelves of America's biggest retailer, it had better ship and deliver that pallet, that case, that 'each' when Wal-Mart wants it delivered, not when it fits the manufacturer's distribution schedule."

Logistics has gone from moving products rather slowly to just-in-time and now to just-this-minute. In years past, a retailer's thinking was, for example, "let's have specific claw hammers in the store just in case a customer asks for one." In the just-in-time scenario, it was "let's have the specific hammer because the retailer might ask for one." We now have "just this minute" because corporate headquarters can forecast, with astonishing accuracy, when that hammer SKU will sell in the Des Moines store. "Logistics today is largely about 'eaches,' minutes, and throughput capacity," Case says.

What makes meeting real estate needs so challenging is that every company's supply chain is different, although there is a universal goal: time-definite delivery of goods. Just-in-time inventory management could mean a scheduled delivery between 9 and 10 a.m. on a specific day. Thanks to technology and the customer's continually growing marketplace clout, the SKUs ordered had better be on the receiving dock at 9:18 a.m. so they can be received, scanned for delivery verification, and stocked, often by the manufacturer's

field sales representatives, says Case. Otherwise another supplier will occupy their prime "real estate"—the shelf or bin space. This is no exaggeration; Case reports that the Home Depot has a vendor-managed inventory program requiring the supplier's sales bin or shelf position to be 100 percent full, 100 percent of the time.

In designing, selling, or leasing distribution centers, warehouses, freight terminals, or other supply chain real estate, the contact within the Fortune 1000 companies is the corporate real estate department, which generally works with property providers that have built a relationship based on past performance. It is difficult but certainly not impossible to break in. "Beyond the Fortune 1000, there is no 'typical' organizational profile for managing real estate issues," Case says. "Many firms, even with multiple supply chain facilities, outsource all their real estate related needs." Consultants such as Case increasingly are functioning as the real estate departments for firms seeking to improve their competitive advantages in the evolving marketplace.

Conclusion

As logistics and real estate continue their symbiotic relationship, development opportunities will be driven by continued infrastructure improvements at prime transport hubs in first-world nations, but will also occur in developing countries as they improve their industrial infrastructure, increase their standards of living, and expand their middle class. U.S. manufacturers and their international shipping partners will be challenged to put greater emphasis on globalizing their supply chain. This globalization will require the same tight delivery schedules and supply chain performance that exist in the United States. Timely, no-excuses worldwide distribution to the receiving dock or selling floor will not be a consignee's expectation—it will be a requirement.

This challenge will put greater pressures on the transportation links in the supply chain. It will also force the providers of industrial real estate—developers, brokers, REITs, private owners/landlords, and property managers—to become knowledgeable, involved partners with their tenants or, in the case of build-to-suits, with clients. The real estate professional seeking to build or expand a customer base among transportation and logistics providers must maintain a close relationship long after a facility is leased or turned over to the buyer. The fluctuations of the U.S. and world economies, new technology, changing distribution channels, product life cycles, greater security, and the continuing trend to outsource logistics will dynamically affect design and demand for industrial properties. Change in distribution channels will accelerate, and the marketplace will not tolerate slow response.

Ongoing improvements in existing and next-generation technology will continue to influence the design configurations of cargo facilities. For example, bar coding and scanner technology already track and trace individual shipments. But new radio frequency identification (RFID) tags—smart bar code labels embedded with integrated circuits—will provide instantaneous remote access on the whereabouts of an individual piece of merchandise anywhere on its distribution route by emitting and transmitting its precise location by radio frequency. Global consumer goods companies and retailers including Procter & Gamble, Wal-Mart, Unilever, and Gillette have pilot programs underway. These miniaturized applications, which have the ability to locate an item anywhere across the supply chain, will likely become widespread within the next few years—at increasingly lower cost. A related technology is "pick by light," a system that electronically beams a light directly to the warehouse or rack location of each SKU on the order sheet. The light is a visual aid to the warehouse employee filling the order and, simultaneously, captures data for inventory control, restocking, ordering patterns, and other management reports. This system could expedite freight flows in fulfillment centers and warehousing.

Domestically, third-party logistics providers will dominate the U.S. commercial warehousing market as manufacturers and other shippers continue to outsource their logistics functions. Armstrong & Associates, a Stoughton, Wisconsin, supply chain management consulting firm and publisher of "Who's Who in Logistics," reports that U.S. 3PLs increased their 2002 gross revenues by 6.9 percent to $65 billion from $60.8 billion a year earlier. That growth was recorded in a weak economic year. (The largest 3PL, Exel, headquartered in the U.K., owns or leases 56.5 million square feet [5.2 million square meters] of warehousing space in the United States.) There are 600 medium-to-large-size U.S. "warehousemen," as these 3PLs are called. But they represent only 10 percent of the total

potential market of $650 billion in the United States alone—and that includes purchased transportation. Trucking operations represent $450 billion, and they require warehousing, terminal, or distribution facilities, according to Armstrong.

There is clearly an opportunity for industrial property companies and professionals, but it is no bonanza. The strong annual growth of U.S. 3PLs does not necessarily mean that their property requirements will increase. Shippers—whether manufacturers, 3PLs, or forwarders—are trying to wring maximum cost and performance efficiencies out of truck, rail, air, and maritime transportation vendors. There is a parallel trend toward consolidating logistics functions at larger distribution centers and repositioning or selling off smaller and intermediate facility locations. With an active customer focus, the real estate professional can play an integral part in the streamlining of this distribution network.

What's driving the fastest-growing sectors in logistics and real estate today—and well into the future—is high-throughput cross-docking facilities, which use the most efficient transportation modes to accelerate the shipment of high-value goods. These goods represent the fastest-growing part of industrial and manufacturing output, observes Armstrong. By eliminating the need for warehousing of high-value, time-sensitive goods, inventory costs fall. The traditional warehouse will not vanish, because low-value goods with lower inventory costs and less time sensitivity will still need to be stored, housed, and secured.

In this decade, the industrial property professional can become a valued partner to manufacturers, distributors, shippers, and consignees by helping them maximize supply chain efficiency. The real estate professional's role: develop and deliver facilities that expedite the flow of goods, and help optimize transportation networks. Such facilities will drive down total inventory costs, including depreciation, obsolescence, and interest expense paid on the goods during transit to the customer's receiving dock or store shelf. At the juncture of real estate and logistics, speed to market has taken precedence over stacking and storing goods.

Notes

1. Data extracted from TortoWheaton Research Fall 2003 Industrial Outlook, www.tortowheatonresearch.com (August 8, 2003).

2. Interview with Pete Robinson, Jevic Transportation, Inc., August 7, 2003.

3. Interview with David Berkowitz, director, public relations, eMarketer, August 6, 2003.

4. Interview with Rich Paongo, director, investor relations, Overstock.com, August 6, 2003.

5. Interview with Patty Smith, director of international public relations, Amazon.com, August 6, 2003.

6. Interview with John H. Langley, Dove Distinguished Professor of Logistics, University of Tennessee, April 17, 2003.

7. Interview with Joel Sutherland, senior vice president, Transplace, August 7, 2003.

8. Interview with John Suerth, managing director, CB Richard Ellis, November 15, 2002.

9. Interview with Blaine Kelley, vice president, corporate services, CB Richard Ellis, October 8, 2002.

10. Interview with Skip Case, chief executive officer, Case Industrial Properties, Inc., March 12, 2002.

Chapter 4

IMPLICATIONS FOR BUILDING DEMAND, DESIGN, AND LOCATION

Luis A. Belmonte

The rapid changes in the supply chain over the past decade have wide implications for industrial real estate demand, design, and location requirements. These changes have been driven largely by new distribution and purchasing patterns and practices such as zero- to minimal-inventory storage, speed-to-market for high-value goods and fashion-cyclical merchandise, vendor-managed inventories, and just-in-time product deliveries that bypass the warehouse and go straight to the selling floor.

Some of these changes can also be attributed to the emergence of e-commerce and business models that promise immediate order fulfillment and express or expedited delivery. Online shopping accounted for only 2 to 3 percent of all U.S. retails sales in mid-2003, but it was growing at 25 to 40 percent a year while off-line retail sales were growing at about 3 to 4 percent.[1] Technology advances in tracking and monitoring shipments, breakthroughs in automated physical handling systems, the ongoing emphasis on outsourcing logistics activities to third-party logistics companies, and the growing practice of measuring the performance of logistical services are additional drivers.

All these forces have helped businesses along the supply chain to create and maintain stronger, long-term customer relationships. Today, companies with slow, inefficient, costly distribution networks will not be able to compete in marketplaces that require "no-excuses" compliance with delivery schedules. Product superiority and vendor loyalty are no substitutes for lax logistics in a customer-first world.

Demand Overview

In the late 1990s, some observers predicted that demand for warehouse space would stagnate as the need for traditional storage space became obsolete. In this scenario, the design of traditional warehouses would no longer be able to serve the specialized needs of e-commerce. Increasingly sophisticated logistics management systems would streamline the supply chain process and reduce the amount of space needed for inventory.

Over the past two decades, manufacturers and distributors have in fact reduced their relative inventory-to-sales ratios by focusing on just-in-time delivery and production processes. The trend toward consolidation of warehouse and distribution facilities also reduces the amount of space required.

Many of the concerns that surfaced in the late 1990s are still valid and should be monitored by investors and developers in this sector. But there are also reasons to expect that demand for certain types of industrial space will not diminish and may actually grow:

- The industrial real estate market is subject to cycles, but globalization of trade will contribute to demand

Figure 4.1 **Historic Inventory to Sales Ratios**

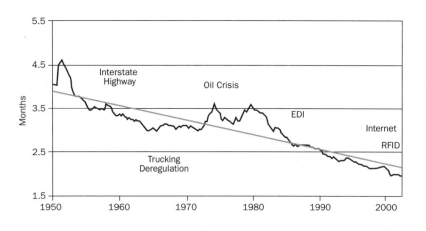

Source: Bureau of Economic Analysis. Chart reflects data through June 30, 2003.
©2003 AMB Property Corporation.

Greater efficiencies in the supply chain process have resulted in the consolidation of warehouse and distribution space, but there is still demand for traditional warehouse space from many small to mid-sized companies.

for space over the long term. Global sourcing of finished goods or components and materials is already leading to the building and filling of direct-to-store containers at Asian factories or assembly plants. This trend may result in a demand decrease for industrial space at U.S. portside locations. However, the rising tide of exports from Asia and Europe may also require more U.S. portside facilities to receive, deconsolidate, and perform value-added assembly and logistics work before forwarding or shipping the products onward.

■ Globalization is also generating demand for regional distribution facilities and new transshipment points. This trend benefits the larger commercial real estate developer, the investor with logistics experience, and joint venture partners. It also builds deep customer and supplier relationships and cross-border expertise.

■ Just-in-time production, delivery, and inventory are integral components of the supply chain process but are not appropriate or practical for all industries. There are still plenty of small to mid-sized companies that require standard warehouse space without the towering clear-height ceilings and other extras that have been added in recent years. In fact, as new technologies facilitate the continual flow of products, the need to stack goods may even diminish, and horizontal movement may prevail over vertical stacking in some transshipment points.

■ Concern is growing about just-in-time distribution systems that do not have the necessary supply backups (called "safety stock") needed when breakdowns in delivery occur for different reasons. Security restrictions resulting from the September 11, 2001, attacks closed and slowed down the flow of cargo at airports and seaports and had a temporary but major impact on the flow of goods. The best just-in-time systems require a provision for "just-in-case" inventory as well.

■ Changes in retailing practices will also influence demand for industrial facilities. The growing popularity of discount retail superstores selling huge quantities of bulk products could increase demand for centralized distribution centers where full truckloads of merchandise are sorted and loaded for direct store delivery. The proliferation of discount superstores in urban and rural locations or clustered at mega shopping centers or malls (known as "power centers") could lead to fewer but larger regional cross-docking cargo facilities.

■ So-called "reverse logistics"—product returns from retailers or consumers—is also growing as manufacturers become more customer-service focused. This activity requires handling centers or expansions of existing buildings in centralized locations or at transportation hubs.

■ The practice of "local finish and customization" offers another facility development and leasing opportunity for industrial property professionals. Major multinationals often import bulk quantities of standard products. They then ship them to nearby local engineering and configuration centers.

A New Tool for Forecasting Demand for Industrial Space

David C. Twist

Predicting demand for industrial property has long vexed commercial real estate professionals. "Office employment" is a strong indicator of office space demand. Household formation, income, and population growth have been reliable indicators of multifamily housing and retail demand for both apartment and shopping center developers. But owner/developers focusing on logistics facilities have lacked proven yardsticks for forecasting the need for industrial real estate.

Traditionally, the predictive indicators for distribution centers and warehouse space have been a collection of statistics linked to manufacturing, warehouse, and distribution employment, gross domestic product, population, inventories, and freight flows. But for years, no system or model was able to achieve any consistent forecasting accuracy.

Some have tried to create an accurate model. In 1990, the real estate analytics firm of Torto Wheaton Research in Boston developed a model that attempted to predict industrial space demand by factoring in manufacturing and distribution employment data. These combined data were portrayed as a profile of industrial employment and therefore a proxy for industrial demand. While such data are timely, cost-effective, and available by metropolitan city/region levels, the Torto Wheaton approach had three inherent limitations.

First, manufacturing employment does not correlate well with actual demand for industrial space. During the last 13 years, for example, manufacturing employment dropped by 13.7 percent, while occupied industrial space rose by 18.5 percent.

Second, employment data tallies do not reflect productivity gains. Logistics and supply chain management have a tremendous impact on manufacturing productivity, which affects industrial space demand and reduces the need for employees. Employment numbers alone do not offer that information. The gross domestic product is not a good barometer either, because this measure of U.S. output is heavily service based.

Third, manufacturing-related businesses are classified with a single employment code. Employees of the Coca-Cola Company, where distribution is a critical activity, are classified as manufacturing employees, even though most of them work in nonmanufacturing roles and offices. Conversely, many employees who perform warehouse and distribution activities are classified as retail employees.

In July 2002, AMB Property Corporation introduced a comprehensive tool for forecasting industrial property demand (net absorption) based on 13 years of quarterly data. Termed the AMB Industrial Absorption Indicator (AMB IAI), it uses the manufacturing component of the Federal Reserve Board's Index of Industrial Production, a prime indicator of industrial demand. AMB has found that changes in manufacturing output affect future changes in demand for industrial real estate. AMB believes that the changes in manufacturing output reflect aspects of broader, more pronounced trends affecting the dynamics of industrial space demand. These include globalization of logistics, airfreight, information technology, supply chain management, and outsourcing/third party logistics. The changes in these broad-based trends affect the long-term health and viability of the industrial real estate sector, including markets, submarkets, and individual industrial assets.

continued on next page

These centers are located in moderate to large population areas, where qualified labor exists for customization, features enhancement, or private labeling of generic products.

- The concern that third-party logistics providers would eliminate the need for warehousing has not been borne out. As noted by Cass Information Systems in its 2003 "State of Logistics Report," third-party logistics companies are actually among the largest users of warehouse space, especially in Europe.

- Average shipment sizes and weights have been declining in recent years, influenced by new product technology, miniaturization, and design efficiencies. Order sizes are also decreasing, but delivery frequencies are increasing. These trends spur demand for close-by, fast-throughput cargo facilities equipped for the swift handling and processing of small packages. This trend reduces emphasis on long-distance trucking as a shipper or consignee cost-saving strategy. The proliferation of shipment sizes and product sizes requires flexibility in facility design to provide adequate space for the staging and breakdown of shipments, as well as other outsourced logistics services.

- The growth of high-value technology and fashion-oriented and perishable products—which are imported and exported internationally and expedited domestically—necessitates infill airport-adjacent or on-tarmac airfreight facilities. The location of their real estate is mission-critical to tenants who place a high premium on quick access to a large customer base and close proximity to ports and airports. Unlike traditional storage users, for whom

The IAI compares the U.S. government's Index of Manufacturing Output—a component of the Index of Industrial Production—with projected future changes in industrial space demand. Since the AMB IAI is a national macroindicator, we consider total employment the best microindicator of industrial space at the metropolitan market level.

The accompanying chart illustrates that the AMB IAI has historically estimated industrial net absorption six months into the future. In reviewing the AMB IAI against 13 years or 52 quarters of historical data patterns, it has shown an 88 percent correlation with the actual demand for industrial space, a higher level of accuracy than other indicators that are used to forecast demand. It would have signaled the downturn in the industrial market between July and September 2000, when it peaked at 119.4. The expected upturn was initially signaled between December 2001 and February 2002, when the index hit 116.0 and continued upward. In mid-2003, the model's forecast pointed to a continuation of a "bounce along the bottom," with absorption over the last two quarters of the year registering the statistical equivalent of net zero.

The AMB Industrial Absorption Indicator

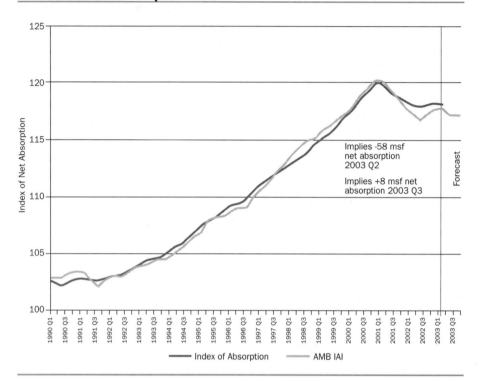

The quarterly AMB IAI projections are posted on AMB's Web site at www.amb.com. No fee or password is required. The index is available and accessible to anyone interested in the demand for industrial space, including investors, developers, brokers, and other REITs. If, as we believe, industrial real estate is an early indicator of the market condition of other property types, this index could be beneficial to the entire commercial real estate industry.

David C. Twist is vice president and director of research at AMB Property Corporation.

rent constitutes 30 to 40 percent of the cost structure, tenants in these close-in facilities often provide a menu of value-added logistical services such as handling and briefly storing perishables, so that real estate is a smaller part of the overall cost/benefit equation. As a result, tenants are more willing to pay for close-in locations and better access. For these types of facilities, demand is expected to increase in a small number of hub and gateway cities that are best positioned to meet the "need for speed" in a global economy.

Future demand will vary depending on the type of industrial real estate. Astute investors must be aware of the entire range of opportunities and be prepared to adapt to market niches.

Location Trends

Traditionally, the distribution of goods has been dependent upon the place of production, for instance in the manufacturing belts of America's East Coast and Midwest or in the old industrialized regions of England and continental Europe. As a result, warehouses and other types of industrial space were concentrated near manufacturing centers. Today, deciding where to locate distribution centers depends largely on access to suppliers and consumers.

Product obsolescence rates and life cycles also dictate location. For time-critical deliveries, access to airports and airfreight facilities is crucial. The shorter the selling cycle, the greater the demand for close-in fulfillment-driven freight facilities with high-throughput configurations to expedite loading and unloading. Retailers that ship and sell products with varying demand can warehouse slower-moving merchandise in a remote or rural located facility. This strategy reduces rent and labor costs and moves goods in full truckloads, achieving additional transportation savings.

Large-scale distribution is also increasingly dependent on major hubs such as airports, seaports, and highway intersections. A major factor for the location of distribution-related facilities is access to these transportation gateways, ideally in a situation where rail, road, port, and air facilities converge. The six hub distribution markets of Los Angeles, New York/northern New Jersey, San Francisco, Chicago, Dallas, and Atlanta, for example, constitute 17 percent of the nation's employment but 44 percent of its industrial inventory in the 53 domestic markets generally tracked by institutional investors.

Secondary hubs have also begun to emerge. Major logistics and integrator companies such as FedEx and UPS handle such a large freight volume that they can afford to operate their own "freight villages." FedEx has established a major hub in Memphis, and UPS has a major facility in Louisville, where it employs approximately 13,000 people, as well as in Hodgkins, Illinois, a southwest suburb of Chicago, with 9,000 additional employees. These sites are reported to be the largest distribution centers in the world.

Inland cities are gaining significance in the supply chain process. As traffic increases at the major hubs and as land becomes scarcer, there is a greater incentive to move cargo out of ports and distribute it from a strategically located inland location. Cities such as Columbus, Ohio; Kansas City, Missouri; Tulsa; and Pittsburgh are positioning themselves as major intermodal distribution hubs. Factors that make a good

An Inland Port in Kansas City

Ann Moline

Congestion at the nation's port and borders means that shipments can be delayed or lost, and only a small percentage of goods can be examined by customs officials. One solution to these logistics and security issues is the development of inland ports that work in concert with operations at traditional ports of entry to improve regional business access to markets. These goals can be accomplished through intelligent transportation systems (ITS) and physical facilities where value-added manufacturing, intermodal transfer of goods, and trade compliance activities can be coordinated and conducted.

In Kansas City, Missouri, an areawide business initiative known as Kansas City SmartPort, Inc., is working to position the region as a major inland port and intermodal center for both domestic and international trade. Situated on the Missouri River, with historic importance as a port of call for barges transporting grain and other bulk commodities, and ranking as the second largest rail center in the nation, the city has long been an important distri-

bution hub for domestic operations. Since the implementation of the North American Free Trade Agreement (NAFTA), the city's location along the so-called NAFTA corridor between Mexico and Canada has taken on even more significance. With federal funding in place, plans are underway to establish Inland Trade Processing (ITP) for freight originating or terminating at the site by preprocessing customs and other agency requirements before the shipments reach the Mexican or Canadian borders.

Kansas City's future as a strategic inland port has received a significant boost from the city's commitment to transform the former Richards-Gebaur Air Force Base into a world-class intermodal terminal, known as the International Freight Gateway. The International Freight Gateway being developed by Kansas City Southern Railway will bring together all the components of freight transportation and distribution into one prime, easily accessible site, located one mile (1.6 kilometers) west off of U.S. Highway 71 via Missouri 150. Improvements to Missouri 150 will convert the previous two-lane road to a divided four-lane highway to expand capacity and ease of travel. A rail

spur, added by Kansas City Southern Railway, will transport freight traffic directly into the site. In addition, the Missouri Department of Economic Development is exploring further economic development incentives that could aid the project.

In addition to customs facilities, additions to the gateway will include intermodal container facilities, brokerage services, and trucking and rail repair services, along with the various other support services exporters and importers would require. The goal? To make this a "one-stop shop" for those involved in international trade.

The site includes 1,200 acres (486 hectares) of undeveloped land and plans call for development of warehousing and transloading facilities. The facilities and adjacent land will be developed into a high-quality, modern business park.

Ann Moline is a business writer specializing in international economic development. She writes frequently about logistics and corporate real estate for a variety of publications.

Sources: www.kcsmartport.com; "Distribution Hubs on a Roll," Plants Sites and Parks magazine, www.bizsites.com/2001/on01/supply.html.

A Guide to Incentives for Warehouse/Distribution Companies

John Skowronski

Warehouse and distribution facilities have long been considered the middle ground when it comes to economic development incentives, with manufacturing and high-tech being on one end and retail being on the other. Since incentives are driven by a project's economic contribution to the state or municipality in which it resides, understanding why distribution straddles the line is an important first step in knowing what to look for and having realistic expectations.

First of all, knowing that a particular jurisdiction has favorable incentive programs for distribution companies, or conversely that they preclude distribution companies from their programs, should give a company a clear indication of how important that industry is to a particular state and therefore what to expect going into a project.

Since economic development incentives focus on economic impact, the more impact that can be projected, the more incentives that are typically offered. Impact is measured in a number of ways and can be direct or indirect. Direct impact, such as tax revenues that are generated by a project, are easy to measure and should be considered the baseline when it comes to any incentive negotiation. Indirect impact, such as the economic spinoff effects of

salaries, is not as easy to measure and therefore needs to be more subjectively analyzed. Nevertheless, direct and indirect impacts are what most economic development agencies use to benchmark what a particular project is eligible to receive in the way of incentives, and it is up to the company to persuade the municipality that the overall impact will be as large as possible.

The first step is to evaluate the direct impact, including items such as sales taxes, property taxes, income taxes, payroll taxes, taxes on net worth, licenses, and so on. The second step is to explore whether any of these taxes can be mitigated or reduced either through statutory provisions or through negotiations. In both cases, eligibility requirements need to be carefully reviewed; possible alternative structures need to be considered in order to meet those requirements, and the pros and cons of those alternatives need to be fully understood.

Once the direct impact has been evaluated and any statutory exemptions or abatements identified, the company then needs to look at negotiable opportunities. For example, some states do not offer property tax abatements. However, those same states may allow an economic development agency to take title to a piece of property and as a result create an exemption that flows through to the company. This arrange-

ment is commonly referred to as municipal ownership or structured finance. In other cases, although no exemption may exist, the company may be able to negotiate that a percentage of the new property taxes being generated by the project be given back to the company to help pay for certain project costs. In some cases new sales tax revenues can be used as well. This strategy is commonly referred to as tax increment financing. In certain cases, when a project has enough impact, jurisdictions will even share the tax revenues coming off of other projects in the area that are clearly attributable to a particular project that spurred the other development. Identifying any such development ahead of time is critical to negotiating such an arrangement.

Besides sales and property taxes, which are factors in virtually every project, income taxes can be important if the company is profitable and paying tax. Although property tax abatements and sales tax exemptions are usually available for a distribution center, income tax credits are not quite as prolific. Income tax credits come in two major categories: capital investment credits and hiring credits, although there can be numerous other credits for training costs, paying certain other taxes, and so on. Within the world of capital investment credits, distribution companies are often left out in the cold, with manufacturing being the primary

location include proximity to a customer base, good intermodal transportation systems, and public sector support.

The price and availability of land, taxes, and incentives also influence location. In recent years, Nevada has become an important location for large-scale distribution centers that serve the western region, owing to its lower land prices and a good infrastructure. Amazon.com is one of the most prominent companies operating in Nevada, with a major distribution facility in Fernley, 45 minutes outside the Reno area.

Large-scale distribution and fulfillment centers have size and access requirements that are pushing

them to the edges of metropolitan areas and beyond. Suburban and exurban locations often offer larger sites and cheaper land than sites closer to the city center or in proximity to transportation hubs. The distance to major markets is a factor, though, and companies must determine the optimal ratio between land prices and the distance to the point of final distribution. How far these facilities can move depends upon local regulations, topography, traffic networks, markets, and labor forces.

The New York/New Jersey metropolitan region illustrates this dynamic. As a consequence of tremendous regional growth and land use changes, ware-

60

target of this type of credit. That's not to say that every capital credit is the same. Some states such as Connecticut and Idaho do allow distribution companies to claim capital-based credits, so each state needs to be researched to determine whether it offers a capital-based credit and, if so, whether distribution qualifies.

Hiring credits are also available to distribution companies, but the industry faces a particular obstacle to overcome. Since so many jobs involve a driver getting into a vehicle and traveling outside the facility's area, many distribution companies fail to qualify for credits when the eligibility criteria require that the employees work at the facility more than 50 percent of the time. It may, however, be possible to reach an understanding with the agency conveying the benefit.

Once the direct impacts of a project are reviewed and ways of recouping costs explored, a review of the indirect impacts and how other costs can be subsidized should occur. For example, an indirect impact of a distribution project may be that 100 new drivers are going to be trained to obtain their commercial driver's licenses. These types of licenses are valuable, and the training that occurs will improve the skills of the citizens of the state and their ability to make a living. This cost should and often can be shared to some degree.

Many states offer training programs that can offset the cost of training employees; in some cases, states may offer training programs themselves through community colleges or state universities that a company can participate in, realizing a dramatic savings.

Besides training, grants of land, cash for equipment, and below-market rents are all incentives that may be available to companies that are proactive in their approach. Some municipalities will give significant non-tax incentives to distribution companies, and some will give nothing. Shopping for the right municipality that wants the project is usually as simple as contacting a state economic development agency that in turn funnels the project through its own pipeline of local economic development agencies. Although what comes back can be challenging, companies usually have more offers than they know what to do with. Too often companies go out looking for sites and then hope that they can strike a deal. If the right deal is out there, it can often find the company if given the opportunity.

When assessing indirect impacts, the key is to create as much impact as possible. If, for example, a company is willing to commit to hiring people from the public assistance rolls, whether for driving trucks, handling administrative work, or filling any

position that gives the person a viable future, the relative impact can be dramatically enhanced. Companies that are aware of the many ways to increase impact or to educate a state or local government about why their project has significant indirect impact are the companies that walk away with the best incentive packages.

The most important thing to remember when beginning a project is to make the incentives a priority. Incentives take many forms, and each project is unique. Having the economic development agency on your side can vastly facilitate many aspects of a project. For example, something as simple as a building variance can often be fast-tracked and save a company time, money, and aggravation when it has the support of an economic development agency. Assembling a team to manage the incentive components of a project and to work with the economic development agencies early on will maximize the vast number of opportunities that are available. Although distribution and warehouse companies may have to work a bit harder than some other industries, the added effort will surely be rewarded.

John Skowronski is a senior manager with the Deloitte & Touche Credits and Incentives team in Parsippany, New Jersey.

---

houses and distribution centers once concentrated in and around New York City are being pushed farther out into the region. The New Jersey Turnpike, which functions as the transportation backbone of this movement, has attracted distribution-related development, particularly at turnpike exits 8A and 10. The area's ports and airports still function as major import and export gateways, but the majority of goods handling now occurs at the region's perimeter. This locational mismatch generates an enormous amount of freight traffic through New York City and could eventually weaken the competitive position of the New York/New Jersey port.[2]

In the San Francisco Bay Area, the East Bay has been the region's traditional industrial and distribution center. Development has clustered along railroad lines and the freeway, and near the port of Oakland's docks and airport. But rising congestion and increasing land prices have pushed warehouses and distribution centers outward to the Central Valley, 50 to 70 miles (80 to 113 kilometers) to the east. This trend is having a major impact on the efficiency of the region's distribution system. Since many customer destinations remain located within the Bay Area's urban core, demand is growing for feeder and delivery trips by truck.[3]

Courtesy IDI Associates

Easy access to suppliers and consumers is a primary factor in the location decision for distribution centers.

There has also been a move toward more consumer-oriented distribution. Demand is thus growing for warehousing that can service home delivery systems. A variety of distribution models are emerging for what is sometimes called "final-mile" delivery.

From the regional perspective, a variety of distribution location trends are in play today. Larger warehouses and distribution facilities will continue to move outward to suburban and exurban areas. The amount of land needed for these large-scale facilities will continue to limit them to locations where large sites are available and land is priced appropriately. Other factors influencing microlocation decisions will continue to include zoning, easy access to transportation infrastructure, proximity to a labor pool, and occupancy costs. At the same time, however, the importance of locating near critical transportation nodes will draw more specialized distribution facilities to prime infill sites near airports, rail terminals, and ports. Companies shipping high-value items will be willing to pay for the advantage of being close to their point of distribution.

Categories of Industrial Real Estate

The supply chain process relies on industrial real estate of all types to ensure its efficient operation. From the initial manufacturing process through storage and distribution, a variety of building types serve its specific functions and needs. These buildings range from large-scale heavy manufacturing facilities to bulk and regional warehouses to R&D flex buildings.

Industrial real estate has traditionally been classified in three main categories—warehouse, manufacturing, and research and development (R&D). These categories cover the majority of the nation's industrial supply, but they are inadequate to describe the diverse range of building types present in today's markets.

A new two-level industrial classification presented in the ULI book *Guide to Classifying Industrial Property* more accurately describes the variations between warehouse, manufacturing, and R&D flex buildings and adds three new categories: freight forwarding, multitenant, and data switch center.[4] The six primary and 12 secondary categories are:

- Warehouse distribution
  - Regional warehouse
  - Bulk warehouse
  - Heavy distribution
  - Refrigerated distribution
  - Rack-supported warehouse
- Manufacturing
  - Light manufacturing
  - Heavy manufacturing
  - Airport hangar
- Flex
  - R&D flex
  - Office showroom
- Multitenant
- Freight forwarding
  - Truck terminal
  - Air cargo
- Data switch center

All these building types play a role in the supply chain process. In addition, new variations on these

Figure 4.2 **Property Categories in the Supply Chain**

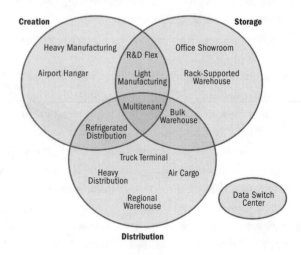

Source: Yap and Circ, *Guide to Classifying Industrial Property* (Washington, D.C.: ULI–the Urban Land Institute, 2003).

building types are emerging to meet changing supply chain requirements: fulfillment centers are a specialized type of warehouse distribution facility designed specially for e-commerce businesses, while high-throughput buildings are warehouse distribution structures without the storage component.

Warehouse Distribution

The five types of warehouse distribution buildings all share common physical and functional characteristics, although each has distinctive features that distinguish them from each other.

Regional warehouses serve a wide variety of tenants involved in warehousing and distributing goods in a local and regional setting. They are mostly rectangular in shape and built for single tenants, although they can be adapted to multiple-tenant use. They generally do not exceed 100,000 square feet (9,290 square meters) in size. A small amount of office buildout, from 5 to 25 percent of the total building size, may be found. A limited amount of space may also be allocated to light manufacturing.

Bulk warehouses are larger than 100,000 square feet (9,290 square meters), and they can exceed 1 million square feet (92,903 square meters). They have extensive loading capabilities—from 5,000 to 10,000 square feet (465 to 929 square meters) of space per loading dock. Ceiling heights often exceed 20 feet (6.1 meters), and in some newer buildings technology advances are pushing them above 30 feet (9.1 meters).

Only minimal amounts of office and manufacturing space are included.

Heavy distribution centers range in size from 100,000 to 500,000 square feet (9,290 to 46,452 square meters) and are geared toward distribution rather than warehousing, although they may also be used to store goods for extended periods. Distinguishing features include the presence of loading docks along more than one wall (also known as "cross docks") and a high ratio of loading docks per square foot of space (less than 5,000 square feet/464.5 square meters for one dock). They rarely include more than 5 percent of office space, and they contain no manufacturing space. Minimum ceiling heights are 24 feet (7.3 meters), but they can exceed 30 feet (9.1 meters). Racking systems may be used for storage, so level floors are necessary.

Refrigerated distribution buildings store perishable goods for only short periods, and so their focus is on the distribution rather than the storage of products. Their interiors include freezers and wheel-in coolers that are incorporated into the design of the building. These buildings have a wide size range, and their ceiling heights vary.

Rack-supported warehouses are configured with separate storage and shipping areas. The storage area has high ceilings and is filled with storage racking systems that also provide structural support for the building. The warehousing operation in these buildings is usually completely automated: tall, computer-

All types of industrial real estate support the supply chain process, from large-scale manufacturing facilities to flex buildings.

Solectron de México: A Model for Continuous-Flow Manufacturing and Distribution

In the global world of high technology, Solectron Corporation is known as one of Silicon Valley's most successful pioneers. It was founded in 1977 by Ray Kusumoto, an electronics engineer who was committed to cutting-edge manufacturing processes. Launched during California's highly publicized solar energy craze in the 1970s, the company hoped to capitalize on the perceived synergy between solar and electronics, hence the name Solectron (www. solectron.com). Early revenues came from providing overflow printed circuit-board assembly services to emerging original equipment manufacturers (OEMs) that supplied components and finished goods to brand-name electronics makers.

As OEM electronics companies boomed, they outsourced more of their manufacturing functions, and Solectron's revenues started soaring even though its name was never on a product or package. By outsourcing manufacturing, Solectron's customers could focus on their core competencies like research and development, sales, and marketing. These OEMs could also benefit from Solectron's state-of-the-art automation, manufacturing, and process technologies and its strong focus on quality.

By 2003, Solectron was a $12.3 billion (in revenues) multinational company, with manufacturing, repair and call centers, warehousing, and distribution facilities covering 21 million square feet (2 million square meters) in 24 countries on five continents. Solectron's approximately 65,000 employees either design, test, manufacture, or repair components and complete assemblies for different consumer and industrial products.

Solectron's advanced continuous-flow manufacturing technologies are linked to a real estate and supply-chain strategy designed to shorten time-to-market and reduce total costs during the distribution and transportation cycles. To remain a competitive low-cost producer, Solectron expanded beyond Silicon Valley in 1992 and began establishing manufacturing and warehousing campuses in strategic locations including Timisoara, Romania; Budapest, Hungary; Suzhou, Shenzhen, and seven other sites in China; Penang, Malaysia; and Guadalajara, Mexico.

Courtesy Solectron

Solectron's manufacturing and distribution facility in Guadalajara, Mexico, is designed to ensure a continuous flow of raw goods moving in and finished goods moving out.

The Guadalajara campus, Solectron de México, S.A. de C.V., was completed in 1998. Guadalajara was chosen as a manufacturing and distribution site for four primary reasons: low labor costs, a well-educated labor force, its centralized location for meeting high-volume requirements of customers in the Americas, and its proximity to major transportation hubs and logistical centers.

The 34-acre (14-hectare), fully fenced facility is located 20 minutes from the airport and has its own power substation. It consists of six 93,000-square-foot (8,640-square-meter) manufacturing modules

operated stacker cranes are used to lift, pull, or grab stored units.

Manufacturing

Light manufacturing and heavy manufacturing buildings are similar in function and appearance, but several differences distinguish these two building types. Light manufacturing facilities generally do not exceed 300,000 square feet (27,871 square meters), the average size of heavy manufacturing buildings. Light manufacturing buildings also rely significantly less on rail transport than do heavy manufacturing and therefore they have a high ratio of docks to square feet of space—10,000 to 15,000 square feet (929 to 1,394 square meters) per dock is the typical range. The lower ceiling heights of light manufacturing buildings—typically ranging from 14 to 24 feet

(4.3 to 7.3 meters) —also distinguish them from heavy manufacturing buildings, which have ceiling heights ranging from 16 to 60 feet (4.9 to 18.3 meters). Heavy manufacturing facilities accommodate tenants that manufacture parts and finished products. Light manufacturing buildings are more compatible with today's high-tech production processes. Increasingly they are being designed and developed with the flexibility to fulfill both manufacturing and distribution functions.

Airport hangars are a specialized type of manufacturing facility used for the repair and maintenance of airplanes. Most space in a hangar is allocated to airplane storage and repair, and the remainder is composed of shops, storage areas, and offices. Loading docks are used for the delivery of airplane parts and materials.

with 32-foot (10-meter) clear-height ceilings and skylights, plus two 34,000-square-foot (3,159-square-meter) jetway warehouses, all attached by an overhead breezeway. The warehouses have 26-foot (8-meter) clear-height ceilings and eight to 12 truck doors and bays. Total square footage under roof is 632,000 (58,713 square meters).

Solectron's senior corporate engineering manager Bruce Field says the Guadalajara facility's jetway warehouses are designed to keep raw goods and manufacturing components moving in and finished goods moving out on a high-throughput basis. While the term "warehouse" connotes storage, the jetways are described as "quick-flow areas" and are not designed to hold inventory for long periods. Inventory typically moves through the jetways within 48 hours.

The jetways are actually way stations or staging centers for parts in Solectron's continuous-flow manufacturing process, Field contends. "They provide points-of-use storage for parts and components for a particular product," he explains. "The worst thing is to not have them available when we need them." The inventoried whereabouts

of virtually every item in the Guadalajara campus is tracked by computer.

Solectron focuses almost 100 percent of its attention and resources in Guadalajara on manufacturing, outsourcing the physical logistics and distribution activities to third-party logistics providers. The 3PLs manage the inventory and all packing, labeling, and transportation scheduling, working out of their own warehouses away from the Solectron campus. The primary 3PL is Kuhne & Nagle, the giant international freight forwarder.

The 3PLs handle both inbound and outbound freight. Inbound, a 3PL receives raw materials and components from foreign suppliers, either by air, truck, or ship. It "detrashes" these materials (removes the packaging), stacking them in high-pile storage or on high-density shelving in their 200,000-square-foot (18,580-square-meter) warehouses. Then it fills orders for components and parts and makes up "kits" that are delivered to the appropriate jetway warehouse at Solectron's campus and then cycled into the attached manufacturing pod.

Outbound, the vast majority of what Solectron manufactures in Guadalajara is shipped north to the United States in convoys of fully loaded trucks accompanied by security escorts, according to Fred Hartung, Solectron's senior director of global logistics. Airfreight is used only for hotshot or emergency shipments, when a customer absolutely must have a product the next day. Solectron does not ship its products by ocean, except in rare circumstances, because it cannot risk exposure of its goods to salt air.

Solectron has outsourced its inventory management to its 3PLs, but the vendor-managed inventory is tracked by an enterprise software program that automatically and continually fills manufacturing kits and integrates other functions to keep product assembly moving. "We try to minimize our own managed-warehousing responsibilities and stay with our core competencies in manufacturing," says Field. The collaboration of manufacturing, real estate, and logistical specialists delivered that solution before the first shovel of dirt was turned in Guadalajara.

Flex

Because of its ability to meet the needs of a variety of users, flex space is the most common speculative industrial building type. Flex buildings can be used for offices, showrooms, distribution, manufacturing, and R&D functions such as laboratories. One definition of flex space is "anything between offices and warehouses." Flex buildings can be categorized as either R&D flex buildings or office showrooms. They are typically one- and sometimes two-story buildings ranging from 20,000 to 100,000 square feet (1,858 to 9,290 square meters). The general pattern for internal use has been about 25 percent office space and 75 percent warehouse/laboratory/light manufacturing, but the proportion of office space has grown considerably in some markets. From the exterior they have appealing facades that feature high-quality materials,

more extensive use of glass, and an upgraded building entrance. Truck doors are likely to be at the rear drive-in level rather than at elevated docks, because goods tend to be received by two-axle trucks and vans rather than tractor semitrailers.

Multitenant

Multitenant buildings are designed to house multiple tenants with functions ranging from small-scale offices and showrooms to production, storage, and service operations. Typically they are one story high and 60 to 100 feet (18.3 to 30.5 meters) deep. Buildings are often configured in L or U shapes, and they may reach about 120,000 square feet (11,148 square meters) in total size. Tenant spaces range from 5,000 to 15,000 square feet (465 to 1,394 square meters). Loading capabilities including docks and drive-in

doors can be either shared or private. Often, loading is available in the front as well as in the back.

Freight Forwarding

Freight forwarding is an integral function in supply chain management, but much of this activity does not involve the use of buildings. For example, rail yards provide a place where containers are off-loaded from trains and loaded onto trucks, and ports host the inter-modal transfer of goods from ships to trains and trucks.

The two major types of facilities used in transshipping are truck terminals and air cargo buildings. In these buildings, configuration is important; they are rectangular and always longer than deeper to minimize the distance that freight must move from one side of the building to the other. Much of the internal space is dedicated to sorting.

Truck terminals generally measure less than 50,000 square feet (4,645 square meters). They are rectangular, with an ideal depth of approximately 60 feet (18.3 meters), and they always have cross-docks. The ratio of docks to building area can be as high as one dock to 500 square feet (47 square meters). Because they transfer rather than store cargo, they have low ceiling heights that range from 12 to 16 feet (3.7 to 4.9 meters).

Air cargo buildings are located on airport property, and their function is to transfer freight from an airplane onto a truck or from a truck onto an airplane. A typical facility is cross-docked, with standard heavy trucks on the outside (the "land side") and smaller airport-type vehicles that use drive-in doors on the inside (the "air side"). Most interior space is devoted to sorting and packaging rather than storage. The size of these buildings depends on the volume of freight that an airline transports.

Fulfillment Centers

Fulfillment centers are a specialized type of distribution facility that is emerging to tackle the specialized distribution challenges of bricks-and-clicks retailers, catalogue merchants, and other e-tailers. At these facilities, employees locate, retrieve, pack, and ship products to individual customers. As expected, the focus is on speed to meet the demands of customers who expect immediate delivery.

Because of the preponderance of individual orders, this kind of fulfillment implies a change in configuration from pallet-sized or case-sized inbound freight (delivered in truckload or less-than-truckload quantities) to outbound individual items ("eaches") destined for the consumer or small business markets, often shipped by a small-package delivery service such as FedEx or UPS. This change in freight configuration has implications for facility design, location (especially for information technology and materials-handling equipment), and timing of building delivery.

These distribution facilities are large, ranging from 250,000 to 750,000 square feet (23,226 to 69,677 square meters). Ceiling clear heights need to be a minimum of 32 feet (9.8 meters) and up to 40 feet (12.2 meters), and floor lengths need to extend a minimum of 300 feet (91.4 meters) deep, in a cross-dock or front-load configuration. The building should be expandable to accommodate growth. Column spacing needs to be a minimum of 40 by 40 feet (12.2 by 12.2 meters). Ideally, additional concrete truck apron space is available for parking excess truck trailers. Floor loads and electrical capacity must be sufficient to accommodate a large amount of mechanization (including sorting equipment and conveyors), much of which will be positioned on a mezzanine level. Employee amenities such as cafeterias, restrooms, and car parking need to be scaled to accommodate several hundred employees on site in round-the-clock operations. Large parcels of land are required to meet expansion, parking, and trailer storage needs.[5]

The first-generation fulfillment centers have gravitated toward the greater Ohio River Valley, encompassing portions of the states of Ohio, Indiana, Kentucky, and Tennessee. Industrial markets such as Columbus, Ohio; Hebron, Kentucky (near Cincinnati); Indianapolis; and Louisville have seen substantial demand from these users. A large majority (more than 70 percent) of the U.S. population is reachable by truck within a two-day drive from these locations. Further, each of the integrated express carriers has its night-time national cargo hub nearby.

Integrated Express Carrier	Hub Location
Airborne Express	Wilmington, OH
BAX Global	Toledo, OH
DHL Worldwide Express	Cincinnati, OH
Emery Worldwide	Dayton, OH
FedEx	Indianapolis, IN
	Memphis, TN
United Parcel Service	Louisville, KY
U.S. Postal Service	Indianapolis, IN

Fulfillment providers seek proximity to a number of these hubs, so they can use alternate providers if necessary to achieve pricing and scheduling flexibility. This proximity also enables them to benefit from later cutoff times (sometimes as late as midnight) in delivering their product to the integrated express carriers.

While this first generation of demand has focused on large, centrally located, multicustomer distribution facilities, maturing fulfillment providers are expected to expand to markets that are accessible to concentrations of consumers. Fulfillment providers will seek outlying locations that offer substantial quantities of available (and inexpensive) land, incentives in the form of property tax and inventory tax abatements, and available (and inexpensive) labor. The biggest challenge facing fulfillment providers today is finding the available labor to staff these large facilities, particularly during the peak holiday season.

Fulfillment companies must commence operations within a narrow timing window each year, well in advance of the all-important holiday selling season. In the future, the goal will be to reduce rollout time frames for new fulfillment facilities. Any delays in commencing operations can be prohibitively expensive. For these reasons, fulfillment companies are increasingly avoiding the longer build-to-suit time frames and instead seeking facilities that are already built.[6]

High-Throughput Buildings

High-throughput buildings are specialized distribution centers designed to move goods as quickly and efficiently as possible from the manufacturer or shipper to the customer/consignee. These buildings differ in design and location based on the transportation

In high-throughput buildings, cargo is unloaded on one side of a building, moved through the facility, and reloaded on the other side.

Design Parameters for HTD Buildings

John T. Meyer

AMB Property Corporation has taken the high-throughput building idea to market with its registered brand of High-Throughput Distribution (HTD). The company's experience has shown different design parameters apply to various HTD facilities, depending on a number of factors—single vs. multitenant use, freight flow volumes, type of on- and off-loading systems and the size of the market served.

On-Tarmac HTD Buildings

A major difference between HTD and off-airport distribution facilities is the amount of column-free space between the air side and the land side. Typically, the building at a major international gateway airport measures 200 feet (61 meters) in depth by approximately 800 to 900 feet (244 to 274 meters), or three football field lengths.

In most cargo facilities, only one set of columns, located 50 feet (15.2 meters) from the land-side doors, is used. The remaining 150-by-900-foot (54-by-274-meter) space is constructed with large span beams to provide a column-free area. The column-

free clear-span is necessary so that forklifts and tugs can move cargoes quickly between the two sides of the buildings without having to dodge vertical support columns. This configuration also adds functionality by enabling users to allocate column-free space for pallet buildup and breakdown areas.

On the air side, door ratios are an important metric in on-tarmac HTD facility design. An aircraft's ability to taxi up and park on an air-side apron close to the building realizes the fundamental advantage of being on an airport. For an FAA Category 5–rated ramp position that can accommodate Boeing 747 and 777 and Airbus 340 wide-bodied aircraft, the recommended door ratio is two doors—for ingress and egress—for every 50,000 feet (15,240 meters) of building space under roof. If the average on-tarmac HTD building is 200,000 to 250,000 square feet (18,580 to 23,225 square meters), it will require eight to ten air-side doors. Each air-side door is typically 12 feet (3.6 meters) wide by 12 feet (3.6 meters) high.

New generation aircraft—including the Airbus 380, slated to debut in 2006 with a 555-seat passenger configuration and

a 150-ton (152.4-metric-ton) freighter configuration—will soon be put into service, altering the design requirements of future on-tarmac airfreight facilities. With 50 feet (15.2 meters) of increased wingspan, these aircraft will certainly need larger ramps. It is impossible to speculate to what extent new buildings will need further changes or whether existing buildings will require modification.

On the land side today, airline tenants want as many truck doors and truck bays as possible to expedite throughput. Truck doors are getting larger as well. Traditionally, they have measured nine feet (2.7 meters) wide and ten feet (3 meters) high, but now they are ten feet by ten feet (3 meters by 3 meters). In some cases the truck door is 12 feet (3.6 meters) tall to accommodate a large loaded container. The door ratio on the land side is typically one door per 3,000 square feet (279 square meters) of space under roof. The facility flooring should be able to withstand a minimum floor load of 250 pounds per square foot (10.5 kilograms per square meter) and up to 350 pounds per square foot (14.7 kilograms per square meter). The largest container allowed on an aircraft weighs approximately 15,000

On-tarmac high-throughput buildings have large column-free areas, a large proportion of doors to total area, and generous exterior truck courts.

pounds (6,804 kilograms); when combined with the weight of a forklift, it exerts extreme force on the warehouse floor.

Another important and often overlooked metric for an on-tarmac HTD building is the truck court. While not materially different than the courts at off-airport buildings, the space required for trucks to turn around, back up, and get positioned to load or discharge cargo is critical. Today's 18-wheel tractor-trailer vehicles measure a maximum of 74 feet (22.5 meters) long. To accommodate these vehicles, it is recommended that a truck court reach at least a minimum of 125 feet (38 meters) in length, with 135 feet (41 meters) preferred. Anything less can easily cause logjams among vehicles either waiting for a bay or trying to pull out of the facility and get on the road. Cargo facilities at major gateway airports are also being designed with truck staging areas to hold vehicles waiting for incoming flights. Such areas are becoming increasingly important as security requirements now focus on searching inbound trucks.

The design of an HTD building has both architectural and functional considerations. The clear height of a single-story on-tarmac building today runs anywhere from 24 to 37 feet (7.3 to 11.2 meters) under roof to the ceiling beam line. Either all or a portion of the building needs a clear height of 37 feet (11.2 meters) so that the airline tenant can stack fully loaded shipping pallets or containers four high using a manual or automated material-handling system. With modifications to the building, a 37-foot (11.2-meter) clear height also enables cargo handlers to load or unload a nose-loading 747 freighter inside the facility.

On-tarmac HTD facilities sit on airport property and therefore must comply with a long list of rules, regulations, approval processes, and zoning requirements often mandated by the airport management, airport commissioners, and municipal government officials (see "How One Developer Landed a Giant Air Cargo Facility at Wash-

ington Dulles Airport" in chapter 3). Architectural design, exterior color choices, landscaping, and other design criteria must often be in visual harmony with other cargo facilities on the airport and even with passenger terminal designs. The entitlement process at an airport is significantly longer, more complex, and costly: Constructing a new facility typically requires a Request for Proposal (RFP) to be sent to a number of developers who have had extensive experience in the development of these types of logistics buildings. The RFP process can take, on average, six months to decide who will receive the rights to develop an on-tarmac air cargo building.

Some cities with jurisdiction near major airports are starting to ban buildings that generate truck traffic or even noise but produce little taxable income for the municipality. The city of El Segundo, California, on the south side of Los Angeles International Airport, where most of its air cargo facilities are based, rejected a proposal by FedEx to build a new on-tarmac cargo handling and distribution facility. Community activists and environmentalists who vocally oppose noise levels and road congestion, among other issues, have mounted persuasive arguments opposing airfreight facilities at or near airports. Real estate investors, developers, and property managers focusing on this niche should undertake exceptionally deep and diligent investigations into potential regulatory and community roadblocks before venturing forward.

The internal configuration of on-tarmac HTD facilities differs from off-airport distribution buildings. Office space can account for up to 20 to 25 percent of the square footage under roof and is usually devoted to housing the airline's cargo sales and administrative staff, plus supervisory staff of ground-handling personnel and other employees. One sound strategy is to create offices separate from the tenant airline's quarters and to market them to federal agencies such as U.S. Customs and the

Department of Agriculture for housing supervisors and senior inspectors. Having these inspectors under roof gives the airline yet another competitive edge by expediting the clearances and inspections required for all international shipments. Office buildouts should be located on a mezzanine level over the truck doors on the land side so that they do not take up valuable floor space.

Opinions differ regarding whether a dedicated refrigerated cooler facility should be part of an on-tarmac HTD. Based on AMB's experience, coolers and chillers are not an asset in a speculative facility unless the gateway airport has an exceptionally heavy volume of perishable cargoes: fruits, vegetables, meats, and seafood. Even then, it can always be added as a buildout if the airline tenant requires it. Portable coolers are also an option.

Security has become a criterion that must be incorporated into the design of an on-tarmac HTD facility. Cargo scanning equipment—giant X-ray machines that electronically inspect boxed cargo as it is tugged through—are becoming commonplace in airfreight facilities. Developers must provide the design flexibility to meet future security technologies that may be required by existing or new transportation-related federal agencies.

Developers of turnkey on- or off-tarmac HTD facilities should consider engaging a security consulting firm to advise and recommend vendors on entry gates, license plate readers, closed-circuit television cameras, and alarm systems. The goal is to ensure that any security systems and procedures can be enhanced and expanded as new regulations and improved technology emerge.

Off-Airport HTD Buildings

The need for speed in handling goods in transit is not confined to air cargo and

continued on next page

on-tarmac facilities. Truckers, particularly expedited motor carriers, watch the clock just as closely and must meet shipper or consignee time-definite delivery schedules or lose lucrative transportation contracts. Off-airport HTD buildings include freight drop-off and distribution centers without the warehouse or storage component. These facilities can be tailored to the differing requirements of airlines that cannot get access to on-tarmac or on-airport buildings, freight forwarders, and customs brokers.

Cross-docked truck terminals, which may have truck bays on both sides depending on the design, have a "door ratio" of one door every 1,500 feet (457.2 meters). These terminals operate essentially as shipment transfer facilities with little consolidation, pallet buildup, or breakdown capabilities. Off-airport distribution centers and terminals generally have a ratio of one truck door per 4,000 to 5,000 square feet (372 to 465 square meters) under roof. Often these facilities are leased by freight forwarders, who use the truck bays for short-haul pickup and delivery. The facilities are also used for drayage hauling of outbound cargo to the airport and for loading and recovering inbound cargoes that are off-loaded and customs cleared.

Clear-span, column-free main floors are not a top priority for off-airport freight handling and distribution because the urgency of airside loading and unloading of parked aircraft is eliminated. Clear heights are lower, too—often 24 feet (7.3 meters), because there are no nose-loading 747 freighters that require higher ceilings. These buildings are generally narrower in design.

The HTD Facility of the Future

The design of on-tarmac or airport-adjacent high-throughput distribution airfreight facilities is driven by a number of factors discussed above, plus one that is often overlooked—the amount of available airport land. The world's ten busiest airports are

In land-constrained Singapore, AMB Property Corporation and Boustead Projects Pte, Ltd., developed a multitenant building with a two-story warehouse and a four-story office component. Ramp access to the second level allows simultaneous loading and unloading on both floors.

Courtesy AMB Property Corporation

almost all land constrained, some more than others. In Hong Kong and Singapore, where land is extremely precious, new airport distribution facilities follow vertical, multiple-floor configurations. One quasi-government-owned airfreight facility at Singapore's Changi International Airport is seven stories tall.

AMB's joint venture at Changi with Boustead Projects Pte., Ltd., its Singapore-based alliance partner, offers an example of the HTD logistics facility of the future at a land-constrained airport. The 233,500-square-foot (21,692-square-meter), multitenant building has a two-story warehouse and a four-story office component. The design and marketing are unusual as well: instead of being a tilt-up concrete structure, it has a futuristic design and is the first third party–owned building in the Airport Logistics Park of Singapore (ALPS I). Although it is not technically on the tarmac, it sits on airport property within a new Customs and Excise Department complex in a designated free-trade zone.

The concept is to give tenants time and cost-savings access on duties, documentation, and customs clearance. While the building does not have direct airplane ramp access, it is located only one minute from the tarmac.

Design parameters for this double-decked off-tarmac HTD building are, not surprisingly, different than for a conventional single-level facility. There are 23-foot (7-meter) clear heights on each story, 44 truck doors, and ramp access to the second level for simultaneous loading and unloading on both floors. The benefit of this configuration is that all tenants can operate as if the warehouse is located on the first floor, resulting in no loss in operating efficiencies—a far preferable alternative to conventional multistory warehouses where staging and vertical transportation is required to move goods within buildings.

John T. Meyer is senior vice president and director of AMB Property Corporation's Airport Facility Group.

modes they serve—airplanes, trucks, or rail cars. But the concept is the same: cargo is unloaded on one side of the building, moved immediately through the facility, and loaded on the other side for uninterrupted distribution.

High-throughput buildings are generally located in infill locations, either in close proximity to major highway arterials or adjacent to or on the tarmacs of high-volume gateway airports such as New York's Kennedy International Airport, Washington Dulles International Airport, Charles de Gaulle International Airport, or Changi Airport in Singapore. (For more information, see Design Parameters for HTD Buildings.)

Supplier Parks

A new twist on an old phenomenon could lead to another business opportunity for real estate professionals. The concept of supplier parks, which first appeared in Europe, is a logical outgrowth of the ever-increasing reliance on just-in-time delivery, zero inventory, and lean, expedited manufacturing. Known in site selection circles as "co-location," supplier parks offer a potentially sensible solution for vendors and suppliers with large customers who have tight delivery windows.

Unlike business parks, where sites are designed and subdivided to house a mix of unrelated companies, supplier parks host different businesses who sell to the same customer. Some tenants share the same facility and cooperate willingly and creatively on subassembly, transportation, and other logistical disciplines. Or several suppliers can receive, inspect, or even finish modules preassembled elsewhere and shipped to the supplier park.

Supplier parks promote collaboration. By sharing, coordinating, and locating near the customer, supplier park tenants can boost their productivity and generate time and cost savings in transportation, manufacturing, warehousing, and distribution. Special processes can be designed and tailored, often in conjunction with the customer, because of the close physical proximity of all participants. Suppliers that share space can reduce their own facility's size and overhead costs. And they can reduce labor expenses, depending on how they structure their collaborative partnership.

European automotive manufacturers, notably Volkswagen, have led the way on supplier parks. But Ford plans to open parks in Brazil and Chicago. The concept is designed for the manufacturer's biggest suppliers but can also attract second- and third-tier vendors who would benefit from the proximity and partnering. So far, existing supplier park models are huge—500 acres (202 hectares) is not uncommon. An early park in Martorell, Spain, designed by Exel, the British-based 3PL and supply chain manager, in concert with Volkswagen, has 35 vendor tenants and 16,000 employees.

Design Evolution

The design of warehouses and distribution centers began evolving ten years ago. Traditionally, these types of buildings tended to be built as one-story structures with short clear-span trusses, simple rectangular or square shapes, few windows, and walls of brick, concrete block, tilt-up concrete, or sheet metal. Storage, however, is no longer the only activity that takes place in today's facilities, and buildings must be designed from the inside out to accommodate a supply chain process that depends on the rapid movement of products. New software programs help companies analyze their freight flows and work backward to design appropriate buildings and interior systems.

Changes to bulk warehouses and distribution facilities over the past decade have included increased floor-to-ceiling heights, better lighting, a higher ratio of dock doors to floor area, wider spaces between columns, and the introduction of superflat floors. At the exterior there are larger truck courts and more area devoted to trailer storage. Many of these changes, such as those related to clear heights and loading capacity, have resulted from advances in the distribution and manufacturing processes as well as innovations in logistics management. The upward push in building height has resulted partly from high-lift forklifts and racking systems that create the possibility for higher pallet stacking.[7]

The flexibility that higher-volume spaces offer for a variety of users has encouraged some developers to go higher, even for speculatively built projects. While it is generally agreed that clear heights of 24 feet (7.3 meters) are a minimum standard, the options for going higher range up to 30 feet (9.1 meters) and beyond. Not all tenants need or want high ceilings, though. At high-speed distribution centers with a focus on moving rather than storing goods, there is no need or time for racking. At these centers, goods must move in and out quickly, and flexibility is crucial in moving shipments swiftly from one part of a building to the other.

Airport Characteristics Needed for an On-Tarmac Cargo Building

John T. Meyer

Not all airports are automatic candidates for a high-speed air cargo distribution center. Certain market factors can make an airport attractive for development or acquisition of an on-tarmac airfreight facility. AMB Property Corporation has identified the following airport market factors that influence its decisions to develop an on-tarmac high-throughput distribution (HTD) center. The key factors include a combination of large absolute growth in facility demand, high facility density, and a large, diverse airline tenant base.

Growth

At an airport with a growing number of flight operations from existing carriers, the addition of new airlines and increased air-freight —in both shipments and tonnage— will require new airfreight facilities. Absolute growth in cargo tonnage, rather than the rate of growth, is the key metric for measuring market effectiveness. For every metric tonne increase in cargo tonnage, there will be an equivalent increase in square footage demand. If a carrier begins new service into a market, resulting in 40,000 additional metric tonnes, the corresponding demand for space would be 40,000 square feet (3,716 square meters). This design rule may vary depending on the airport, the predominant cargo carried into that airport, and future security rules. While mature market airports will grow more slowly in percentage terms, their incremental space requirements significantly exceed faster-growing smaller airports. Examining an airport's absolute cargo growth provides a window into the future demand of cargo facilities.

Scarcity

The density of on-airport airfreight facilities, or square footage per acre, is an indicator for the scarcity of airport land. The more freight facility space per acre, the higher an airport's "scarcity." This measure enables developers to compare off-airport industrial developments in greenfield versus infill locations. Lower-density airports such as Denver International (34,000 acres/13,760 hectares) will be less stable and will not see higher rents, owing to the abundance of vacant land that can accommodate future competing projects. On the flip side are airports such as New York's John F. Kennedy International and Miami International, which will enjoy minimal competition because land at these air-

Incremental Airfreight Facility Space Forecast for Top International Cargo Airports: 1999–2005

New airfreight facility space required in millions of square feet

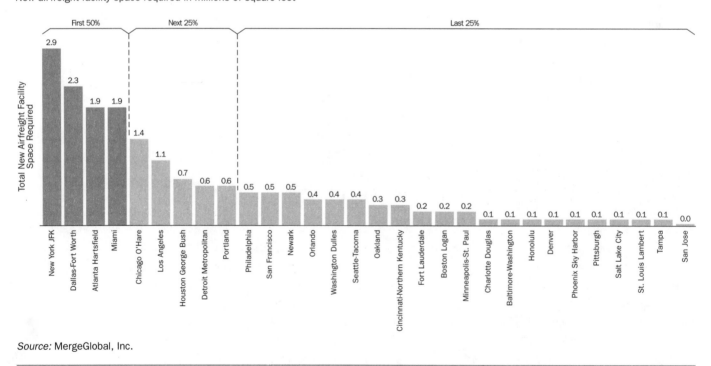

Source: MergeGlobal, Inc.

ports is completely developed. As illustrated in the accompanying graph, some of the most land-constrained airports in the nation move the largest amount of freight. Higher-density (-scarcity) airports will enjoy higher rents and less competition. Both these characteristics are attractive to landlords, whether they own on- or off-airport facilities.

Diversity

This third factor, diversity, refers to the number of airlines—passenger and all-cargo—offering international service at the airport. This variable is a key driver of market attractiveness because air carriers require more space-per-unit of capacity. High diversity also creates demand for off-airport forwarder freight-consolidation facilities where cargo from a number of shippers can be combined to achieve a

lower rate. The more airlines serving a particular airport, the more fragmented the tenant base. A fragmented tenant base is good for a landlord because it reduces dependence on a few large customers and increases the ability to rent the same

space to another air carrier should an existing tenant move out, be acquired, or drop service at the airport.

John T. Meyer is senior vice president and director of AMB Property Corporation's Airport Facility Group.

Highest Density Airfreight Facility Markets: 1999, 2005

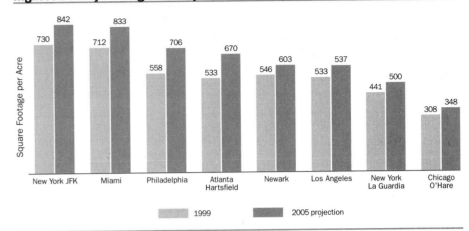

Carriers Offering Nonstop Overseas Service

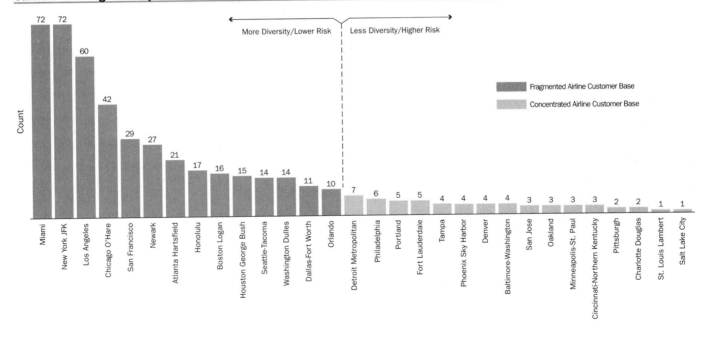

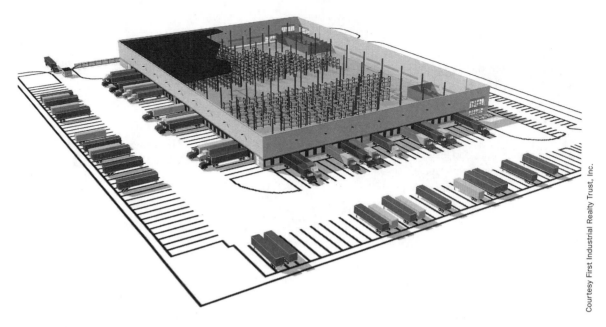

In distribution buildings, floor-to-ceiling heights are generally at least 24 feet (7.3 meters) and can be higher.

Higher stacking requires superflat floors with high loading capacities. Today the use of laser screed allows for larger areas of floors to be finished simultaneously, thus reducing the number of construction joints.

Bay spacing (the space between structural columns) is another design feature that is receiving greater attention. Requirements by large users have grown to bays of 50 feet by 50 feet (15.2 by 15.2 meters) or larger to accommodate racking and storage systems. Wider clear-span areas make buildings much more adaptable to different internal configurations, but it costs more to build the structural systems to support these widths.[8]

Power requirements are also growing for all industrial uses. In warehouses, more automated equipment and machinery, as well as more widespread use of HVAC systems, means greater demand for electrical power. An important change to life-safety systems has been the introduction of early-suppression, fast-response (ESFR) equipment.

More attention is also being paid to elements of the overall site plan. Roadways and parking areas are being configured to provide sufficient flexibility for contracting or expanding in the future. The challenge of site planning for an industrial facility is to provide the most convenient truck maneuvering and trailer storage space on the least amount of land, so that the site does not resemble a huge staging area. This goal is increasingly difficult to achieve as the old width standard of 120 feet (36.6 meters) has increased to 130 or 150 feet (39.6 to 45.7 meters) and is expected to grow to as much as 185 feet (56.4 meters) in the coming years.

A higher-quality workplace environment is also increasingly important for warehouses as well as manufacturing facilities, which tend to have more employees per building area. Natural lighting from skylights, operable windows, and air conditioning help provide a more pleasant work atmosphere. Other amenities such as lunchrooms and exercise facilities are becoming more common as a way of retaining trained workers.

Aesthetic appeal is becoming a design objective for some warehouses and distribution centers. Developers of build-to-suit industrial buildings are finding that certain owners demand style along with efficiency, flexibility, and functionality, in an effort to distinguish themselves from big, boring boxes with truck bays and roll-up doors. Attractive architecture and distinctive facades can certainly help revitalize neglected infill locations or can assure local government and zoning officials that a new industrial development will visually enhance a property or comply with community design guidelines and restrictions.

While a particular architectural style or extensively designed facade may please municipalities and first-generation users, however, the extra investment may not add sustained value to the building or command a higher price on resale. Subsequent-generation users are likely to be more focused on functionality and cost containment than curb appeal. As supply chain management, logistics services, and transportation providers as well as consignees continue to be more time- and throughput-sensitive, greater emphasis will be placed on the interior design of industrial buildings.

Design that maximizes the flow of goods is—and will continue to be—the first priority for a distribution center, freight transfer facility, truck terminal, or warehouse. Optimal use of space is directly linked with facility pass-through efficiencies. Such efficiencies, in turn, attract new customers and help retain existing ones, contributing to bottom-line profitability. The trend toward high-cube interior space volume also affects the design, sophistication, and selection of package and material handling systems—whether customized or off-the-shelf, computerized or manual. Investing in an industrial facility's interior space planning and infrastructure is probably more cost effective as owners and tenants expand their operations from single-day shifts to swing shifts and, in some cases, to partially or fully staffed round-the-clock 24/7 operations.

Investing effort and dollars in an industrial building's facade or architectural detailing may be worthwhile to get a project approved by a municipality, or for a build-to-suit for sale or long-term lease. Another justification is when a warehouse or distribution center is integrated into a multiuse industrial facility located in an office park or business campus. For an industrial facility that will be owned and leased, however, dollars are better spent on design that incorporates flexibility and enhances the flow of goods.

Size is also changing. Many national marketers are consolidating their smaller, older regional distribution and subdistribution centers into one, two, or three "megacenters" or "campuses" to capture transportation and labor efficiencies and to simplify their supply chain.

This logical trend is starting to accelerate. Companies originally built smaller distribution centers to serve two or three states and to maintain inventories. The goal was to keep high-value shipments on the ground and to use costlier airfreight for out-of-stock and hotshot shipments. But with the advent of express trucking—the ability to cover one-third of the United States within a day or overnight—and the measurable benefits of just-in-time inventory management, smaller distribution centers suddenly became expensive, unproductive, and redundant. Shippers and contract 3PLs could slash inventory, labor, real estate, equipment, and other overhead costs by combining operations into several strategically located facilities.

Historically, there have been variations in the locational decision-making process. In tough times, a company's CFO may drive the location decision, pushing for the larger, regional distribution center on cheap land. In better times, the marketing department's criteria for smaller warehouses, closer to stores for faster response and better service rise to the top of the requirements list.

Large public and private real estate owners/ operators are leading the move into king-sized distribution centers:

- Duke Realty Corporation built 500,000-square-foot (46,452-square-meter) centers in Indianapolis and Portland, Oregon, for Epson America. Epson consolidated the operations of 20 smaller centers (average size: 40,000 square feet/3,716 square meters) into the two new buildings.
- In 2002, ProLogis, a large industrial REIT, announced it was investing over $200 million to construct a national distribution network for Unilever Home and Personal Care division. Unilever HPC was created in 1997 through the mergers of Lever Brothers Company, Chesebrough-Ponds, and Helene Curtis, but the three distribution systems were not integrated. By 2005, Unilever HPC expects to save 7 percent annually in transportation, administrative, and facility costs by consolidating 15 smaller facilities into five regional DCs, totaling 4,865,630 square feet (452,032 square meters).
- USAA Real Estate Company was the developer for Sweetheart Cup Company, the $1.3 billion food-service manufacturer, when it combined five smaller distribution centers in the Middle Atlantic region into one massive distribution center. Sweetheart plans three more facilities covering 800,000 square feet (74,322 square meters) on the property as needed.
- Atlanta-based Industrial Developments International (IDI) used 55-foot (16.8-meter) clear heights in the 832,000-square-foot (77,295-square-meter) distribution center it built for Toys"R"Us near Dallas. Advancements in computer technology for processing throughput were cited as one reason for the new development.

The trend toward cavernous distribution facilities with a warehousing component is also driven by the proliferation of different products, packaging, sizes, or other distinguishing factors within a brand. Each requires its own shipping/tracking designation or

Stock Keeping Unit (SKU) and often requires separate handling or stacking.

Committing to follow these trends holds inherent risks. Historically, trends toward consolidation and decentralization in logistics facilities have ebbed and flowed, driven in part by the providers of logistics services. Nevertheless, speed to market and proximity to the customer—whether a manufacturer or a marketer—are likely to continue to be important trends influencing facility location and design. The days of building (or buying and leasing), staffing, and managing 20 different regional distribution centers may be gone.

Building for anticipated growth on sites that are not easily expanded requires a deep knowledge of logistics and transportation economics. AMB Property Corporation built two nearly identical high-through-put distribution air cargo distribution centers on the tarmac at Dallas/Fort Worth International Airport. Recognizing that DFW is a centrally located cargo gateway from the United States to Latin America, Europe, and Asia Pacific, AMB configured the combined 430,000-square-foot (39,948-square-meter) cross-dock centers with 100 truck bays and parking positions for eight 747–400 freighters on the tarmac.

The shift away from smaller facilities to half-million-foot (152,400-meter) new distribution centers could lead to redevelopment opportunities. As mid-sized companies grow and expand their supply chains, and as smaller 3PLs add services and customers, they will both be candidates for industrial properties that can be reconfigured to meet their distribution or storage needs. Some manufacturers or 3PLs do not need full occupancy and can start by leasing portions of an older or existing distribution center in a quality market with proximity to different transportation modes and infrastructures.

Security Design Considerations

Corporate America has always been at the mercy of natural disasters and sociopolitical catastrophes. Fires, earthquakes, tornadoes, floods, hurricanes, and surprise attacks can devastate businesses as well as communities. The supply chain is particularly vulnerable to catastrophic events that disable public and private infrastructures and disrupt the flow of goods and commerce. But while large companies—financial institutions and governmental agencies—invest in

disaster-preparedness plans, data redundancy, and quick-response emergency operations, the logistics function commands only secondary attention. There is little that the real estate professional can do about it.

Industrial property developers, investors, landlords, and brokers can, however, be of assistance in addressing another major but largely unknown threat to the supply chain: cargo theft. The National Cargo Security Council in Washington, D.C., whose members include Fortune 500 retailers, shippers, and tenants leasing millions of square feet nationwide, estimates cargo losses from warehouses, distribution centers, truck hijackings, and stolen tractor-trailer rigs to be nearly $15 billion annually. (These losses rank second only to the estimated $25 billion in health care fraud, which is said to be the largest drain on the U.S. economy.) The value of cargoes lost does not include the expensive ripple effects: Companies victimized by thieves have already paid material, labor, financing, manufacturing, marketing, and transportation costs to make and promote a product that is stolen. Not only do they lose the sale, but they do not recover their original costs or profit margins. And their market share is at risk when empty shelves and out-of-stocks drive their customers to competitors. Security experts contend that manufacturing and warehousing employees are responsible for more than 60 percent of the cargo thefts and merchandise losses.

The cargo theft epidemic is only worsening, with new impacts on logistics and property professionals. The September 11, 2001, attacks prompted the federal government to redirect its crime-fighting resources and beef up homeland security, pulling FBI agents off cargo theft task forces in high-crime areas. Economic slowdowns have squeezed the budgets of local law enforcement agencies. Major cities like Los Angeles, a gateway city to Asia and Latin America—and the number one market for stolen trucks loaded with cargo—have cut back on freight theft prevention and investigations. Now, more resources are devoted to high-profile and violent crime. Clampdowns by the U.S. Transportation Security Administration (TSA), which is now part of the Department of Homeland Security, and by manufacturers paying the freight bills have also put new constraints on containerized shipments and on marine, truck, and airport freight facilities. These restrictions can bite deeply into the owner's or tenant's revenue stream and profit margins. The TSA's authority is likely to expand, and real estate professionals involved in any aspect of cargo should learn more about the regulations and people who administer them.

For example, manufacturers and shippers of high-value goods must conduct security inspections of a transportation vendor or freight forwarder's cargo handling, warehousing, and distribution facilities. If they flunk, shippers are likely to boycott the airline or motor carrier until the facility's security meets their standards. Another powerful prod for importers and exporters to strengthen security is the federal Customs Trade Partnership against Terrorism program (C-TPAT). If a company fails to register for C-TPAT because it cannot meet some tough security standards, its international shipments are the last to clear U.S. Customs. In a global economy where supply chain speed is measured in minutes, a two- or three-hour delay is costly.

Traditionally, facility security has not been a concern of the industrial property professional. Security consulting firms and alarm companies have always focused on these priorities. Today, though, developers and brokers can add value for owners and tenants by recognizing and incorporating security considerations into the facility's design and construction, saving significant retrofitting costs. By demonstrating an awareness of the importance and nuances of cargo theft prevention, real estate specialists can reinforce their role as valued members of the client's team, not simply vendors.

One specialist in asset protection for logistics and industrial real estate facilities is Barry Wilkins, director of global transportation and supply chain security for Pinkerton Consulting and Investigations, the world's largest security consulting firm. His counsel may not win architectural awards for landlords or leaseholders, but it should control losses, reduce insurance premiums, and possibly make self-insurance more advantageous.[9]

Regardless of facility location, he advises his clients with warehouses, distribution centers, or any logistics facility with merchandise flow-through that they must have a secure perimeter. Best practices include a steel fence at least six feet (1.8 meters) high, topped with three strands of heavy-gauge barbed wire. The property must have a vehicle control system with a single entry and exit gate, monitored by an employee or by reputable contracted security guards. This is the bare minimum recommended by Wilkins.

A secure and well-lit perimeter is the first line of defense in securing an industrial facility.

Courtesy ProLogis

While developers of infill industrial buildings often have to comply with aesthetic requirements and codes, landscaping for a logistics facility should be neither lush nor extensive, according to Wilkins. He specifies clear sightlines, with neatly trimmed low shrubbery and no obvious places to hide loose merchandise or a shipment that could be stolen later. Landscaping can be aesthetically pleasing without providing opportunities for terrorists or thieves.

Wilkins recommends that a building's facade should have minimal glass on the ground or lower floors, thus discouraging potential thieves from canvassing the facility to study employee and vehicle movements. A logistics facility needs only one main entrance for employees, salespeople, vendors, truck drivers, and other transportation providers, and it should follow a "man-trap" configuration. This access-control strategy gives people entry to the lobby, but restricts nonemployees from entering the building's interior without a secondary log-in verification and clearance. Another design idea: bollards or giant cement flowerpots can be incorporated into the entry so that thieves cannot drive a vehicle directly into the building.

Wilkins does not suggest that commercial real estate professionals conduct security audits or specify products for tenants and landlords. But they should demonstrate a concern and understanding of the security exposures in design planning and marketing. Emergency exits should obviously be locked, with alarms tied to a central station. Closed-circuit television cameras and a backup motion detection system in the warehouse, particularly in high-value product storage areas, are recommended. CCTV cameras should be focused on loading docks and the front gate to monitor movement and to capture license plates on all vehicles entering and leaving

Global Variations in Distribution Facility Design: The Toys"R"Us Example

Jeff Ashcroft

A variety of real estate market factors around the world directly influence the size, design, and operation of warehouse and distribution facilities. As land becomes more scarce and costly, the footprint of these types of facilities must shrink to minimize costs. At the same time, in order to maintain the same storage and throughput capacities, building heights and more advanced and costly technology must be employed.

Design concepts such as multistory logistics facilities and 90-foot (27.4-meter) ceiling heights that are largely unheard of in the United States and Canada are already in use in some Asian and European cities. As land costs and availability issues intensify in North America, it is expected that these new building formats and technologies will increase in attractiveness.

Toys"R"Us across the Globe

A comparison of three Toys"R"Us distribution center facilities in different regions reveals the potential design implications for these types of facilities located in the more densely developed and costly markets of Europe and Asia.

The Toys"R"Us sites selected for comparison were in Concord, Ontario (north of Toronto); the Lodge Farm Distribution Center in Coventry, England; and the Ichikawa Distribution Center in Ichikawa, Japan. Detailed sales figures are not available. Rough estimates, however, indicate that sales at the Coventry and Ichikawa facilities are approximately twice and three times the volume, respectively as at the Concord center.

The Concord facility was built on a greenfield site and measures 398,000 square feet (36,974 square meters). The building's clear height is 36 feet (11 meters), with a capacity of 15,538,380 cubic feet (440,000 cubic meters). Sixty-four Toys"R"Us "big-box" specialty retail toy stores are serviced by this distribution center, catering to roughly 26.8 million people across Canada.

The Concord, Ontario, facility is the smallest of the three sites in both square footage and cubic capacity. It is a conventional, single-story building with relatively low ceiling heights and straightforward materials-handling methods using standard-reach forklift equipment. For its storage configuration, the center employs standard single- and double-deep pallet racking and standard straddle-reach trucks. Conveyors move packing units from receiving through to the shipping/staging area, and a sorter system is in place, as at the other two distribution centers.

The Toys"R"Us distribution center in Coventry, England, is representative of European logistics land use practices and differs significantly from the North American example. The size of this facility is 667,000 square feet (61,964 square meters), or 67 percent greater than at Concord. The building height is also greater at 52.5 feet (16 meters). The difference is magnified even further relative to total cubic capacity; at 29,664,180 cubic feet (840,000 cubic meters), the Coventry facility represents a whopping volumetric capacity

increase of 91 percent over Concord's. Maintaining the cubic capacity of this U.K. site at the same 36-foot (11-meter) building height used in Canada would require the building footprint of the U.K. site to be expanded by over 157,000 square feet (14,585 square meters).

There are also distinct differences in the materials handling solutions used for storage racking and in the mobile materials-handling equipment. The racking in the U.K. facility is configured in a seven-pallet-high fashion, versus four-pallet-high in the North American facility. In Coventry, a narrow-aisle, high-bay layout of six-foot (1.8-meter) -wide aisles is used for the racking, versus standard aisle widths in Canada of eight to 12 feet (2.4 to 3.6 meters). These configurations affect the mobile materials-handling equipment selected for operation at each site. In North America, standard straddle-reach trucks are used, while in the U.K., Crown TS Turret Trucks operate in the narrow aisles, lifting loads safely to roughly 50 feet (15.2 meters).

Carton sorting methodologies differ as well. In the Coventry location, a Matthews Sliding Shoe sorter is used, with a throughput of 8,000 cartons per hour. Conversely, the Concord facility is equipped with a pop-up wheel sorter that can process 4,500 cartons per hour.

Even greater differences are apparent at the Toys"R"Us distribution center at Ichikawa, which reflects the changes resulting from significantly costlier and scarcer land. The two most striking differences are the facts that this facility houses multiple com-

the facility. Physically secure, visible cameras are effective crime deterrents.

Other facility design considerations include separating the truck court and loading docks from the employee parking area and creating a separate lounge for truck drivers—with its own restroom and vending machines—so that drivers do not need to use the general office facilities or interact with employees. Trash compactors should be secured inside the loading dock, eliminating any need to haul refuse, and possibly merchandise, across a yard to a dumpster.

Incorporating these security considerations and configurations should include hard wiring the facility at the design stage. "Retrofitting," contends Wil-

Comparative Data for Toys"R"Us Distribution Centers

Site Variables	North America Concord, Ontario	Europe Coventry, U.K.	Asia Ichikawa, Japan
Sole tenant	Yes	Yes	No
Stories	Single	Single	Multiple
Material-handling equipment type	Standard reach	Turret truck	Crane
Building size	398,000 square feet (36,974 square meters)	667,000 square feet (61,964 square meters)	350,000 square feet (32,515 square meters)
Building height	36 feet (11 meters)	52.5 feet (16 meters)	98 feet (30 meters)
Building volume	15,538,380 cubic feet (440,000 cubic meters)	29,664,180 cubic feet (840,000 cubic meters)	14,478,945 cubic feet (410,000 cubic meters)
Indicative sales	1x	2x	3x
Cartons shipped	4,250,000	7,400,000	5,250,000
Pallet positions	31,150	57,750	27,070
Stores served	64	64	121
Managers	7	10	7
Staff off season	40	80	45
Staff in season	125	300	130

Source: Toys"R"Us.

panies in separate portions of the facility and that it is a multistory or stacked distribution warehouse. Basically, three different distribution centers are stacked on top of one another in the forward part of the building, with the Toys"R"Us 98-foot (30-meter) -high crane storage area using the entire complex height for its rack-clad pallet storage area in the rear.

The Ichikawa facility is much taller than both the European and North American buildings. With its storage area height at 98 feet (30 meters), it reaches nearly 62 feet (18 meters) higher than its North American counterpart. In other words, to build a storage area with similar capacity using the North American model would require a building footprint of more than double the size of this Japanese facility.

The increased building height results in different solutions for storage racking and mobile materials-handling equipment. The racking in the Japanese facility is 15 pallets high, more than three times the four-pallet-high configuration in the North American facility.

An automatic narrow-aisle crane system is built into each aisle. Mobility is, of course, limited, but the only way to lift and lower palletized products from such great heights safely is with an extremely stable crane system. This variance in materials-handling equipment illustrates the impact of cost on basic building features.

The accompanying table summarizes the differences between the three Toys"R"Us facilities in North America, Europe, and Asia.

This comparison of Toys"R"Us distribution facilities in North America, Europe, and Asia provides insights into the future design and materials handling features of warehouse and distribution facilities. It suggests that flexibility in design is crucial. Building designs that can be converted to different configurations, including multistory use, should be considered. Developers, logistics providers, and local governments should be aware of the issues, impacts, and planning variables involved in the future introduction of multistory distribution facilities in advance of future needs.

Jeff Ashcroft is president of Strategic Logistics Partners, a logistics consulting and information services business.

kins, "is a lot more expensive than doing it right the first time."

Indeed, providers of logistics and transportation services have an even more pressing reason to secure their cargo terminals and freight facilities: their customers—manufacturers and shippers—are demanding it. The Technology Asset Protection Association (TAPA)—a group of 65 multinational high-technology manufacturers including Intel, IBM, Hewlett-Packard, and Matsushita—have established a set of freight security requirements for all cargo-handling facilities owned or occupied by airlines, trucking lines, ocean liners, railroads, 3PLs, and freight forwarders. If a vendor/supplier's facility fails a risk assessment audit and does not meet TAPA's standards, the provider is excluded from the member's supply chain. This hammer has been effective in motivating landlords and tenants to comply and seek TAPA certification.

Richard Bernes, a retired FBI agent, director of TAPA, and president of the Bernes Group, a San Jose, California, security consulting firm advising technology manufacturers such as Phillips, Fujitsu, and Amdahl, says that securing the physical facility is the first priority but not the only procedure. Other basic strategies include investigating the backgrounds of employees and contract labor, and strengthening the entire supply chain. He contends, however, that a company's real estate adviser, developer, or broker "can provide a valuable service by thoroughly understanding a building's potential exposures to theft or loss. They can then point out to the client what should be immediately addressed on either new construction or retenanting."[10]

Like Wilkes, Bernes suggests a variety of physical security amenities to make a new warehouse or distribution center resistant to both burglaries and physical attack. He advises that all exterior and interior posts be made "ram proof" by burying them deep in concrete. He also says that windows should measure 96 square inches (619 square centimeters) and be covered with bars or steel mesh. Prewired for an alarm, the property should also have floodlighting and card-key access systems. A transportation vendor's terminal should have locked high-value cages or even vaults with a secondary access system requiring a personal identification number or card-key activation. All truck bays should be alarmed and, if possible, monitored by an exterior-mounted CCTV. A property owner, however, must strike a careful balance here: a for-lease building covered with burglar bars may convey a message to prospective lessees that the location is unsafe—rather than simply well secured.

Bernes contends that "hardening" the facility to prevent loss is the most crucial consideration, because recoveries of stolen merchandise are rare. Recovered goods are often damaged, outdated, and of little value. "Building owners or tenants need to invest time at the front end," he says. "I've found that an experienced real estate broker who understands logistics, transportation patterns, the local markets, and even the neighborhood can have solid input on security concerns."

Senior management's increasing awareness that facility security and loss prevention procedures are an investment, not an expense, will continue to grow. It has already become a chief concern for the industrial real estate professional. A deeper understanding of the challenges and possible solutions will pay dividends in stronger client relationships and referrals.

The potential for U.S.-based industrial real estate builders, developers, and brokers is substantial. Site experts predict that supplier parks will be developed in the Southeast to support new or expanded Japanese, Korean, and European automobile manufacturing sites in the region. Italian and French automobile manufacturers and automotive parts suppliers are also considering North American supplier park locations.

But there is also a risk for the suppliers and for the businesses that service them. A prime vendor can always fall out of favor and off the procurement lists after making a hefty capital investment at a supplier park. On the other hand, agile real estate professionals can always capitalize on this change by redeveloping or re-leasing the property, particularly if they understands the manufacturer's business well enough to pinpoint the supplier's likely successor.

Notes

1. Interview with David Berkowitz, director, public relations, eMarketer, August 7, 2003.

2. Markus Hesse, "Distribution Centers," unpublished paper, p. 6.

3. Ibid.

4. This system was developed by First Industrial Realty Trust and is described in Johannson L. Yap and Rene M. Circ, *Guide to Classifying Industrial Property* (Washington, D.C.: ULI–the Urban Land Institute, 2003), pp. 15–76.

5. Douglas Abbey, David Twist, and Leo J. Koonmen, "The Need for Speed: Impact on Supply-Chain Real Estate," *ULI on the Future: The Real Estate and Technology Link* (Washington, D.C.: ULI–the Urban Land Institute, 2001), pp. 4–19.

6. Ibid.

7. Anne B. Frej et al., *Business Park and Industrial Development Handbook,* 2d edition (Washington, D.C.: ULI–the Urban Land Institute, 2001), p. 134.

8. Ibid.

9. Interview with Barry Wilkins, director of global transportation and supply chain security, Pinkerton Consulting and Investigations, January 27, 2003.

10. Interview with Richard Bernes, president, the Bernes Group, November 21, 2002.

Chapter 5

AIRPORTS: SHORT-
AND LONG-TERM TRENDS

Margery al Chalabi and John D. Kasarda

Although recent events slowed the growth of cargo in most markets around the world, air cargo traffic and volumes are expected to benefit over the long term from an increasingly global economy, thriving just-in-time industries, and growing demand for high-value commodities that require fast delivery. Airports are increasingly important hubs that both support and attract logistics and distribution activities. An understanding of the dynamics of the air cargo industry and a look at the future of airport development can help guide real estate professionals who want to remain on the cutting edge of supply chain trends.

THE IMPACT OF CHANGES IN
AIR CARGO ON AIRPORT REAL ESTATE

Margery al Chalabi

Prior to September 11, 2001, growth in the U.S. and world economy helped create strong, sustained demand for world aviation services, both passenger and cargo. A seven-year boom period with unprecedented growth in demand and profitability came to an abrupt halt with the terrorist attacks, and demand for air travel within the United States and in other world travel regions entered a period of stagnation. The tur- bulence inflicted by the attacks of September 11 and their aftermath has had a considerable impact on the air cargo industry. Recovery will require that a hard look be taken at airports and aviation-related facilities and the trends affecting them. The capacity and design of existing and new facilities must be examined in light of continuing pressures to move goods faster and more efficiently.

Recent Air Cargo Trends

Prior to 2001, air cargo demand had grown at a faster pace than passenger demand, with worldwide freight tons[1] and revenue ton kilometers (RTKs) growing an average annual rate of 8.6 and 8.0 percent over the 1994–2000 period.[2] A variety of factors, including the events of September 11, the slowdown in U.S. economic activity, and the collapse of the high-tech industry, resulted in significantly reduced demand for air cargo services worldwide and record losses in 2001.

Air cargo traffic staged a moderate rebound in 2002, but the recovery was spread unevenly around the world. There were double-digit growth rates in the Asia/Pacific region (13 percent) and the Middle East (11 percent). Cargo volumes were also up slightly in Africa (2 percent) and Europe (1 percent), but they declined in Latin America/Caribbean (down 3 percent) and remained flat in North America. Overall, there was a 4 percent increase in cargo volumes worldwide.[3]

Near-term predictions for air cargo traffic remain uncertain, given current economic and political conditions. Growth forecasts by the Federal Aviation Administration (FAA), however, are optimistic. Air cargo traffic is expected to grow at rates higher than those predicted for passenger traffic, with domestic and international revenue ton miles (RTMs) increasing at annual rates of 3.9 and 5.8 percent, respectively, over the period 2003 to 2014.[4] The FAA predicts that most increased demand for domestic cargo services should occur among all-cargo carriers because of the stricter security restrictions for transporting cargo on passenger aircraft and the faster growth of freight/express services relative to mail.

Some of the changes that the air cargo industry is experiencing today were already underway before September 11, 2001. The decline of belly cargo, initially precipitated by the increased use of narrow-body passenger aircraft, has accelerated owing to the need to segregate unsecured cargo from passengers; there seems to be no reversal of this trend in the mid- to long-term. One of the FAA's first steps after the terrorist attacks was to prohibit the transport of all U.S. mail as belly cargo; that restriction was later modified to all mail weighing more than 16 ounces (453.6 grams). Furthermore, sharp cutbacks in passenger operations have dramatically affected the share of air cargo that travels in belly holds; currently, that portion is 50 percent of international freight express. In addition, both the real and imagined dangers of flying over unsurveilled cargo trouble much of the traveling public;

these concerns may be justified, since little cargo is X-rayed or subjected to other security measures.

The fact that many passenger aircraft will not be providing double duty to deliver cargo means greatly increased operations for the same traffic, not counting the forecasted growth. Much of this operations growth will materialize during night-time hours, with the possibility of greatly increasing noise levels. On-field conflicts can also be expected to rise sharply.

All-cargo airlines, on the other hand, are expected to benefit from the current turmoil. Air cargo itself has no fear of flying, and manufacturers are anxious to continue their just-in-time parts and inventory practices. Much of this cargo already is carried on all-cargo aircraft. It is expected that much more will travel that way to lessen delays caused by increased security (now) and increased traffic (later). However, a sustained recession could flatten a cargo growth curve that—for a decade—exceeded that of all other aviation sectors and that was expected to rebound from a disappointing 2000 as the global economy improved and global trade escalated.

Cargo Capabilities at Large and Medium Airports

Over the past decade, as major airports accommodated greater numbers of passenger operations and as cargo separated itself from the belly holds of those operations, overall airport operations increased. In most instances, the airport expansions required to

Figure 5.1 **Changes in Enplaned Tonnage Carried**

Airport	1993 Hub Size	Rank	Share of U.S.	Airport	2000 Hub Size	Rank	Share of U.S.
Memphis	Medium	1	9.13%	Memphis	Medium	1	8.02%
Chicago O'Hare	Large	2	5.32%	Louisville	Medium	2	4.98%
Los Angeles	Large	3	5.06%	Detroit Willow Run	—*	3	4.78%
Anchorage	Medium	4	4.62%	Los Angeles	Large	4	4.23%
Miami	Large	5	4.18%	Anchorage	Medium	5	3.90%
New York JFK	Large	6	3.60%	Indianapolis	Medium	6	3.60%
Atlanta Hartsfield	Large	7	3.21%	Dallas/Fort Worth	Large	7	3.40%
Dallas/Fort Worth	Large	8	3.19%	Newark	Large	8	3.22%
San Francisco	Large	9	3.04%	Chicago O'Hare	Large	9	3.10%
Newark	Large	10	2.96%	Miami	Large	10	2.88%

*Detroit Willow Run is a freight-only airport.

Sources: Compiled by ACG from Data Base Products, Inc., and U.S. Department of Transportation, combined T3/T100 tables.

Note: 1993 data for many smaller airports appear to be incomplete.

accommodate such growth did not materialize. This deficiency contributed significantly to the massive delays and aviation gridlock of the three years prior to the September 11 attacks. While weather was often cited as the cause, it was lack of capacity that was the true culprit. Congestion grew until the gridlock-producing delays of 1998–2000 prompted serious complaints from the flying public and their elected representatives.

In the ensuing public outcry for a "passenger bill of rights," the legitimate concerns of the cargo industry were scarcely heard. Many air express and cargo concerns had simply moved or were in the process of moving to less congested venues. FedEx, UPS, DHL, and the U.S. Postal Service had located their hubs at medium-sized and underused airports; they also created subsidiary hubs in even smaller airports. The result is a U.S. cargo industry that is more diffused now than it was in 1990.

The growing congestion at the nation's leading hub airports has had a profound effect on air cargo operations. In general, the major trends of the past decade have been:

- Large hub airports have watched their shares of the nation's cargo traffic decline and their rank slip, while medium and freight-only airports have grown—particularly in recent years. O'Hare International Airport has lost the greatest share (in tonnage forgone) of cargo traffic.

- The traffic lost or forgone to the larger hub airports continues to be served—for the most part—within their regions by smaller airports (medium hubs) with excess capacity.

- Belly traffic has slipped as a share of total cargo traffic. Cargo-only carriers have taken over larger portions of the traffic. This trend has produced increased total operations for the same delivery volume.

- Cargo operators are demanding larger, more accessible loading facilities and access to uncongested runways to avoid delay and to secure storage. The events of September 11 have intensified these concerns and the consequent demands.

- Cargo travels primarily at night, and cargo hubs have pushed operations well into the late night and early morning hours. The consequent noise impacts have increased dramatically.

Over the past eight years, for which there is consistent and reasonably comprehensive data, most large hub airports have declined in rank and in share of U.S.-enplaned cargo carried. The accompanying table, compiled from U.S. Department of Transportation data, shows the ten airports with the greatest volume of enplaned tonnage in 1993 and those in 2000.

Whereas large airports comprised four of the top six airports in 1993, there was only one (Los Angeles) in the top six in 2000, and it had dropped in both

Figure 5.2 Changes in Enplaned Cargo/Freight (percentage of U.S. freight carried)

	1975		1998	
	Freight	**Mail**	**Freight**	**Mail**
Large hub	82	76	53	72
Medium hub	13	17	33	21
Small hub	4	5	9	6
Nonhub	1	2	5	1
Total	100	100	100	100
Tons (in 000s)/ Metric Tons	2,764/ 2,808	896/ 910.4	11,786/ 11,975	2,300/ 2,337

Source: U.S. Department of Transportation.

rank and share. Both Louisville and Indianapolis benefited from the location of major express mail carriers at their sites, but they also served medium-sized populations and had reasonable capacity. Detroit Willow Run (a freight-only airport) supplemented Detroit Metro in supplying just-in-time cargo to the globalized auto industry. Willow Run was Detroit's main passenger airport until Metro Airport opened in 1955, and it served Ford's production of B-24 bombers. With the metropolitan area's greatly increased JIT cargo operations for the auto industry, it was pressed back into service. Louisville and Indianapolis have excellent central locations and good surface transportation.

While medium-sized hubs supplanted large hubs in enplaned cargo ranking, both small and medium hubs often benefited from capacity constraints at the large hubs. For instance, Chicago O'Hare's drop from the second to the ninth or eleventh spot (depending on the year) accompanied large drops in the U.S. share. Luckily, its excellent great circle routes to Europe and Asia helped O'Hare's international growth to offset its domestic losses. A survey conducted in 2001 by CRESA Partners noted that FedEx had canceled an on-airport development at O'Hare because of the airport's congestion.[5] Fortunately, the nearby Rockford Airport grew by 133,657 enplaned tons (135,802 metric tons) over the same (1992–2000) period, and Indianapolis International Airport also grew by 401,200 enplaned tons (407,638 metric tons) to help take up the slack.

In transfers not quite as stark, Sacramento's Mather Field and Oakland Airport grew to compensate for San Francisco's constraints; Boeing Field was pressed into service to compensate for Seattle's lack of capacity; Philadelphia and, to a lesser extent, Newark grew

to serve New York's losses; and Miami and Tampa–St. Petersburg's losses may have been taken up by smaller airports, including two freight-only airports: Fort Worth's Alliance and Houston's Ellington Field. (This analysis is derived from tables compiled by ACG: The al Chalabi Group, Ltd., from Data Base Products, Inc., which give the latest standing and rank changes for the top 100+ airports.)

U.S. Department of Transportation data from 1975 to 1998 show that large hubs have lost share of both airfreight (which grew by 326 percent) and mail (which grew by 157 percent). Medium hubs and nonhubs were the major gainers; freight changed venue more than mail; and large hubs lost one-third of their share. These data are summarized in the accompanying table.

Cargo operators, shippers, and users are always concerned about congestion at major hub airports, particularly the ability to get on and off the runway. Mid-sized hubs are less likely to have major congestion issues, and they often provide truckers the potential for direct speed-limit access to interstate highways. Another reason that mid-sized hubs look attractive is that they often offer more space for cross-docking facilities. All these factors, plus the need for freighters to pick up and consolidate at night (after the business day), and to sort and deliver early the next day (at beginning of business), has made location at mid-sized hub airports on the fringes of urban development more desirable.

Space is also needed for security purposes. The September 11 attacks have reinforced and expanded the need for both secure facilities and segregation of cargo from passenger operations. A secure airport perimeter, with adequate on-site space for cargo, is perceived as a major selling point. One measure likely to be adopted by airlines is the "known-shipper requirement," which means that many shipments will be held for 24 hours, increasing the need for storage space.

Adding a major cargo component to a small- or medium-hub airport provides substantial opportunities for operational efficiencies; building from the ground up, rather than retrofitting, offers a decided advantage. The broader economic benefits can be enormous for the mid-sized communities that attract cargo facilities. The environs of the airports at Cincinnati, Louisville, and Indianapolis have grown and prospered from their cargo development, as have the surroundings of major cargo/freight facilities at the Los Angeles, Miami, Chicago O'Hare, and Memphis

airports. Cargo development at certain mid-sized airports has enabled cities to participate in the expanding global economy and to revitalize stagnant or transitional economies. (See also "Characteristics Needed for an On-Tarmac Cargo Building" in chapter 4.)

Growth in Cargo-Focused Airports

As a result of space and operational constraints at large hub airports, new security concerns, and the increasing emphasis on separating passenger and cargo operations, there is growing interest throughout the world in cargo-focused airports. Some early success stories have fueled interest in cargo-focused airports. Huntsville International Airport in Huntsville, Alabama, has been successful in attracting all-cargo operations. Alliance Airport near Fort Worth, Texas, is an industrial airport that serves as the centerpiece of billions of dollars of public and private investment.

The availability of former military sites in the United States and Europe (many with existing runways), combined with local economic development incentives, has also encouraged the creation of airports with a cargo focus. Rickenbacker International Airport in Ohio is a former military base that has become a strong outpost for cargo service, enabling goods flown in from domestic and international sites to be distributed by truck throughout the Midwest and Northeast. In its early development stages, the airport pursued air carriers as well as retailers and distribution center operators by providing development parcels in an adjacent business park.[6]

The area surrounding Rickenbacker International Airport now features 13 industrial parks, including the 11-million-square-foot (1,021,933-square-meter) Rickenbacker Industrial Park. There are more than 13,000 jobs, and private investment totals nearly $1 billion. With Rickenbacker's development into a logistics center, four key business types have emerged: e-commerce fulfillment; international airfreight; freight forwarding; and distribution.

Another model for cargo-focused airports is the Global TransPark (GTP), which combines modern manufacturing and distribution facilities with multimodal transportation, advanced telecommunications, sophisticated materials-handling systems, and commercial support services that link tenants to domestic and international customers. The first Global TransPark in the United States is being developed 80 miles (128.7 kilometers) east of North Carolina's Research Triangle Park, near major highways, rail corridors, and ports. The initial phase is fully permitted, and a major runway extension and cargo building have been completed. Foreign-Trade Zone status has been awarded, and highway improvement projects are being put into place. The GTP's existing buildings consist of a 58,000-square-foot (5,388-square-meter) cargo building on a 50-acre (20-hectare) site and a 210,000-square-foot (19,510-square-meter) facility situated on 46 acres (19 hectares). Both facilities are adjacent to the Kinston Regional Jetport, minutes from major highways and 90 minutes from both Raleigh and two deepwater ports.

Development Attractions, Conflicts, and Constraints at Three Midwest Airports

Margery al Chalabi

While Chicago's O'Hare has gradually slid from the second largest cargo airport in the United States to a position that hovers around tenth place, the fortunes of Indianapolis and Louisville took off in the mid-1980s.

Growth and Congestion at Chicago O'Hare Airport

Chicago and its O'Hare International Airport long held claim to the title of the "world's busiest airport." Centrally located and well-positioned for international routes, the city has always been a logical transportation hub. It originated as a portage between the Great Lakes and the Mississippi River network and evolved successively into a rail, highway, and aviation hub. When it opened in 1960, O'Hare International Airport supplanted Midway Airport as the nation's busiest. It retained that title until 1998, when it outgrew its physical facilities and could no longer compete for growth with unconstrained airports such as Hartsfield Atlanta International Airport.

For nearly 40 years, O'Hare attracted not only the nation's largest number of air passengers, but also hundreds of thousands of jobs, millions of square feet of development, and hundreds of thousands of households. By the late 1990s, the greater O'Hare area had eclipsed the Chicago central business area as a focus for job growth and economic development. The al Chalabi Group (ACG) has analyzed this development at ten-year intervals by measuring the region's "excess jobs." Areas of excess jobs are those with a higher ratio of jobs per household than the regional average. The growth around O'Hare from 1960 to 1990, measured by this yardstick, is illustrated in the accompanying maps.

This growth, which has continued to the present, has significantly affected real estate taxes. Assessment rates in the southern portion of Cook County now stand at 1.8 times that of the north, reflecting the migration of revenue-producing jobs from the south to the north and the need to make up the shortfall. The increased tax burden falls on the southside residents.

When it opened as a replacement for Midway Airport in 1960, O'Hare was near the edge of existing development. "The Land beyond O'Hare" was a popular derisive phrase used to describe an area where nothing existed. But all the elements for growth were in place. Already located on the airport's perimeter was a major industrial development, Centex, which had anticipated O'Hare's opening. The airport's traffic volumes and the readily available space on and off the airport offered considerable incentives for the development of a major cargo industry. The city of Chicago had built several expressways to serve O'Hare, and funds from the Interstate Highway Bill, passed in 1956, supported their extension into the suburbs. This road system made the O'Hare area extremely accessible and prime for development. Because the expressways that focused on O'Hare and the northwest portion of the region were among the first to be built, they also influenced the region's major growth direction.

With these incentives in place, development at O'Hare took off in tandem with the growth of its operations. By 1990, the area generally considered to lie within the primary influence zone of O'Hare Airport (within three miles/4.8 kilometers, and including O'Hare itself) had the following concentrations of economic activity:

- 15,000,000 square feet (1,393,500 square meters) of offices
- 10,000 hotel rooms
- 15,000 square feet (1,393,500 square meters) of retail
- 4,500 acres (1,821 hectares) of manufacturing
- A total of 616,191 employees, not all of whose jobs were related to O'Hare (1989 figures)

The area within the secondary zone (within 12 miles/19 kilometers) had the following concentrations:

- 30,000,000 square feet (2,787,000 square meters) of offices
- 20,000 hotel rooms
- 125,000 retail employees
- 1,085,993 employees (1989 figures)

The development of air cargo facilities on site at the airport began in earnest in the

Job Migration in the Chicago Region: 1960–1990

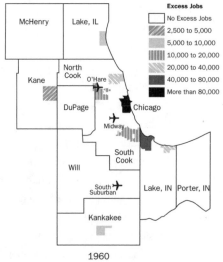
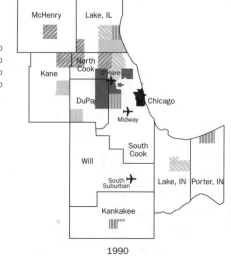

Source: ACG: The al Chalabi Group, Ltd.

O'Hare International Airport Freight and Mail Tonnage

Year	Domestic Long/Metric Tons	International Long/Metric Tons	Total Long/Metric Tons
1990	738,350/750,198	349,493/355,101	1,087,843/1,105,299
1991	706,318/717,652	382,195/388,328	1,088,513/1,105,980
1992	839,374/852,843	390,080/396,339	1,229,454/1,249,182
1993	840,718/854,208	423,362/430,155	1,264,080/1,284,364
1994	863,509/877,365	521,104/529,466	1,384,613/1,406,831
1995	819,972/833,130	542,341/551,043	1,362,313/1,384,173
1996	824,956/838,193	564,084/573,138	1,389,040/1,411,329
1997	882,687/896,851	668,919/679,653	1,551,606/1,576,504
1998	896,655/911,053	693,012/704,132	1,589,667/1,615,176
1999	890,559/904,849	797,358/810,105	1,687,917/1,715,002
2000	816,447/829,548	824,077/837,300	1,640,524/1,666,849

Sources: City of Chicago and Landrum & Brown; compiled by ACG.

mid-1980s, and the area around O'Hare has grown to be one of the largest air-freight distribution areas in the world. Although it has slipped in rank in all-cargo activity, O'Hare continues to move large volumes of freight/cargo and mail.[1] By most sources and surveys and its own statistics, O'Hare annually enplanes and deplanes 1.4 to 1.7 million tons (1,422,465 to 1,727,279 metric tons) of mail and freight. "Goods are shipped to and arrive from more than 140 domestic and 30 international nonstop destinations," reports the airport's Web site. The accompanying table shows the enplaned and deplaned cargo shipments for O'Hare Airport from 1990 to 2000.

A large and varied group handles this cargo, including the following airlines:

- Air Canada/DHL
- Air France
- Alliance
- American Airlines
- Bax Global
- British Air Cargo/Alliance
- Delta
- El Al Israel Airlines
- FedEx
- FedEx (Metroplex)
- KLM Royal Dutch Airlines
- Lufthansa Airlines
- Lynxs Chicago Cargo Port
- Northwest Airlines
- U.S. Postal Service
- United Airlines
- United Parcel Service

Few travelers or visitors—indeed, few Chicagoans—are aware of the mammoth cargo facilities that surround O'Hare. The cramped quarters originally used by the airport's cargo carriers and freight forwarders were long ago recognized as too limited to handle even nominal growth. That recognition led first to the design and construction of the facilities known as Cargo City. Begun in 1985, the site encompasses approximately 240 acres (97.1 hectares), nearly double the size of the original cargo area. Located in the airport's southwest quadrant, Cargo City offers 1.2 million square feet (111,480 square meters) of space in buildings designed to move freight and mail quickly and efficiently, well into the 21st century.

In 1996, the O'Hare Express Center was developed to meet the additional demand created by cargo operations. It covers 50.2 acres (20.3 hectares), includes five buildings, and offers approximately 850,000 square feet (78,965 square meters) of

space. To date, more than 600 jobs have been created by the development of the Express Center.

In spite of these massive existing and proposed cargo facilities, O'Hare continues to lose share of U.S. cargo, down from 5.32 percent in 1993 to 3.10 percent in 2000. In September 18, 1999, the *Chicago Sun Times* reported that the number of overnight cargo flights leaving Chicago had dropped significantly, while passenger-flight departures between 10 p.m. and 7 a.m. had increased. Chicago Department of Aviation figures showed that those flights had dropped by 17 percent—from 3,791 operations to 3,164—during the first four months of 1999, compared with those of the previous year. The number of passenger operations had risen by 7 percent, from 12,166 to 13,060, during the same period.[2] The net increase in total nighttime departures was thus 2 percent. Aviation growth in Chicago—as shown in the accompanying figure—had stalled; in spite of Midway's efforts, regional growth was stagnant and O'Hare's domestic traffic since 1998 had declined. This exchange in operation use could mean only one thing: O'Hare was being forced to relinquish its cargo operations to accommodate its growing passenger operations.

Without further expanding the aviation capacity of the region and the space availability near O'Hare Airport, Chicago will be hard-pressed to maintain its share of U.S. cargo operations. With a forecasted doubling of revenue ton miles by 2012, O'Hare's cargo tonnage would double as well. Furthermore, aircraft operations would more than double because of the decline of belly cargo.

Plans to expand Chicago's aviation capacity have been ongoing for more than 15 years. O'Hare is one of four airports in the United States whose operations were capped in 1969 under the federally imposed High Density Rule (HDR); LaGuardia

continued on next page

Aviation Trends in Chicago: 1983–2001

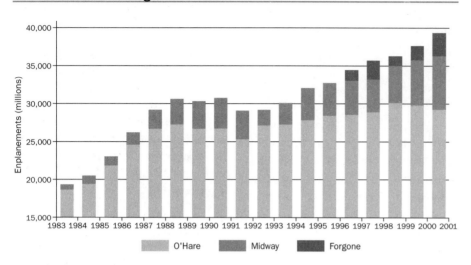

Source: ACG: The al Chalabi Group, Ltd.

and John F. Kennedy International Airports in Queens, New York, and Ronald Reagan Washington National Airport were the others. In the late 1990s, in a triumph of political correctness over reason, the HDR was lifted at LaGuardia and was scheduled for lifting at O'Hare. Lifting LaGuardia's cap resulted in aviation gridlock across the nation. The lifting of O'Hare's HDR would have been equally serious, but flight cutbacks caused by the September 11, 2001, terrorist attacks forestalled the problem. Capacity constraints are expected to resume as aviation recovers. Chicago's traffic has already rebounded, and operations are at record high levels.

Plans to build a South Suburban Airport at Peotone (38 miles/61 kilometers) south of downtown Chicago, in Will County), to serve the growing needs of the region's south and southwest areas, have been hampered by political infighting for years. The South Suburban area has a population of 2.5 million residents within 45 minutes' commute, and components of this population (Will and South DuPage counties) rank among the fastest growing in the state. For the interim, increased cargo demands for the Chicago region and Midwest will need to be met elsewhere. Rockford Airport,

75 miles (121 kilometers) northwest of O'Hare, has functioned as a reliever cargo facility for several years and will continue to serve the region's northern sector. Until the South Suburban Airport or O'Hare expansions are built, however, Indianapolis, Louisville, and Willow Run–Detroit will continue to be the principal beneficiaries of the congestion at O'Hare.

Indianapolis International Airport Thrives on O'Hare's Constraints

Indianapolis International Airport, 198 miles (319 kilometers) from O'Hare Airport and a three-and-a-half-hour drive from its environs, has been a major beneficiary of O'Hare's congestion—in the air, at on-site facilities, and on highways leading to it. Furthermore, the major industrial development focus of the Chicago region now lies on its south/southwest side; this factor makes the trip to Indianapolis more competitive as an alternative to driving the congested highways to O'Hare.

Between 1994 (when O'Hare began to hit capacity) and 2000, Indianapolis's share of U.S. cargo increased from 2.37 percent to 3.60 percent. In 1999, at the height of its cargo hubbing, it served 4.93 percent.

That year, it overtook O'Hare, ranking fourth to O'Hare's seventh in cargo/freight volume. Indianapolis has snared at least three major facilities that probably would have located at O'Hare had there been adequate space in the air and on the ground. In addition, it captured a new airline's headquarters and maintenance. These developments included:

- FedEx (sub-hub);
- ATA Airlines: headquarters and maintenance facility;
- United Airlines maintenance facility (now closed); and
- U.S. Postal Service hub (now closed).

Since the first air cargo hub was established at the airport in 1984, Indianapolis has played an important role in the development of the overnight air cargo industry. Although the overnight air cargo industry has consolidated through mergers and acquisitions, Indianapolis has retained its prominence with the FedEx hub located at the airport.

In 1999, the FedEx sub-hub opened a $250 million expansion, increasing the sort capacity to 79,000 packages per hour. The aircraft ramp was enlarged to park 68 aircraft. On the airport's north side, the U.S. Postal Service also expanded its ramp area by 560,000 square feet (52,024 square meters). Together, the hubs served 79 aircraft in a night sort and another 29 aircraft during a day sort. In February 2001, FedEx introduced "extra hours" service, including an additional sort cycle that created a virtual 24-hour operation. Future planned expansions may increase local employment to 7,000.[3] Today, Indianapolis is FedEx's second largest hub, after Memphis. It features 70 gates serving 36 wide-body jets, 26 narrow-body jets, and eight feeder planes. The facility currently employs 4,000 people.

In August 2001, the U.S. Postal Service (USPS) facility closed its overnight package hub. Owing to a new nationwide arrangement between FedEx and the USPS, FedEx is now providing all airport-to-airport transport of priority, express, and first-class mail. As a result, Indianapolis Airport lost many of its USPS employees (although some were hired by FedEx), as well as a third of its air mail and several million dollars in landing fees. FedEx will process most of this mail and package volume at its Memphis facility; Indianapolis will serve as a collection point for the USPS's overnight packages only. In the long term, FedEx may shift some of the USPS shipments back to Indianapolis. Plans call for USPS to remain an Indianapolis Airport tenant, with a potential increase in regional truck operations.

Prior to this contraction of express mail services, Indianapolis had been the fastest-growing cargo airport among the world's top 30 airports in 1998. According to figures released by the Airports Council International (ACI), Indianapolis experienced a dramatic 23.1 percent increase in air cargo from 1997 to 1998, easily outpacing the runner-up. Air cargo growth continued into 1999 and 2000; according to the ACI, Indianapolis cargo increased by 28.2 percent in 1999 and by 12.4 percent in 2000. David Roberts, the airport director for BAA Indianapolis LLC, claims a slightly lower growth for 2000 (an increase of 10.4 percent); this discrepancy is due to the minor inconsistencies in keeping cargo data mentioned in note 1. Roberts also states that this growth pattern was "consistent with our projections in the planning for the new midfield terminal and future airfield improvements."[4]

With its total cargo volume of 1,115,272 tons (1,133,168 metric tons), Indianapolis ranked 17th in the world in 2002. In this capacity, "the air cargo industry not only provides over 3,500 jobs at the airport, but is a critical part of the infrastructure supporting thousands of other jobs in the distribution business throughout the region," according to ACI.[5]

Indianapolis International Airport is operated in its entirety by BAA-USA, the world's foremost and most expert airport management firm, which has contributed toward its visibility and traffic growth. The airport is unusual in that it has no dominant commercial airline tenant. Passenger service is well distributed among competing carriers.

In spite of its small share of airport traffic, United Airlines' bankruptcy has had a major negative impact on Indianapolis. In 2003, UAL, the parent company of United Airlines, filed a motion in federal bankruptcy court in Chicago to reject its lease at the Indianapolis Maintenance Center. The city of Indianapolis has countered, asking for the return of $100 million owing to UAL's inability to deliver jobs as promised (all 4,500 are lost). ATA Airlines has also relocated its maintenance operation to Midway International Airport in Chicago.

The Indianapolis Department of Metropolitan Development, recognizing the importance of its airport and transportation resources, commissioned the preparation of a strategic development plan to help Indianapolis become an "inland port." This study, the *Indianapolis Intermodal Freight System Plan: Airport Deployment Study,* summarized its recommendations as follows:[6]

> The Indianapolis region is uniquely positioned to emerge as one of North America's critical freight transportation and distribution centers. Continued investment in the Indianapolis International Airport, Avon Yard, and the regional highway system can enable the region to expand its role as a world-class distribution center, creating new jobs and income for central Indiana. The Intermodal Development District or Inland Port, once fully developed, might include the following assets:
>
> - An expanded Indianapolis Airport, with a new midfield terminal, ground transportation center, and third runway;
> - Expanded air cargo and small package operations at the airport, through contin-

ued growth of FedEx and USPS and the location of new air cargo carriers and related facilities at the site of the existing airport terminal;
- Expanded aircraft maintenance facilities, through continued growth of UAL, ATA, or other carriers;[7]
- A redeveloped Avon Yard with a state-of-the-art rail/truck intermodal terminal serving critical customer markets in the Northeast and Southwest;
- High-speed rail service connecting the Airport district with Chicago, Cincinnati, Louisville, and other Midwest cities and carrying both passengers and small package freight;
- Regional transit service connecting the Airport district with downtown Indianapolis and the Northeast corridor, with service to both the midfield terminal and major employers in the district;
- Extension of Interstate 69 as a NAFTA (North American Free Trade Agreement) superhighway linking Indianapolis and the Airport district to both Canada and Mexico.

Louisville International Airport Takes Flight

Louisville International Airport is a medium hub airport that began operations in 1947 on the site of a U.S. Corps of Engineers runway used for manufacturing and converting military aircraft during World War II. The then-named Standiford Field served a relatively small passenger demand that has grown modestly to the present.

In 1982, however, a new level of activity at the airport was set in motion. At that point, United Parcel Service (UPS) initiated its next-day air service and launched hub operations at a UPS site located at the south end of Standiford Field. In 1987, UPS announced that it would take direct control of its entire fleet and maintenance operations based in Louisville. It began with a 35-acre (14-hectare) aircraft parking apron and 135 employees, and its subsequent growth and impact on Standiford Field and the city of Louisville have been nothing less than spectacular.

continued on next page

In 1989, UPS announced plans to construct an $18 million aircraft hangar. In 1991, it completed its headquarters office building. In 1992, it opened a 95,000-square-foot (8,825-square-meter) facility to warehouse aircraft parts and spare engines. In 1998, it announced plans to construct a major expansion of its Louisville Air Hub. By that year, the airport—now named Louisville International—had grown to be the sixth largest cargo/freight airport in the United States, with nearly 1 million square feet (92,900 square meters) of UPS operations.

By the late 1990s, the cargo facilities and operations at Louisville International Airport included the following:

- a 986,381-square-foot (91,635-square-meter) air park;
- 317 acres (128 hectares) at the airport;
- 220,000 packages/documents sorted per hour;
- 100+ flights per day; and
- 15,438 air employees; 1297 ground employees; 16,737 total Louisville employees.[8]

Louisville's success as a major cargo/express-mail facility took many—including the city's, region's, and UPS's own planners and forecasters—by surprise. Regional planners, accustomed to a less-than-robust local economy, continued to forecast only tepid growth, if not out-right declines. The airport's own master plan update in 2000 monitored the development, but forecast 2002 results from a proposed $1 billion construction program that were exceeded several years before that time.

Few people equate the simple brown boxes of UPS with the global economy and the Internet-based revolution of commerce, but they do deliver the goods. New industries have been located at Louisville International Airport that reflect the critical need for information and expedited service. For instance, computer repairs are carried out on site with 24-hour turnaround times.

While e-commerce has fueled the growth of UPS and the Louisville economy, the relatively light demands of passengers have permitted this growth to flourish. The following statistics are taken from the airport's 2000 master plan update.[9] Enplaned passengers have increased from 1.645 million in 1994 to 1.845 million in 1998. Passenger operations increased from 49,312 to 49,368 over the same period, and they are expected to increase to 64,600 by 2020. Air cargo operations, on the other hand, grew from 52,160 in 1993 to 55,444 in 1998 and are forecasted to grow to 82,232 by 2020.

UPS has been able to expand its facilities at Louisville as demand materializes. To accommodate UPS's initial major expansion and peak period aircraft arrivals and departures, the airport began an ambitious and extensive expansion of the airfield in 1988. That program involved the acquisition and relocation of major segments of residential neighborhoods, including Standiford, Highland Park, Prestonia, and Tuberose. This first relocation effort concluded in 1993.

The airport expansion was successful in allowing more operations, but it created significant noise problems that affected large numbers of nearby neighborhoods. Residents began to request noise buyouts (subsidized relocations); the community of Aston Adair's requested buyout of 1994 was completed in 1997. Other Louisville neighborhoods and the entire small city of Minor Lane Heights followed with buyout requests in 1995. A tight housing market, plus numerous complaints that the airport was insensitive to the concerns of relocatees and the cohesiveness of the neighborhoods being demolished, prompted one solution that was both original and creative. The residents of Minor Lane Heights worked together with the airport and its consultants to plan a completely new community, Heritage Creek, for relocatees. As summarized in the Holmes Report, "the

airport purchased a 287-acre (116-hectare) site for relocation. A model home village was constructed in June 1999; the first families moved to their new homes in February 2000."[10] The entire city of Minor Lane Heights, including its government and at least 90 percent of its residents, planned to move as a unit; Phase 1 consisted of 350 homesites, and Phases 2 and 3 will have 500 homesites. As a result of all such relocation efforts since the airport's major expansion program began, and those expected to be completed by the end of 2003, approximately 3,500 Louisville households will have been relocated.

In 1997, FedEx announced plans to invest $10 million on a major expansion of its Louisville Airport Express cargo operations, aiming to compete head to head with UPS. Louisville has long been attractive to truck-based and intermodal distribution enterprises because of its central location and transportation infrastructure. In addition to its air/highway transshipping of computer parts, Louisville is a key center for automotive parts owing to its central location within "Auto Alley" (a region stretching from Michigan down to Alabama with 56 automobile plants scattered in 14 states, all within a 500-mile (805-kilometer) radius of central Kentucky; interconnecting these plants with numerous suppliers are interstate highways 64, 65, 71, and 75). All these intermodal facilities would benefit by improved I-65 and I-264 access; a draft environmental impact statement has been released for a proposed new bridge crossing the Ohio River. This project would greatly improve highway access for Kentucky, Indiana, and beyond.

Increasingly, air cargo operators are moving their product by truck. As Stephen Schapiro has reported for *Air Cargo World Online*, "Many experts point to United Parcel Service's decision to guarantee its ground service as a defining moment in pressing truckers to offer their own time-definite domestic delivery. Jim Delong, general manager of Louisville International Airport, UPS's primary hub, said, 'Before the economy softened, UPS and FedEx recognized anything (shipped) less than 300 miles (483 kilometers) made as much if not more sense to go by truck.' In fact, Louisville and the FedEx hub at Memphis International Airport have seen gains in air cargo traffic in recent years even as express carriers . . . move more traffic over highways."[11]

To accommodate this trend, Louisville has made significant improvements to its highway network near the airport. Two proposed Ohio River bridges (one supplementing downtown Louisville; one serving as the missing link in the eastern circumferential highway) are expected to be further contributors to the regional highway network. Schapiro quotes Larry Doak of Aviation Facilities Company: "Airports are the catalyst for everything to come together: the airline, the trucker, and the forwarder. Airports that have property to include cross-dock operations are at a distinct advantage because some of the truck freight is going to end up on an airplane."[12]

A Search for Space

Chicago's O'Hare has run out of space—in the air and on the ground—for aviation activity, and cargo consumes great amounts of both space. Consequently, until the region is able to expand its facilities, cargo destined for the Midwest will look for space elsewhere. Indianapolis International Airport has grown rapidly and could have outstripped its own facilities had it not been for a major FedEx/USPS consolidation and the postal service's decision to ship mail traveling less than 1,000 miles (1,609 kilometers) by surface transportation. Consequently, the airport has time to complete its proposed midfield expansion. It then will be positioned for considerable new growth and additional contributions to the city and state economies. Louisville Inter-

national Airport's growth has been dramatic and has provided the essential ingredient for the economic turnaround of the city. While the airport started its expansion rather callously, it has grown to respect its neighbors. Considerable operations growth is most probable, and surrounding industrial development related to distribution should grow commensurately.

The Chicago region, on the other hand, cannot afford to further compromise its locational advantages as a national and international transportation hub. It must begin—and quickly—to expand its aviation capacity to accommodate the expected growth of passenger and cargo demands. Increasing capacity at O'Hare cannot, however, be accomplished rapidly; it will take eight to ten years. Reconfiguring and adding runways will consume most of the land currently available on site. Adding off-site parcels to the cargo inventory would require acquisition of developed facilities and provision of unimpeded access; both are expensive prospects.

Meanwhile, land acquisition continues at the site of the proposed South Suburban Airport. The FAA has approved a first-phase environmental impact statement, and additional studies are underway. The South Suburban Airport site fulfills all the requirements and desirable elements sought by the cargo industry, including:

- an uncongested airport with major growth and development potential;
- location at the nation's center;
- ready access to the nation's highway and rail networks;
- unobstructed access to runways and taxiways;
- location at the edge of a vibrant metropolis;
- large, secure on-site land availability (24,000 acres/2,230 hectares); and
- opportunities to provide input into the airport layout plan.

National freight/cargo forecasts indicate a doubling by 2015. With a regional demand for an additional 1.6 million tons (1,625,675 metric tons) of enplaned and deplaned cargo just to meet existing share, the Chicago market is both ample and enticing. By developing South Suburban Airport, Chicago should be able to retake its 5-plus percentage share of national freight/cargo.

Notes

1. Freight and cargo rankings over the past decade vary greatly by source and measurement. Although there is fairly general agreement as to the top 15–20 cargo airports, internal rankings and longitudinal trends vary considerably.

2. "O'Hare Overnight Flights Up but Cargo Takeoffs No Longer to Blame," *Chicago Sun Times,* September 18, 2001.

3. Cambridge Systematics, Inc., "Indianapolis Intermodal Freight System Plan: Air Deployment Study," June 2001.

4. Ibid.

5. "ACI Cargo Traffic Reports: Cargo Traffic 2002 Preliminary," Airports Council International, www.airports.org (June 9, 2003).

6. Cambridge Systematics, "Indianapolis Intermodal Freight System Plan."

7. With UAL and ATA gone, new users must be secured.

8. "UPS Facts," www.ups.com (May 12, 2002).

9. PB Aviation, Inc., "Louisville International Airport: Master Plan Update," June 8, 2000.

10. "An Innovative Way to Escape Airport Noise: Relocating a City," www.holmesreport.com/holmestemp/story.cfm?edit_id=287&typeid=4 (April 20, 2001).

11. Stephen Schapiro, "Airports Getting Grounded," www.aircargoworld.com/archives/feat1_aug01.htm (July 20, 2002).

12. Ibid.

AEROTROPOLIS:
THE FUTURE FORM

John D. Kasarda

A catalytic convergence of digitization, globalization, aviation, and time-based competition is creating a new economic geography, with international gateway airports driving and shaping business location and urban development in the 21st century as much as did highways in the 20th century, railroads in the 19th, and seaports in the 18th.

Today, major airports are becoming key nodes in global production and commercial systems and engines of local economic development, attracting air commerce–linked businesses of all types to their environs. These include, among others, time-sensitive manufacturing and distribution, e-commerce fulfillment, and third-party logistics firms; hotel, retail, and exhibition complexes; and office buildings that house air-travel intensive professionals such as consultants, auditors, and high-tech industry executives.

As more aviation-oriented businesses cluster near such airports and along corridors radiating from them, a new urban form—the aerotropolis —is emerging.

With the airport and its immediate area serving as a multimodal transportation and commercial nexus, strings and clusters of aviation-oriented business parks, logistics parks, industrial parks, distribution centers, information-technology complexes, and merchandise marts are forming along connecting transportation corridors stretching as far as 15 miles (24 kilometers) from the airport itself.

These airport-integrated urban complexes play a role analogous to the function that central business districts (CBDs) play in the traditional metropolis. Indeed, under the rubric of "airport city," some of these airports have become regional intermodal surface transportation nodes and major employment, shopping, meeting, entertainment, and distribution destinations in their own right.[7]

Forces Supporting Aerotropolis Growth

The Imperatives of Speed and Agility

A variety of macroeconomic forces have contributed to the growing importance of airports. Over a decade ago, futurist Alvin Toffler argued that by the beginning of the 21st century one indisputable law would determine competitive success: survival of the *fastest*.

Aerotropolis schematic.

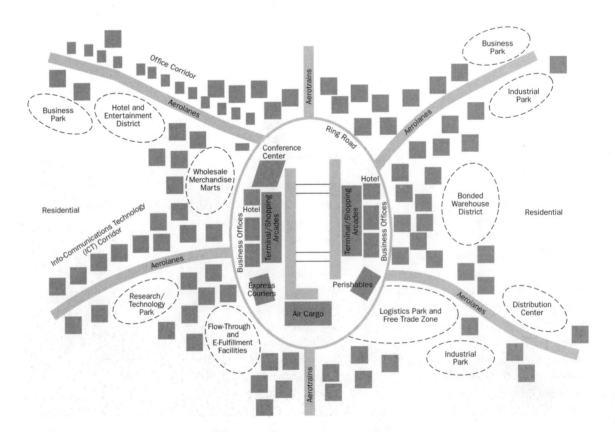

In Toffler's view, producing high-quality goods at competitive prices would still be necessary, but no longer sufficient for commercial success. Speed and agility would take center stage, as industry increasingly emphasized accelerated development cycles; international sourcing and sales; and flexible, customized production and rapid delivery.

How right he was. As we have entered the 21st century, the most successful companies are using advanced information technology and high-speed transportation to source parts globally, minimize their inventories, and provide fast and flexible responses to individual customers' needs, nationally and worldwide. They seek international partners, just-in-time suppliers, and sophisticated distributors and logistics service providers. By combining flexible production systems with information systems that connect companies simultaneously to their suppliers and customers, firms can time manufacturing much closer to customer ordering (thus reducing inventory and uncertainty), shorten their cycle times, and customize products to create additional value. They can also offer the same speed and flexibility in the delivery process from the time finished goods leave the factory until they arrive at the customer's doorstep.

Mandating such changes are rapid and relentless worldwide technological, political, and economic transformations. Modern transportation, telecommunications, and goods-producing technologies have spread throughout the globe. Trade policies are being liberalized and new markets opened. Huge wage differences between advanced industrial and developing countries have resulted in much wider geographic dispersion of component manufacturing sites, places of assembly, and distribution centers. With rising workforce skills and rapid cross-border technology transfer, what were previously known as Third World countries in Asia and Latin America have achieved much higher levels of output and now produce more sophisticated goods and services.

International customers (including those in developing countries, which many observers believe pose the best long-term markets) have also become far more sophisticated and demanding. They can choose from an unparalleled variety of products from all over the world. They are able to assess and identify value, and are therefore highly selective in purchasing. They expect quality, reliability, and competitive pricing. They also want customization of the products they buy, and they want these customized products right away, not in two to six months. For many purchases, not even two to six weeks is fast enough.

The importance of time has been heightened by the rise of e-commerce. As late as 1995, sales through the Internet were essentially zero. By 1999, U.S. Internet-based business-to-consumer (B2C) sales had grown to nearly $7 billion. Despite the death of thousands of dot-coms between 2000 and 2002, the consensus among economic and business forecasters is that e-commerce, which now accounts for about 1.5 percent of total retail sales, will continue to grow and flourish in the future.[8]

Most growth in e-commerce is expected to be in business-to-business (B2B), supply-chain transactions,

The increasing importance of speed and reliability has made airports desirable locations for distributors, air cargo, air express, less-than-load trucking, freight forwarders, and third-party logistics providers.

93

where materials and components will be ordered via the Internet and shipped to next-stage producers. Manufacturers already are able to electronically access an international network of suppliers to acquire the best-quality materials and parts at the lowest possible price. The introduction of e-marketplaces (auctions, aggregators, bid systems, and exchanges) is greatly expanding B2B e-commerce. In 2001, 93 percent of e-commerce related to B2B transactions.[9]

The expansion of B2C e-commerce and direct-to-customer Internet orders has placed a particular premium on speed and reliability in the delivery process. To meet the imperatives of speed and reliability in order fulfillment, e-commerce distribution centers are being built near gateway airports with extensive flight networks, a location trend that is sure to accelerate in the decades ahead. This is especially the case at major air express hubs such as Memphis International (FedEx) and Louisville (UPS). Air cargo express hubs actually extend the business day for e-commerce fulfillment by enabling shippers to take orders for next-day delivery as late as midnight. Dozens of e-tailers have thus already located their fulfillment centers near Memphis International Airport, including barnesandnoble.com, Toysrus.com (now teamed with Amazon.com), and Williams-Sonoma.com. The same story holds for Louisville International Airport, where such companies as Nike.com and Guess.com have sited e-commerce fulfillment centers.

Complementing airport-linked e-commerce fulfillment centers are flow-through facilities for perishables (either in the physical or economic sense), just-in-time supply-chain and emergency parts provision centers, and reverse logistics facilities for the repair and upgrade of high-tech products such as computers and cell phones. The clustering of such time-critical goods facilities around airports (often within air logistics parks), is stimulating further expansion of air cargo, air express, less-than-load (LTL) trucking, freight forwarders, and third-party logistics providers along major arteries leading into and out of gateway airports.[10]

Speedy, reliable delivery of products over long distances has become so critical to the new economy that air commerce is quickly becoming its logistical backbone. Already, air cargo and air express are the preferred modes for shipping higher-value-to-weight B2B transactions in microelectronics, automobile electronic components, aircraft parts, mobile telephones,

fashion clothing, pharmaceuticals, optics, and small precision manufacturing equipment, as well as many perishables such as seafood and fresh cut flowers. Even lower-value-to-weight B2B product distribution such as apparel, shoes, and toys are becoming time sensitive and increasingly shipped by air. As just one example, Nike chose a site near the FedEx hub in Memphis for its only apparel distribution center and one of its two footwear distribution centers. If a major athletic-shoe retail chain like Foot Locker offers a special on a new Nike product and sales are running high, its stores can make replacement orders at closing time and have them in stock by the time they open the next morning.

Further evidence of the growing imperative of speed is offered by data showing that nearly two-thirds of all U.S. air cargo is transported via 24- to 48-hour door-to-door express shipments, with Memphis International Airport becoming the world's leading air cargo airport.[11] Billions of dollars of time-sensitive goods processing and distribution facilities have been attracted to the vicinity of the FedEx hub, transforming once sleepy Memphis into a global air commerce gateway.

Information and Accessibility

Knowledge networks and air travel networks are also increasingly overlapping and reinforcing each other. With intellectual capital supplanting physical capital as the primary factor in wealth creation, time has taken on heightened importance for today's knowledge workers.

As the world's service economy shifts into fast-forward, gateway airports are becoming magnets for regional corporate headquarters, trade representative offices, and professional associations that require officers and staff to undertake frequent long-distance travel. Airport access is likewise a powerful attraction to information-intensive industries such as consulting, advertising, legal and financial services, data processing, accounting, and auditing, which often send professionals to distant customers' sites or bring in their clients by air. Business travelers benefit considerably from access to hub airports, which offer greater choice of flights and destinations, more frequent service, more flexibility in rescheduling, and generally lower travel-related costs. For example, hub airports make it easier to avoid the time and expense of overnight stays; when overnight stays are required, these airports offer clusters of on-site or nearby hotels, restaurants, shopping, fitness centers, and entertainment facilities.

The accessibility and travel flexibility hub airports offer have become essential to attracting business meetings and conventions, trade shows, and merchandise marts. Two U.S. megafacilities—Infomart and Market Center, both located on the I-35 corridor between Dallas Love Field Airport and the Dallas/Fort Worth International Airport—offer good examples of the latter attraction. Infomart is a huge, ultracontemporary merchandise display building for information and communication technology (ICT) companies. Market Center—a cluster of six large buildings containing nearly 7 million square feet (650,321 square meters) of display space for fashion clothing and home merchandise—is the world's largest wholesale merchandise mart. Hundreds of thousands of buyers and vendors fly into Dallas annually to conduct business at Infomart and Market Center.

Some observers have suggested that advances in Internet access, videoconferencing, and other distributed communications technologies will diminish the need for air travel. The evidence so far indicates that telecommunications advances often promote additional air travel by substantially expanding long-distance business and personal networking. Indeed, innovations in telecommunications technology have generated spatial mobility at least since the days of Alexander Graham Bell—whose first words over his newly invented telephone were "Watson, come here, I need you."

Others have suggested that prolonged global economic downturns, exacerbated by catastrophic events such as the September 11 attacks and the constant threat of terrorism, will permanently diminish air commerce in general and business travel by air in particular. This outcome does not seem likely, since the business imperatives encouraging the growth of air commerce and business travel (speed, mobility, and global access) are increasing in importance. Air commerce and air travel are expected to rebound from their 2001 and 2002 cyclical dip to record levels in the decade ahead.

Aerotropolis Functions and Forms

Reflecting the new economy's demands for networking, speed, and reliability, the aerotropolis is optimized by corridor and cluster development, wide lanes, and fast movements. In other words, form follows function.

Although aerotropoli have so far evolved spontaneously—with previous nearby development often creating arterial bottlenecks—in the future they will be improved through strategic infrastructure planning. For example, dedicated expressway links (aerolanes) and high-speed rail (aerotrains) will efficiently connect airports to nearby and more distant business and residential clusters. Special truck-only lanes will be added to airport expressways, and highway interchanges will be improved to reduce congestion. Seamlessly connected multimodal infrastructure will accelerate intermodal transfers of goods and people, improving transport system effectiveness and further influencing nearby land values, business locations, and resulting urban form. Advanced information-processing technologies and multimedia telecommunications systems, served by high-density fiber-optic rings and satellite uplinks and downlinks, will instantly connect companies in the aerotropolis to their suppliers, distributors, and customers and to their branch offices and partners around the globe. Multimedia technologies will also produce aerotropolis-themed electronic art along transportation corridors, highlighting culture, economic characteristics, and other features of the region served by the airport.

The metric for determining land value and particular business locations will be time-cost access to the airport. Firms of various types will bid against each other for airport accessibility, predicated on the utility each gives to the related combination of time and cost of moving people and products to and from the airport and—via the flight networks—to regional and global markets. Land values, lease rates, and commercial use will no longer be measured by traditional bid-rent functions that decline linearly with spatial distance from the primary node (the airport) but by speed to the airport from alternative sites via connecting highway and rail arteries.

This new land use and structure may initially resemble additional sprawl along main airport transportation corridors. Yet an aerotropolis will actually be a highly reticulated system based on time-cost access gradients radiating outward from the airport. In short, the "three A's" (accessibility, accessibility, accessibility) will replace the "three L's" (location, location, location) as the most important business location and commercial real estate organizing principles.

Air commerce clusters and spines are already taking distinct spatial form around major gateway

Amsterdam Airport Schiphol: The Airport City

John D. Kasarda

Amsterdam Airport Schiphol offers an excellent example of an airport city. Its grounds employ 54,000 people daily—more than the 50,000-resident criterion to attain metropolitan central city status in the United States. Two major highways link the airport to downtown Amsterdam and the broader urban area. A modern train station, directly under the air terminal, efficiently connects travelers to the city center, the rest of the Netherlands, and much of western Europe.

Schiphol Airport's passenger terminal, incorporating retail mall design elements, contains expansive, well-appointed shopping and entertainment arcades accessible both to travelers and the general public. By combining terminal design with mall design, Schiphol has substantially increased revenues through rents and passenger purchases. In fact, the airport regularly attracts many Amsterdam residents who come to shop and relax in its public section, especially on Sundays and at night when most city retail stores are closed.

Directly across from Schiphol's passenger terminal is the World Trade Centre, with meeting and commercial facilities and regional headquarters of such firms as Thomson-CFS and Unilever. Two five-star hotels adjoin this complex. Within a ten-minute walk is another complex of high-quality office buildings housing aviation-related businesses and companies offering international financial and commercial services. The commercial value of this property is reflected in its office rents, which command a solid premium in the Amsterdam area. Research by the international real estate firm Jones Lang LaSalle showed office rentals in the immediate airport area in 2000 were averaging 363 euros ($320) per square meter per year, compared to 250 euros in the Amsterdam city center and 226 euros in other Amsterdam suburban areas. Between 1997 and 2001, lease rates of prime space in the Schiphol area rose by 65 percent.

The A4 and A9 high-speed highways lie within 500 and 1,000 meters (1,640 and 3,281 feet) respectively of the airport center. Radiating from Schiphol along these roads are strings and clusters of business parks, logistics parks, high-tech industrial parks, distribution centers, information and telecommunication complexes, and merchandise clothing marts—all of them airport-intensive users.

Air cargo is largely separated from passenger operations at Schiphol. To ensure that the limited land around the airport is used most efficiently, a system of classifying cargo-related activities and regulating their locations in zones or "lines" has been in effect since the 1980s. First-line activities situated adjacent to the runways include the cargo handlers, and the second line is reserved for large freight forwarders that receive goods. The third line, situated just outside airport boundaries, includes warehouses and distribution centers.

Maintaining the proper mix of land uses in these zones and beyond is major concern. Many offices are attracted to the Schiphol area, and it is home to 10 to 12 percent of the regional supply. Because not all businesses have a pressing need to be in direct proximity to the facility, restrictions have been imposed that limit businesses in the area to those related to aviation, telecom, consultant work, and logistics.

In the face of rapidly changing logistics practices, and the need to use the limited amount of land adjacent to the airport as efficiently as possible, airport planners are now studying the classification system and reviewing whether cargo facilities' design should be based on the flow of goods rather than traditional logistics activities. They are also exploring ways to create a more seamless connection between air

Amsterdam Airport Schiphol is at the center of an expanding area of airport-linked industrial and commercial development.

cargo coming in to the airport and the rail and trucking systems that distribute it. Fully automated underground logistics systems are in the planning stage.

The pressures created by the need for speed, combined with constraints in land availability, are typified by Schiphol's flower auction. Goods are received, unloaded, and taken by truck to the flower auction facility (approximately five miles/eight kilometers away from the airport), where they are recombined or packaged as bouquets and distributed by truck to major markets. Not only does this time-sensitive process lead to congestion at the airport, but it also contributes to increased road traffic. To remedy this overload, an underground logistics system to carry preloaded air cargo containers is being planned. The project is estimated to take ten years for completion and is being undertaken in phases.

The intensification of land use activities at Schiphol is a major concern. For the proposed Schiphol Logistics Center, plans call for almost total site coverage by buildings and parking. The possibility of high or multistory distribution facilities has been researched but rejected in the near term because of cost. Observers expect that in the next five to ten years, as land prices skyrocket, this more expensive type of construction will be justified.

airports such as Chicago O'Hare, Dallas/Fort Worth, Miami, New York Kennedy, Washington Dulles, Los Angeles, London Heathrow, Paris Charles de Gaulle, and Amsterdam Airport Schiphol. In the United States, even smaller, specialized air cargo airports—such as Fort Worth Alliance Airport and Rickenbacker Airport in Columbus, Ohio—are generating mini-aerotropoli in the form of low-density cluster and spine development. Alliance Airport has attracted over $4 billion in commercial real estate investments since its inception.

Those in the air cargo industry know that the competitive battle is won on the ground—not in the air—with multimodal surface connections. This is why most of the world's leading air cargo airports also have excellent on-site or nearby intermodal interfaces. Many of the largest centers are quadramodal, possessing efficient access to all four transportation modes of air, highway, rail, and water.

Commercial growth surrounding southern California's Ontario Airport—an emerging aerotropolis that cornerstones a major logistics complex 40 miles (64 kilometers) east of Los Angeles—offers an excellent illustration of such quadramodality. The airport occupies the nexus of major east-west and north-south interstate highways I-10 and I-15, with the Burlington Northern and Santa Fe intermodal rail yard nearby. The ports of Los Angeles–Long Beach are connected to the Ontario Airport by interstate highways and rail lines.

Over 25 million square feet (2,322,576 square meters) of warehouse and distribution space were added in 1999 and 2000 adjacent to the airport and on Interstates 10 and 15, radiating out from it. In 2001 and 2002, another 30 million square feet (2,787,091 square meters) were added, led by e-commerce fulfillment and distribution facilities ranging up to 1 million square feet (92,903 square meters) in floor space for companies such as Toys"R"Us, Staples, and Home Shopping Network.

Enhancing Ontario's position as a leading logistics and e-commerce fulfillment center is the growth of express transportation services at and around the airport. During 2001, UPS, whose West Coast hub is at Ontario Airport, handled over 700 million pounds (317,514,659 kilograms) of freight, while FedEx carried over 100 million pounds (45,359 kilograms). This express service was boosted by another 100 million combined pounds (45,359 kilograms) carried by BAX Global, Emory Worldwide, and Airborne Express. Ontario's development as a multimodal logistics-based aerotropolis has greatly contributed to making the surrounding "Inland Empire" (Riverside and San Bernardino counties) the fastest growing urban complex in the United States.

In Brazil, one can observe an emerging aerotropolis centered around Viracopos International Airport in Campinas, located 50 miles (70 kilometers) northeast of São Paulo, where high-tech manufacturing, distribution, and logistics industries are clustering. Viracopos is quickly becoming the air cargo and e-commerce fulfillment center of South America, with aviation-driven urban form resulting from logistics and high-tech clusters along major highways radiating outward from the airport.

Aerotropoli are also emerging in distinct patterns around new international airports in Asia. One example is Lantau Island, where the new Hong Kong International Airport is spawning business and commercial clusters directly linked to the airport. Ten million square feet (929,030 square meters) of commercial land is being developed adjacent to the main passenger terminal. This area, known as Hong Kong Sky City, will contain office and retail, a business park, and a large hotel, leisure, and entertainment complex. In addition, a $500 million international exhibition center for trade shows is being developed.

Hong Kong International Airport's urban impact will eventually include southern China via high-speed ferries and cargo water shuttles, efficiently connecting 14 nearby coastal mainland manufacturing and commercial centers to the airport. Lantau's quadramodality (aerolanes, aerotrain, airplanes, and sea/air links) will be integrated and enhanced through mixed-use passenger/commercial terminals, business centers, and logistics parks at and near the airport.

Another major planned aerotropolis is under development at Incheon, South Korea, where the government is creating a 24-hour "winged city" on the land mass between Yeongjong and Yongyu Islands, about 35 miles (50 kilometers) southwest of downtown Seoul. The new international airport (which opened in 2001) will anchor an expansive urban agglomeration composed of commercial, industrial, residential, and tourism sectors. Its centerpiece will be Songdo Media Valley, Korea's version of Silicon Valley. Designed as a center for global high-tech industries, Songdo is being constructed adjacent to the airport on a 3,600,000-

Alliance is a major high-technology logistics, fulfillment, and trade complex in North Texas focused on multiple integrated transportation services, including Fort Worth Alliance Airport (FWAA), a 450-acre (182-hectare) industrial airport. The airport is surrounded by 9,600 acres (3,885 hectares) of privately owned land entitled for manufacturing, distribution, and office-related development. Alliance has been developed by a public/private partnership that included the Federal Aviation Administration (FAA), Texas Department of Transportation (TXDOT), and the city of Fort Worth; it was been spearheaded by Hillwood, a private developer.

Site

Alliance's development plan capitalizes on the Dallas–Fort Worth metropolitan area's transportation and other infrastructure resources, as well as its central location within the North American Free Trade Agreement (NAFTA) area. The complex is located 15 miles (24.1 kilometers) north of downtown Fort Worth, 15 miles (24.1 kilometers) northwest of Dallas/Fort Worth International Airport (DFW), and 30 miles (48.2 kilometers) northwest of downtown Dallas.

The site has exceptional transportation assets. It is well served by interstate highways and railroads. It features access to the main lines of two railroads—Burlington Northern and Santa Fe (BNSF) and Union Pacific (UP)—and interstate and state highway frontage of 18.6 miles (30 kilometers). Fort Worth Alliance Airport provides runway access to 2,600 acres (1,052 hectares), which is available on a fee simple basis.

Between 1984 and 1994, Hillwood secured a total of 15,000 acres (6,700 hectares) north of Forth Worth in an area that has become known as "AllianceTexas." Alliance is the most mature of the three components of AllianceTexas; the other two are Circle T Ranch and Heritage. The development plan for the 2,500-acre (1,012-hectare) Circle T Ranch calls for a mixed-use, master-planned community with open space, recreational facilities, and corporate campuses. Corporate campuses for Fidelity Investments and DaimlerChrysler, as well as the gated private golf community of Vaquero, already have been developed. Future plans call for additional golf courses and corporate facilities, well as a regional shopping center and medical campus.

Heritage provides the residential components of AllianceTexas. All 2,700 homes in this 2,300-acre (931-hectare) development are built with high-tech bundled wiring that allows for immediate networking of computers and video equipment. Fiber-optic wiring also enables the highest connection speeds available to a homeowner.

Development and Construction

Alliance was born in 1987, when the FAA approached Ross Perot, Jr., regarding a 2,600-acre (1,052-hectare) parcel that he owned and that the FAA had identified as a potential site for a new airport to relieve the congested air traffic at Dallas/Fort Worth International Airport. Perot recognized the FAA's interest as a real estate opportunity and pushed for the development of the parcel into a multimodal transportation hub, including an industrial airport. Perot created Hillwood, a privately owned and operated company, to lead the development of the project. Hillwood worked with various public/private partners to develop the transportation infrastructure for the project, including partnerships with the city of Fort Worth and the FAA to develop the FWAA and with TXDOT and other private landowners to build an 18-mile (29-kilometer) segment of outer-loop freeway and other highway expansions and improvements. A BNSF main line on the property's western boundary has led to the development of one of the nation's largest intermodal centers and an off-loading facility. A

Circle T Ranch at Alliance is a large-scale master-planned community with luxury residential, retail, recreation, and corporate campus uses.

Courtesy Hillwood

UP main line provides a direct connection to the companies on the development's east side. Since 1990, the public sector has invested $168 million in infrastructure development, which has leveraged $4.3 billion of private development.

The development of Alliance has involved teams of planners, economists, landscape architects, environmental consultants, and real estate professionals who worked together to create a flexible planning model that put the land's resources and attributes at the center of every development and marketing decision.

The city of Fort Worth and Hillwood negotiated an annexation and infrastructure corridor agreement that expanded the municipality's land area to encompass Alliance, extending the 1987 city limits by 12 miles (19.3 kilometers). The project has encountered few zoning and land use constraints. Fort Worth zoned a majority of the industrial park as "K–Heavy Industrial," which is the city's most encompassing land use designation. Development controls; covenants, conditions, and restrictions (CC&Rs); a comprehensive set of development guidelines; and a design review board temper the flexibility of this designation.

Commercial Development

From 1988 to 1991, Hillwood focused its efforts primarily on infrastructure development and land sales. As the Alliance project progressed, Hillwood expanded its involvement to include building development and asset management as well as land development. To date, the company has sold more than 2,100 acres (850 hectares). In 1992, it began offering real estate development services and engaging in development for its own account, and in 1994, the company expanded its speculative development efforts.

Alliance contains a total of more than 22.4 million square feet (2,081,028 square meters) of commercial, office,

and industrial space, of which Hillwood owns and manages 10.3 million square feet (956,901 square meters) (41 percent). Other owners have developed the remainder.

Because a wide variety of corporate tenants are attracted to Alliance, Hillwood has divided the site into districts catering to specific business needs. Six distinct districts are under development: Alliance Center, Alliance Gateway, Westport at Alliance, Alliance Commerce Center, Alliance Advanced Technology Center, and Alliance Crossing, which is designed to provide business and retail conveniences for Alliance area employees and residents.

The key to the project's long-term success is the synergy between the three available modes of distribution. Alliance Center, Alliance Commerce Center, Westport at Alliance, Alliance at Gateway, and the Alliance Advanced Technology Center are each linked to one or more of the transport modes offered at the park.

Fort Worth Alliance Airport, opened in 1989, ranks among the top 25 airports in the nation for air cargo traffic. It was finished in 18 months, shattering FAA design and construction records. Located in the center of the park, the airport features a 9,600-foot (2,926-meter) -long primary runway and an 8,200-foot (2,499-meter) parallel runway. It already can accommodate the world's largest aircraft, but upon completion of a primary runway extension, large cargo carriers with a full load of fuel and cargo will be able to fly nonstop to practically any destination in the world. The airport is owned by the city of Fort Worth and managed by Alliance Aviation Services, which operates a corporate aviation center and fixed base operations unit (FBO) for corporate and general aviation operations. The Alliance FBO, which has been named one of the top five FBOs in the country for seven straight years, offers various services to the airport's customers, including planning and weather briefing rooms and

conference and meeting space. Alliance Aviation Services provides all the services offered at traditional airports, including hangar spaces, cargo handling, and fueling. The airport also has its own U.S. Customs service office staffed by full-time customs personnel.

The 2,600-acre (1,052-hectare) Alliance Center is one of the districts anchored by the FWAA. The majority of the tenants in Alliance Center are air-related companies offering tenants direct runway access. American Airlines' maintenance and engineering center was the first aviation-oriented firm to locate to Alliance Center, partly because of a tax-exempt financing structure that the Alliance partnership was able to devise using Forth Worth's bond issuance abilities. To serve its fleet of Boeing 757s and 767s, American constructed a $481 million maintenance and engineering hub that encompasses 1.7 million square feet (157,930 square meters) on 200 acres (80.9 hectares) and employs more than 2,000 workers. FedEx, another notable tenant, chose a 158-acre (63.9-hectare) parcel in Alliance Center for its new $300 million sorting hub, completed in 1997. The facility, which currently employs 900 workers and ships over 175,000 packages daily, grew by 600 percent in its first three years of operation. Alliance Center also houses a Gulfstream sales and design center and Bell/Agusta Aerospace Company's corporate headquarters, which includes the delivery center for the BA609 Civilian tiltrotor aircraft. In 2004, the airport will open the Alliance Air Trade Center, an 80,000-square-foot (7,432-square-meter) cross-dock facility, which will increase the speed of multimodal transactions. More than 2,000 acres (809 hectares) are still available for development in Alliance Center.

Westport at Alliance is a 1,500-acre (607-hectare) district designed to offer tenants access to rail and other modes of transportation. Situated along the development's

continued on next page

western edge and directly on the BNSF railway's main north–south line, Westport offers development sites for distribution and industrial operations. In late 1988, BNSF selected Westport as the site for a 25-acre (10-hectare) auto unloading facility for its client, American Honda Motor Company; later, the railroad also brought Ford Motor Company and Hyundai Motor America into the Westport auto distribution center. BNSF also developed a $115 million cargo hub and rail complex on 700 acres (283 hectares) here. Completed in April 1994, the state-of-the-art facility includes a rail yard—for through trains, connecting trains, and switching cars—and an intermodal transportation center that handles large cargo containers and freight trailers. It encompasses approximately 42 miles (67.5 kilometers) of rail line, two fueling stations, and six buildings totaling 100,000 square feet (9,290 square meters) that are used for maintenance and office space. The 24/7 facility sits on BNSF's main north–south transcontinental rail line and handles over 450,000 containers a year. Companies such as Volkswagen, Michaels, Kraft, and S.C. Johnson take advantage of the efficient rail to truck distribution facilities offered by BNSF. In 1999, J.C. Penney Company opened a 1.2-million-square-foot (111,484-square-meter), highly automated retail products distribution facility at Alliance Center, employing 500 workers and moving 19,000 containers annually. In 2002, Hyundai opened its first inland processing center here. Westport at Alliance also is home to Alliance Operating Services, a Hillwood subsidiary that provides foreign-trade zone expertise and overflow industrial

Fort Worth Alliance Airport, the world's first industrial airport, serves as the centerpiece of an international trade and logistics center.

Courtesy Hillwood

space; it also houses a new centralized examination station that provides a more convenient place for U.S. Customs to inspect import shipments. Approximately 850 acres (344 hectare) remain available for development in Westport at Alliance.

Alliance Gateway, a 2,400-acre (971-hectare) industrial district, is designed to provide sites for warehouse facilities serving large-scale distributors and manufacturers. Situated on the eastern edge of Alliance about halfway between FWAA and DFW, Alliance Gateway is bisected by state highway 170 and is bordered by a UP rail line. It opened in 1992 and currently contains more than 12 million square feet (1,114,836 square meters) of warehouse and distribution facilities. Alliance Gateway's tenants include AT&T Wireless, Mitsubishi, UPS Supply Chain Solutions, Motorola,

Hewlett-Packard, Philips Electronics, General Motors, Nokia, Bridgestone/Firestone, General Mills, Nestlé, Ryder, and Honeywell. More than 1,500 acres (607 hectares) are still available for development in Alliance Gateway.

Alliance Commerce Center, a 300-acre (121-hectare) business park for office, distribution, light manufacturing, and high-tech facilities, offers a corporate environment, excellent visibility, and easy access to Interstate 35. I-35, known as the NAFTA superhighway, is the only central existing interstate corridor linking the three NAFTA nations. To date, almost 624,000 square feet (57,969 square meters) have been developed within the center, of which about 571,000 square feet (53,046 square meters) are owned and managed by Hillwood. Tenants include AdvancePCS, Ander-

square-meter (38,751,345-square-foot) site that will include a large technology park and a university research center. A new town is being developed to provide a residential base for those employed in this emerging aerotropolis. Dedicated expressways and planned aerotrains will connect to downtown Seoul and give both Songdo Media Valley employees and

the new town residents high-speed access to Incheon Airport. A teleport is under construction, and the airport also will soon be complemented by a seaport leisure port and business port.

An even more ambitiously planned aerotropolis radiates northward from the Kuala Lumpur International Airport in Malaysia. This massive new airport sen Windows, Pitney Bowes, Patterson Dental Company, Recaro, and Kimley-Horn and Associates. Approximately 260 acres (105 hectares) are available for development.

Alliance Advanced Technology Center, a corridor for technology-oriented businesses, occupies a 1,400-acre (567-hectare) site northeast of FWAA and bisected by I-35. Approximately 900 acres (364 hectares) are still available for development in the Alliance Advanced Technology Center.

Economic Incentives

There are three primary economic incentives offered at Alliance. The free-port exemption allows firms to pay no property tax on inventory that leaves the state within 175 days. Alliance offers a triple free-port tax exemption, meaning that all three primary taxing jurisdictions—school, city, and county—honor the inventory exemption.

All of Alliance's 9,600 acres (3,885 hectares) fall within a foreign-trade zone (FTZ). Foreign trade zones are secure sites where foreign and domestic merchandise are considered to be outside U.S. Customs territory. The taxable value of items produced within the FTZ does not include labor, overhead, profit, or domestic materials used during production; therefore, a savings on production costs is realized. Alliance Operating Services President Steve Boecking estimates that firms operating within the FTZ save anywhere from $75,000 to $1 million simply from using the foreign-trade zone properly.

A portion of Alliance also lies within Fort Worth's enterprise zone. Part of the Texas enterprise zone program, Fort Worth's zone provides incentives such as one-time refunds of state sales and franchise taxes. Local incentives include reduced development fees and permit fee waivers.

Experienced Gained

- To minimize land-carrying costs, large-scale land developers must position themselves as resource managers and work to generate profitable interim yields on land being held for future development.

- It was an uphill struggle to convince potential corporate tenants that Alliance is a diversified transportation and communication facility offering state-of-the-art strategic assets—in other words, that it is more than simply an airport. Many manufacturing and distribution tenants are just beginning to learn how to exploit the property's strategic assets, and Hillwood is continually providing the facilities, infrastructure, services, and support systems to serve existing and potential corporate residents. As distribution continues to become more multimodal, the transportation infrastructure and services provided at Alliance will become more crucial.

- In such a massive project, the developer must assume some managed risk in order to stimulate activity and to achieve credibility for the project. Although initially reluctant, Hillwood developed speculative warehouse space in concert with local economic development officials. The reward for taking this risk was solid absorption that stimulated job growth and gave the project momentum. Hill-

wood currently owns 42 buildings in the park totaling more than 10 million square feet (929,368 square meters). When companies need flex space, Hillwood allows them to use existing buildings on a long- or short-term basis.

- An effective public/private partnership is critical to the success of a one-of-a-kind project like Alliance. Fortunately, the local community shared Hillwood's vision and was willing to participate in its realization. Hillwood positioned itself not only as a developer but also as a public service provider and economic developer, and as such it garnered strong public support.

- The relationship between the various firms located in Alliance adds to the success of the project. A network of third-party logistics companies and supply chain operators located at Alliance provides quick access to services and products. In addition, Hillwood has helped to establish service-oriented businesses specifically for its corporate residents. Companies such as Alliance Operating Services and the Alliance Opportunity Center provide foreign-trade zone services, third-party logistics, and education services to Alliance customers, helping them compete successfully in a global economic environment. Other ancillary firms provide services or components to Alliance's largest businesses. These opportunities are fostered by Hillwood, which helps organize human resource, facility management, and security groups to provide better collaboration between companies.

is designed to provide the aviation foundation for Malaysia's Multimedia Super Corridor, a high-tech government, commercial, education, and residential zone about the size of the city of Chicago. Promoted internationally as the future information and communications technology center of Asia, the corridor will contain two new cities—Putrajaya, the relocated gov-

ernment capital, and Cyberjaya (Cybercity), each of which will house about a quarter of a million residents —along with a multimedia university to train information technology workers. The corridor's hard infrastructure is being complemented by a soft infrastructure of laws and policies, with the objective of creating a distinctive commercial environment for developing and merging new audio, video, and data transmission technologies.

Perhaps the most efficient and aesthetically appealing emerging aerotropolis is Singapore's Changi International Airport. At its land-side core, the passenger terminals house extensive arcades designed around thematic retail, restaurant, and entertainment center concepts. Open 24 hours a day, Changi's arcades also include lounges, business centers, transit hotels, fitness centers, saunas, and local area networks (LANs) that provide computer-equipped passengers with free wireless access to the Internet.

Changi's wide, uncongested aerolane to downtown Singapore will soon be complemented by an aerotrain going directly from the city center to the air terminals. An air logistics park adjacent to the airport is designed to further improve Singapore's rapid fulfillment functions and allow third-party logistics providers (3PLs) to offer distant customers highly customized products at minimum response time. Virtually every major 3PL in the world is active in and around Changi.

Real Estate Opportunities

Amsterdam's Schiphol, Hong Kong's Lantau Island, South Korea's Incheon, and Singapore's Changi demonstrate that international gateway airports have the ability to drive dynamic new forms of urban development. In so doing, they are increasing nearby transportation-accessible property values at rates faster than those at virtually all other metropolitan locations.

The commercial real estate community has already begun to take serious notice. For example, both the Trammell Crow Company and Hines have established airport property divisions in their corporate structures. The Perot Group has spun off Hillwood Development to focus on maximizing real estate returns on the acreage surrounding its Alliance Airport and offers Hillwood Strategic Services to replicate the Alliance model elsewhere. Hillwood was selected as the master developer for a 2,000-acre (809-hectare) business park to be anchored by the San Bernardino International Airport. San Bernardino is marketing itself as a hub for the Inland Empire's logistics/transportation industry, serving as a magnet for further industrial and warehouse development.

Real estate investment trusts such as ProLogis and AMB Property Corporation are likewise giving primary emphasis to airport-linked logistics and distribution properties. In fact, AMB disposed of nearly all its traditional warehousing and retail properties to focus its investments on high-velocity flow-through distribution facilities and air-commerce property at or near America's largest airports. At the same time, specialized commercial real estate companies including International Airport Centers in Birmingham, Michigan, and Craig Davis Properties of Raleigh, North Carolina, are concentrating on building business and distribution parks around the nation's top airports, while firms such as DAMG of New York and Aris of Houston are introducing innovative public/private financing instruments to develop air cargo facilities and commercialize cargo complexes at existing airports.

Airports are even buying other airports (for example, Frankfurt Airport has purchased nearby Hahn Airport) and, under concession, managing commercial property at other airports. Schiphol manages JFK's new terminal and retail outlets, the British-based BAA manages Pittsburgh International's highly acclaimed retail AirMall terminal, and the Vancouver International Airport Authority operates 14 airports in six countries. Major airports are joining hands and forming property companies; Amsterdam Schiphol and Frankfurt airports forged a joint-venture company (Pantares) to purchase equity and manage air-side and land-side assets at airports around the globe. Pantares is part of the consortium chosen to develop, build, and manage Hong Kong's Air Logistics Park.

Finally, multinational engineering and construction enterprises are establishing partnerships with airport management groups to purchase privatizing airports worldwide and develop on-site and adjoining real estate. An example is Alterra Partners, which is owned by Bechtel Enterprises and Singapore Changi Airport Enterprise, a wholly owned subsidiary of Singapore's Civil Aviation Authority. Another Bechtel subsidiary, Fremont Realty Capital, is aggressively seeking airport-linked property for investment purposes. These firms understand the powerful role airports and air commerce will play in business strategy and location in the 21st century. They are placing their bets accordingly.

Challenges Ahead

While the accessibility, connectivity, and speed the aerotropolis provides to business will enhance the competitiveness of urban places, its emergence presents a number of planning challenges. First, as

Reasons for Interest in Commercial Airport Privatization

In spite of the paucity of privatization attempts or successes to date, there remains considerable interest in the possibilities for privatization of U.S. airports. The reasons are:

- Commercial airports generate significant revenues.
- Well-capitalized firms, with worldwide experience in airport development and management, are eager to expand into the world's largest aviation economy.
- Developers believe airports have considerable untapped potential.
- Large construction firms have spun off a company to build, own, and operate airports worldwide, focusing on international business.
- Large real estate firms have established airport-specific subsidiaries.
- Aviation demand will continue to grow at a substantial pace, in spite of a worldwide economic downturn and the impact of the September 11 attacks.
- Federal funding levels continue to drop for expansions and improvements.
- Additional security increases costs.
- Capacity constraints have caused increased costs to airlines, higher fares for passengers, and economic losses to regions.
- States and municipalities are facing budget problems and are beginning to view airports as significant revenue and economic development sources.
- Airports, airlines, and municipalities are eager to seize new private sources of funding both for airport expansion and for economic development.
- Cargo operators in particular are well financed and seeking airports in which they can operate more freely.

Obstacles, however, remain. According to the General Accounting Office, the Federal Aviation Administration itself remains one of the most difficult hurdles to overcome. Many of the controversies concerning privatization involve revenue diversion, and the FAA responds to each proposal as a case-by-case study. These problems are most severe in the sale of an existing facility in which substantial public funding has been consumed. A new facility may have fewer problems, but timeliness, reasonable schedules, and a commitment to complete the project remain necessities to any private developer.

Source: ACG: The al Chalabi Group, Ltd., Issues in Airport Finance and Development: A White Paper on Public/Private Partnerships, 2003.

---

pointed out by Güller and Güller in *From Airport to Airport City*, land-side development beyond airport perimeters is rarely coordinated, since the territory frequently crosses numerous jurisdictions. In absence of aerotropolis-wide coordination and planning, the efficiency and true functional integrity of the aerotropolis is often compromised, limiting businesses and cities from achieving their full competitive potential.

Other challenges confront efficient aerotropolis evolution, especially around mature gateway airports. The existing development, which sometimes took place many decades ago, in the immediate vicinity of such airports is often unsightly and inconsistent with current best-use functions and efficiency. Numerous older airports are surrounded by low-grade warehouses and truck depots, strip commercial establishments (such as fast-food establishments, budget motels, and adult entertainment facilities), and large non-aviation-oriented businesses (such as lumber yards and heavy equipment sales and service). It may take many more decades for these to be replaced by new airport-intensive businesses. Complicating the process is that many small parcels around airports are privately and independently owned, making large contiguous land assemblage too costly and difficult to attract the major commercial real estate developers that typically drive integrated cluster projects such as business and logistics parks.

In many parts of the world, uncoordinated planning continues to permit residential development under aircraft noise contours. This oversight frequently leads eventually to restrictions on flights even when excess airport capacity exists, while lowering the value of the residential properties and eliminating more appropriate commercial uses of the land. Tax dollars are thereby lost, residents are disturbed, and commercial efficiencies are diminished.

Recognition by local jurisdictions in the Netherlands that Amsterdam Schiphol Airport was at the center of an expanding territorial complex of airport-linked industrial and commercial development led to the establishment of a public/private partnership to oversee the development of available sites near the airport. This organization—the Schiphol Area Development Corporation—directly manages some of these projects while coordinating all of them. It operates like a quasi-development authority for the broader Schiphol aerotropolis.

Shown here is Schiphol-Rijk, a master-planned office/industrial park next to Amsterdam Airport Schiphol.

Although it appears unlikely that many such development authorities will be created in the near future to coordinate and optimize broader land use development near most major airports, measures can be implemented to encourage such outcomes. One strategy would be to institute periodic working sessions with local jurisdictional officials and planners in an aerotropolis area to inform them about the nature of airport-linked development and to explore how each specific jurisdiction might complement and leverage this new form of development. A larger view of the aerotropolis and local governments' roles in its evolution could reduce unproductive jurisdictional competition, encourage more effective and mutually beneficial marketing and branding for business recruitment, and lead to more coordinated actions addressing airport-induced problems.

A related tactic would be to periodically convene all land use decision makers within an aerotropolis area (including airport executives, planners, developers, and community officials) for discussions and information exchange regarding all stakeholders' real and perceived needs and goals. Such discussions may prevent (or at least reduce) future conflicts and improve the prospects for sustainable aerotropolis development. Arterial congestion, pollution, noise, unsightly construction, and other factors negatively affecting the image of an aerotropolis and the quality of life of nearby residents must be addressed. Appealing design, high-quality building standards, improved site planning, adequate green space, signage regulations, attractive thoroughfare lighting, and other amenities should be incorporated into a consistent development process. Aerotropolis gateways defining the project area should be planned and designed with appropriate signage, and the area's corridors should be beautified with attractive lighting, themed electronic art, and landscape design that includes screening of large parking areas and unsightly buildings. Consistent with aerotropolis principles, cluster rather than strip development should characterize commercial land use planning, with maintained green space between clusters.

Longer-range planning should emphasize the eventual smooth transition of existing inconsistent buildings and land uses to functions that better leverage overall aerotropolis productivity and sustainable development. Where feasible, regulations or incentives should be implemented to speed this transition process.

One cannot ignore the widening and deepening impact of major airports on urban growth and form in the coming decades. Aerotropoli will increasingly emerge. The critical question is: will they form and grow intelligently, achieving the maximum potential benefits to people, businesses, and places, or will they persist in following the spontaneous, haphazard, less-than-efficient pattern that has characterized much airport-related commercial real estate development to date?

Notes

1. U.S. domestic tons weigh 2000 pounds, but most of the world measures cargo volume in metric tons (tonnes), which weigh 2204.62 pounds.

2. "FAA Aerospace Forecast: Fiscal Years 2003–2014," p. I-3, www.apo.faa.gov/foreca02/content_5.htm (May 15, 2003).

3. "ACI Cargo Traffic Reports: Cargo Traffic 2002 Preliminary," Airports Council International, www.airports.org (June 9, 2003).

4. "FAA Aerospace Forecast," p. I-15.

5. Ed Riggins, "Landed Cost," *Air Cargo World Online*, March 2001, www.aircargoworld.com (April 16, 2002).

6. "Airport's Industrial Cargo Strength," *Air Cargo World*, April 2002, pp. 33–39.

7. Mathis Güller and Michael Güller, *From Airport to Airport City* (Barcelona, Spain: Airport Regions Conference, 2001).

8. "E-Stats," U.S. Census Bureau, www.census.gov/mrts/www/current.html (July 23, 2003).

9. "E-Stats," U.S. Census Bureau, www.census.gov/eos/www/papers/2001/2001estatstext.pdf (July 23, 2003).

10. John D. Kasarda, "Time-Based Competition and Industrial Location in the Fast Century," *Real Estate Issues* (winter 1998/99): 24–29.

11. Airports Council International, "ACI Cargo Traffic Report Final 2001," www.airports.org (June 10, 2003).

Chapter 6

RAIL INTERMODALISM AND NEW INDUSTRIAL LOCATION DYNAMICS

Jon B. DeVries

The emergence of containerization as the dominant mode of moving international goods, coupled with the growth of U.S. rail and truck intermodal shipping, has affected the location choices of major industrial distribution developments. For decades, industrial distribution facilities were decentralized to scattered locations as freight traffic—particularly high-priced merchandise traffic—shifted to trucking, which allowed greater flexibility in distribution patterns. Recent trends in manufacturing and in intermodal shipping, however, seem to support recentralization trends in the location of major manufacturing and regional distribution facilities:

- Development of major new intermodal freight facilities is occurring in select major markets—particularly port cities and inland cities with strong growth dynamics and multiple intermodal connections.
- Urban brownfield sites are becoming attractive for new intermodal yards in some markets, creating new economic development opportunities for these areas.
- Large-scale intermodal yards being developed in suburban areas are replacing older, smaller facilities in scattered locations.

These trends have important implications for corporate location decision makers, transportation planners, economic development professionals, and developers.

Railroads and the Growth of Intermodalism

Historical Background

When intermodal rail/truck shipping began in the 1950s, the railroads were struggling to compete with common-carrier trucking firms that were rapidly capturing most high-value merchandise traffic. In response, the railroads started rolling trucks onto flatcars (a practice known as "piggybacking") and opened ramps at hundreds of locations where they thought they could capture some truckloads. Piggyback loads were often carried in regular freight trains and did not represent a significant improvement in timely service.

The emergence of major international ocean carriers with dedicated container ships (pioneered by SeaLand) revolutionized the international shipping industry. As globalization increased, the ocean carriers started investing in railroad container equipment to move in solid trainloads and maintain strict shipping schedules. The introduction of double-stack trains (cars with the capacity to stack two containers atop one another) in the 1970s and 1980s brought a major technological breakthrough in shipping efficiency. The 1990s thus saw a decline in trailers moving on rail and an explosion in container traffic. In addition to being stackable, containers move without the weight of undercarriages and wheels, resulting in significant train fuel savings. The result of combining ocean container shipping with dedicated double-stack trains has been a significant decrease in the cost of shipping and transit times.

The railroads have responded by building major new facilities at key shipping centers and subsequently abandoning hundreds of underserved ramps at every railhead. Clearly, there are both winners and losers among American cities in this location shift.

Rail Carrier Facility Expansion Plans

The four major U.S. railroads have concentrated their resources at 30 to 40 rail yards each and are signifi-

Railroad companies are developing major intermodal freight facilities in selected markets throughout the United States.

cantly increasing their operating capacities at key gateways. The location characteristics and expansion plans of each carrier have dramatic implications for manufacturers and distributors who rely on access to dependable, cost-effective international and domestic shipping resources.

CSX currently has 35 U.S. facilities, all located east of the Mississippi River. Nearly 75 percent of these facilities have been expanded in the past five years. New facilities have been opened in Cleveland, Atlanta, and Chicago (59th Street) since 1997. In Atlanta, CSX has opened the first phase ($32 million expenditure and 175,000 lift capacity—i.e., number of containers or trailers that can be transferred annually between trains and trucks) of a 500-acre (202-hectare) facility on I-285 and has seen a wide range of regional distributors locate nearby. New facilities planned for the next five years include those in Charlotte, North Carolina; Chicago (a third yard); Buffalo; Detroit; and Jacksonville, Florida.

Norfolk Southern (NS) owns 31 U.S. facilities and operates a total of 39 facilities (eight facilities are owned by different railroads or port authorities). In the past five years, more than 35 percent of the facilities have experienced major expansions, and six new facilities have been added in Harrisburg and Bethlehem, Pennsylvania; Atlanta, Savannah, and Decatur, Georgia; and Cleveland. Austell Yard, opened in July 2001, gave Atlanta its second new facility in the past two years. NS has also announced plans to build a $16 million intermodal terminal on the site of the former Philadelphia Navy Yard. The 160-acre (64.7-hectare) site will open in 2004 with 60,000 lift capacity on a 50-acre (20.2-hectare) first phase. It is expected to stimulate significant new industrial development.

Union Pacific (UP) has 40 U.S. intermodal facilities in 31 markets. There are four facilities in Chicago, and a fifth facility in Rochelle, Illinois, west of the city, is underway.

Burlington Northern and Santa Fe (BNSF) currently has 35 U.S. intermodal facilities. Major expansions have occurred at Alliance, Texas; Houston; San Diego; Memphis; and at two yards in Chicago. In the past five years, BNSF has opened new facilities in Stockton and San Bernardino, California, and in Joliet, Illinois. In conjunction with the Alameda Corridor project in southern California, BNSF will also be developing a major intermodal facility somewhere in the Los Angeles market in the next five years.

The two Canadian carriers, Canadian National and Canadian Pacific, have major U.S. facilities as well, with more planned. Regional carriers such as Kansas City Southern (KCS) are also major intermodal players—particularly with the expansion of KCS into Mexico, which promises to vastly expand U.S./Mexico intermodal traffic. Gateway traffic to Canada (through Detroit; Port Huron, New York; and Buffalo) and Mexico (through Laredo, Texas; El Paso, Texas; and Otay Mesa, California) is experiencing significant new levels of growth in the wake of the NAFTA agreement.

Line haul capacity is also under major expansion. As part of the breakup of Conrail, NS and CSX spent more than $200 million each to reduce delivery times between Chicago and New York from 32 hours to 26 hours. BNSF and UP have double-tracked hundreds of miles of western lines to increase train capacity.

Recentralization Trends

New Intermodal Facilities

Container-based intermodal shipping adds a cost-effective, relatively weatherproof, vandal/theft-proof and increasingly speedy form of transit to the range of freight transportation options available to U.S. companies. This option is affecting many location decisions being made for markets that have high-quality intermodal capacity and connections. After decades of decentralization of industrial development encouraged by the trucking industry and the interstate highway system, a decided recentralization trend is resulting in a new clustering of industrial/distribution facilities in select U.S. markets with intermodal capabilities. In particular, Chicago, Atlanta, Kansas City, and port cities such as Los Angeles; Charleston, South Carolina; and the New York/New Jersey metropolitan area have been big early winners.

Chicago, which has long been the Midwest's principal transit hub, is seeing a new surge of activity because it has six rail lines: America's four biggest freight-carrying railroads (BNSF, UP, CSX, and NS), as well as Canadian National and Canadian Pacific. Within the city are 21 intermodal sites—with more on the way—that could spur job creation and real estate development in surrounding areas. Four new yards have been completed in recent years and a fifth is in planning. The city of Chicago and the Association of American Railroads both have major task forces and study efforts underway to plan an updating of

The San Pedro Bay ports at Long Beach and Los Angeles are well connected to the rest of the country by rail and highway links.

Courtesy Port of Los Angeles, Nick Souza Photographer

the railroad infrastructure to handle expected traffic growth in the coming decade.

Coastal cities like Los Angeles, where ports, rail lines, and interstate highways come together, also are part of the recentralization trend. The San Pedro Bay ports at Long Beach and Los Angeles, for example, the leading points of entry for the Pacific Rim, offer extensive rail links to the rest of the nation. The Alameda Corridor, a 20-mile (32-kilometer) dedicated rail line now connecting the ports to the major rail yards in central Los Angeles, is expected to greatly speed up the shipment of Pacific Rim goods to the rest of the United States, strengthening Los Angeles's dominance as the West Coast's key transportation center and creating opportunities for new warehouse/distribution and other industrial and commercial facilities along the line and at the central rail yards.

Cities along intermodal corridors can be expected to be centers of additional railroad intermodal investment and related spin-off manufacturing and distribution activity.

Chicago has encouraged the retention and expansion of industries in the city through the use of incentives such as tax increment financing.

Redevelopment of Urban Brownfield Sites

Over the last several decades, many developers of factories, warehouses, and distribution centers fled America's inner cities in favor of suburban locations near major highways. Once-flourishing inner-city industrial areas became virtual ghost towns, and the surrounding blue-collar neighborhoods deteriorated. Factories and warehouses that had hummed with activity were demolished or left to become ruins. Weeds grew over rusting train tracks.

Now, despite repeated doom-and-gloom predictions by market experts, the expansion and development of new intermodal nodes and the spin-off of new industrial and distribution facilities in nearby areas is resulting in the revitalization of some inner-city industrial areas.

Because of the sustained surge in intermodal shipping over more than the past decade, railroad companies are expanding their existing intermodal centers or building new ones in once-abandoned rail yards. Industrial land owners are using intermodal centers to transform deserted mills and factories into major mixed-use centers around which developers are constructing a wide variety of products, primarily distribution/light industrial facilities. Though this recentralization trend remains in its infancy, it could achieve a profound impact on U.S. cities by drawing development back to the historical industrial sites where major rail corridors are concentrated, thereby creating jobs and increasing city revenues.

Chicago's economically depressed South Side, for example, is already reaping the benefits of recentralization. In September 1999, CSXI, the intermodal division of CSX Corporation, opened a new \$40 million 59th Street Terminal at the long-abandoned, 132-acre (53.4-hectare) Penn Central Railroad rail yard. The terminal has an annual lift capacity of 600,000. In addition to providing a new link between the primary East Coast railroads (CSX and NS) and the primary western railroads (BNSF and UP), the 59th Street intermodal center provides 800 jobs to the surrounding economically depressed neighborhoods and is spurring ancillary development. CSXI also agreed to contribute a fee per container to city projects in the area, enabling several much-needed road, traffic light, and community projects to be funded. The yard also resulted in the removal of over 100,000 trucks per year from Chicago streets.

Ford Motor Company has made a commitment to infill development by creating the nation's first auto supplier park in the distressed Calumet region of south Chicago. The 155-acre (62.7-hectare) park is under development by CenterPoint Properties and will contain a dozen auto supplier manufacturers producing parts for the nearby Ford auto assembly plant. Chicago competed with several Sunbelt locations for this park and assembled a \$100 million brownfield site, road infrastructure, and workforce training package to attract it. The site is strategically located near CSX and NS intermodal facilities that will bring in parts from other suppliers and a regional "car-mixing" facility on NS for shipping cars to dealers. The site, once occupied by a steel mill, offers another good example of how intermodal shipping and JIT production are making former brownfield sites attractive development locations.

Concentrated Intermodal Facility Development

The growth of intermodal traffic is also spurring the development of a new generation of large intermodal facilities in suburban locations. This type of concentrated development in certain metropolitan markets contrasts sharply with the hundreds of small ramp facilities the railroads opened in the 1960s. Some of the new large yards are becoming anchors within new industrial parks, while others are spawning new industrial parks within close proximity.

The CenterPoint Intermodal Center outside Chicago represents a new type of suburban business park development: anchored by a major intermodal rail yard and surrounded by businesses that rely heavily on seamless international and national container shipping. Such projects also represent a new scale of industrial development, with millions of square feet of new facilities oriented to swift assembly and transshipment operations. (See the CenterPoint Intermodal Center feature box.)

To the west in nearby Rochelle, Union Pacific Railroad is building a state-of-the-art terminal to serve as a critical interchange hub and loading/unloading terminal for intermodal rail shipments moving through the Chicago region. The Greater Rochelle Economic Development Corporation (GREDCO), a nonprofit economic development effort of the city of Rochelle, identified intermodal as a growth sector, commissioned a study of the potentials, and worked closely with UP to attract this facility. Since construction started in mid-2001, Ken Wise, director of GREDCO, reports daily inquiries from manufacturers, developers, trucking companies (such as Schneider and H.L. Hunt), and others seeking locations near the facility. Activity has picked up in the existing Interstate Transportation Center, and a major developer has been seeking options on up to 1,000 acres (404.7 hectares) of adjacent farmland.

The opening of new intermodal yards (and the anticipation of new yards to come) is stimulating new industrial/distribution park development, is increasing activity in existing parks, and is providing anchors for a new generation of transportation-oriented parks. For example, the new CSX yard on I-285 in south Atlanta has been joined by a large number of new business park and new regional distribution operations in nearby locations.

Catalysts for Recentralization

Four central and interconnected growth dynamics have jump-started the recentralization trend: international trade, new railroad investment, logistics companies, and just-in-time manufacturing.

International Trade

U.S. international waterborne freight nearly doubled in the past two decades—most of this growth being in containerized freight. Trade patterns have seen a shift from East Coast to West Coast ports and significant increases in shipments between Mexico and Canada. The combination of international container shipping and domestic intermodal shipping has reduced shipping costs and times, and has in turn increased the

ease of conducting manufacturing and distribution operations on a global level.

New Railroad Investment

The railroad industry has greatly increased the speed and efficiency of container shipments by improving roadbeds, transforming single-track lines into double-track lines, and introducing unit and double-stacked trains. The four major U.S. rail companies (CSX, NS, UP, and BNSF) have each been investing over $1 billion per year in capital expenditures largely related to expanding intermodal capacity. In the current business recession, however, railroad stock prices have declined, which is slowing capital investment.

Rail intermodal shipments started on a small scale in the 1950s and have grown dramatically in the 1980s and 1990s. Lifts increased from 6 million in 1990 to an estimated 9 million in 1999, and they are anticipated to reach 11 million to 12 million by 2003. The largest intermodal shipper is United Parcel Service, but major trucking firms such as Schneider and H.L. Hunt now predominantly use intermodality for distances exceeding 600 miles (965 kilometers).

"This is not a new transit mode," says Jack Kyser, chief economist of the Los Angeles County Economic Development Corporation. "It's a new way of using what we have, combining the best of the trains and trucks. One transportation mode now does not exclude the other. Competitors in the past must now work together in a seamless, time-sensitive manner."[1]

Logistics Companies

Recentralization owes a great deal to the recent rise of third-party logistics companies that perform nonessential functions such as warehousing and distribution. Logistics companies are heavy users of rail intermodal facilities. A logistics company, for example, will transport parts from a client's factory to the client's assembly plant, and then ship the client's final products to stores or outlets for sale. Many large companies, such as car manufacturers, now outsource their warehouse/distribution functions to logistics operators that provide those services, often to support just-in-time manufacturing processes.

To perform these services, logistics companies are building large-scale, state-of-the-art warehouse/distribution facilities near major intermodal shipping centers in order to cost-effectively store the goods

CenterPoint Intermodal Center: Joliet, Illinois

CenterPoint Intermodal Center is a 2,200-acre (890-hectare) project, one of the nation's largest private developments, anchored by a 621-acre (251-hectare) multi-modal rail facility. It is designed to integrate direct rail, truck, transload, and intermodal services with distribution and warehousing in a single location. When fully completed, the center will encompass up to 15 million square feet (1.3 million square meters) of buildings, including specialized cross-dock truck facilities.

The CenterPoint site was formerly the Joliet Arsenal, once a munitions manufacturer and one of the largest employers in the Chicago metropolitan area. When the 25,000-acre (10,117-hectare) military base was decommissioned in 1976, more than 8,000 jobs were lost. Labeled as

excess property by the U.S. Army, the site was neglected until 1995, when Congress created the Joliet Arsenal Development Authority (JADA), the catalyst in initiating legislation to rescue and reuse the base.

The arsenal property encompassed nearly 25,000 acres (10,117 hectares) but the CenterPoint Intermodal Center only required 2,200 acres (890 hectares). Thus, use of the remaining land became a critical component of the entire redevelopment plan. The U.S. Army transferred 19,000 acres (7,689 hectares) to the Midewin National Tallgrass Prairie and 2,000 acres (809 hectares) to the Department of Veterans Affairs for a national cemetery. Extensive environmental remediation and land improvements ensured that the massive industrial park would successfully coexist

with the prairie and the cemetery, while not compromising the integrity of the historic surroundings. Since the property is designated a Superfund site, the U.S. Environmental Protection Agency (USEPA) was key in the remediation process and cleanup of the former arsenal. The developer established a memorandum of agreement among the JADA, CenterPoint, USEPA, Illinois Environmental Protection Agency (IEPA), and the Army to define the rights, duties, and assurances needed to proceed with converting the property.

The Site and Development

Situated roughly 40 miles (64 kilometers) southwest of Chicago, the CenterPoint site is strategically located to access the region's immense transportation infrastruc-

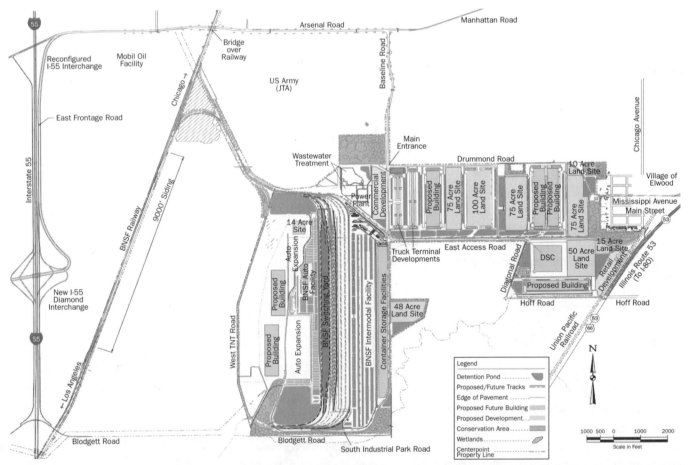

CenterPoint Intermodal Center in Joliet, Illinois, integrates intermodal transportation services with modern warehouse and distribution facilities. It is a model for the conversion of a brownfield site into a large-scale development.

ture. It provides access to intermodal facilities as well as major road and rail connections, with proximity to Interstate 55, Illinois Route 53, Interstate 80, and Chicago's expressway system. Major area waterways and port authorities are also nearby. Most buildings constructed on the site will be adjacent to the park's rail services, with direct access to the Burlington Northern and Santa Fe Railway (BNSF) logistics park. The area is also open through reciprocal switch to Union Pacific (UP) and the Elgin, Joliet, and Eastern Railway Company (EJ&E).

In 1997, CenterPoint Properties Trust learned of the availability of acreage at the site and set out to acquire it. After disposition of the preserve and cemetery acreage by the Army, 1,850 acres (749 hectares) were left for private development, and the developer acquired the land well below market rate. In addition to this property, CenterPoint also purchased 350 acres (142 hectares) of a farm adjacent to the arsenal's eastern boundary to bring the total acreage to 2,200 (890 hectares). By August 2000, the land transfer was made and the remediation process had begun. By the middle of 2001, the developer started infrastructure work for the site, which is being completed on an as-needed basis throughout the life of the development. A critical component of the plan is the 621-acre (251-hectare) intermodal rail facility operated by BNSF, which occupies one-third of the site and serves as the project anchor.

In addition to the BNSF rail facility, which was completed in October 2002, two build-to-suit facilities owned and managed by CenterPoint Properties Trust have been finished. These facilities include a 300,000-square-foot (27,870-square-meter) warehouse/distribution space completed in January 2003 and leased by Partners Warehouse (as part of a 600,000-square-foot/55,740-square-meter multidistribution warehouse center), and a 408,000-square-foot (37,903-square-meter) multidistribu-

Project Data: CenterPoint Intermodal Center

Land Use Information

Site area	2,200 acres (890 hectares)

Gross building area	Completed as of 1/03	At buildout (12/08)
Intermodal yard	621 acres (251 hectares)	650 acres (263 hectares)
Warehouse	1.1 million square feet (102,190 square meters)	12 million square feet (1.1 million square meters)
Distribution	0	2 million square feet (185,800 square meters)
Light manufacturing	0	1 million square feet (92,900 square meters)
Office	0	0
Container yard	50 acres (20 hectares)	100 acres (40 hectares)
Ancillary rail/commercial	0	0
Total	1.1 million square feet (102,190 square meters)	15 million square feet (1.3 million square meters)

Land Use Plan

	Acres (hectares)	
Office	approx. 20	(8)
Warehouse	approx. 600	(242)
Distribution	approx. 200	(81)
Light manufacturing	approx. 200	(81)

Developer/Owner

CenterPoint Properties Trust
1808 Swift Drive
Oak Brook, Illinois 60523
630-586-8000
www.centerpoint-prop.com

Development Schedule

October 2002	BNSF rail yard Phase I completion
December 2002	Village roadway, utility, water tower, and well house completion
December 2003	Village of Elwood waste-water treatment plant completion
December 2004	Industrial park Phase I (640 acres)
December 2006	Industrial park Phase II (245 acres)
December 2008	Industrial park Phase III (170 acres)

tion warehouse center completed in 2003 and leased by the Potlatch Corporation. Potlatch retains an expansion clause in its lease giving it the option to acquire additional space at the site.

Another tenant, Container-Care International, Inc., has completed a small repair and maintenance shed as well as made improvements to its 50-acre (20-hectare) container storage and repair facility, which

lies on a parcel that is leased from the developer. CenterPoint Properties Trust is in the final stages of a deal with InDEC regarding the leasing of 150 acres (14 hectares) for a three-year buildout of a power plant, and a 57-acre (23-hectare) parcel of land was sold to DSC Logistics in 2000 (although it has not yet been built upon).

continued on next page

Aside from the 621 acres (251 hectares) that constitute the BNSF logistics park, the facilities and projects discussed above lie within the 1,100-acre (445-hectare) industrial park situated on the CenterPoint intermodal site. The typical anticipated use of the remaining acreage is build-to-suit for lease space, but the parcels are currently available and use remains negotiable. Future phases of the industrial park will include a commercial area with restaurants, hotels, truck stops, and ancillary office facilities.

Financing

Total investment for CenterPoint Intermodal Center will approach $1 billion upon completion, making it one of the nation's largest private developments. CenterPoint Properties Trust aims to fund the project from rents provided through space that it owns and manages and through the sale of mature developments, as well as a revolving credit line and $125 million in the form of tax increment financing (TIF) provided by the municipality of Elwood.

Since spring 2002, when CenterPoint announced the buildout plan, the company has made deals involving approximately 45 percent of the 2,200 acres (890 hectares), with the 621-acre (251-hectare) BNSF site already committed at that point. These transactions have included the BNSF logistics park (the underlying land of which is owned by CenterPoint), completed for $243 million; the Potlatch Corporation facility, which cost $11.8 million; and the Partners Warehouse project, finished for $18.1 million.

In December 2002, the acreage housing the BNSF logistics park was sold to a private investor group. The BNSF ground lease had been secured in June 2002 through the issuance of $90.2 million of nonrecourse bonds, as well as leveraged lease financing of the intermodal rail improvements situated on the leased land and built for the BNSF (the latter arranged by

CenterPoint Capital Funding LLC). The total transaction proceeds were $91.1 million, which included assumption by the new owner of the nonrecourse debt. The gain from the sale could increase if realization of TIF proceeds is made in 2003 (strategies for which include the sale of all or a portion of the development notes), which would result in a reduction of the land's cost basis.

Public support amounting to approximately $200 million has provided significant needed investment at the site. Of this amount, the Illinois Department of Commerce and Community Affairs provided $25 million in grants and loans for infrastructure on the site; the Illinois Department of Transportation committed roughly $50 million toward upgrading area roads, bridges, and other essential aspects; and the town of Elwood annexed the site parcel and instituted a plan that provided for a maximum of $125 million of tax increment financing for infrastructure development, thus permitting tax-exempt debt to fund such improvements.

Marketing

The center is configured to take advantage of Chicago's rank as one of the nation's premier transportation centers for industrial goods. CenterPoint seeks to attract additional distribution centers and manufacturing operations that would benefit from the on-site intermodal facilities. Potential industrial park users include manufacturers, food processors, warehouses, lumber companies, paper companies, injection molding companies, auto distributors, and logistics firms. Businesses with access to BNSF's state-of-the-art, high-capacity intermodal facility can eliminate several steps in the freight transportation cycle, achieving efficient inventory and warehouse control as well as significant time and cost savings.

The marketing of the center has proceeded on several fronts. The project's unusual

scale has made it the subject of feature articles in major newspapers and commercial real estate trade publications. Print advertising campaigns have targeted real estate professionals at both the local and national levels, and marketing brochures have aimed to attract potential customers and investors.

Economic Development/ Community Impacts

CenterPoint serves as a national model for the conversion of a closed, environmentally tainted military installation into a large-scale development providing jobs, business opportunities, and tax revenue. Upon completion of the buildout in 2014, the $1 billion project is projected to create as many as 8,000 to 12,000 permanent jobs and more than 20,000 union construction jobs. Annual tax revenues of $27 million are expected, as well as significant sales tax proceeds from construction material costs.

Remediation of the site has worked to eliminate environmental contaminants, as well as to establish berms and forestation in the surrounding area. In addition to these ecological efforts, CenterPoint Properties Trust has participated in community improvement initiatives that have included donations to area school districts, the village of Elwood, and the town fire department.

Experience Gained

- The commitment of key government officials and agencies is crucial to ensuring that the necessary resources are available for a project of this magnitude and complexity.
- Collaboration on the federal, state, and local levels is critical to financing such a venture and actualizing its success.
- Flexible zoning permits a wide array of industrial and manufacturing uses and build-to-suit facilities that can meet specialized customer needs.

before moving them around the country and the world. Those facilities, in turn, are helping to raise property values, create jobs, and build demand for ancillary commercial and retail services.

Just-in-Time Manufacturing

Large manufacturers such as auto companies are big supporters of intermodal shipping and recentralization. The automobile industry led in just-in-time production and has also led in using international intermodal shipping to globalize car production.

City and State Support

Recentralization requires the active support of city and state governments, which need to expand and improve highways and connector streets to those highways to support the new intermodal traffic. Cities also must provide rezoning, site assembly, and tax benefits to help jump-start the development of intermodal centers. Another important form of public/private assistance can ease and speed the cleaning up and redevelopment of often contaminated inner-city industrial properties.

The city of Chicago, which has made industrial retention and expansion a major priority, has been particularly aggressive in establishing authority and incentives to attract intermodal users and ancillary industrial facilities. Its strongest incentive is the use of TIF for industrial development.

Through the use of TIF, which typically lasts 23 years, Chicago offers financial incentives to companies that want to expand existing industrial facilities or build new ones by dedicating the tax revenue from new development to area redevelopment. The city eventually will recapture its investment through greater tax revenues generated by the new facilities, while helping to generate jobs and stimulate ancillary development in inner-city areas. The TIF mechanism broadens the city's authority for land assembly through the power of eminent domain and provides funding for infrastructure and site preparation.

Challenges to Intermodal Growth

A number of challenges and obstacles can slow or derail intermodal growth before it can help to spur the redevelopment of inner-city industrial areas and large-scale suburban developments.

Inconsistent Railroad Service

Railroads need to provide consistent, fast, and competitively priced service if they are going to attract intermodal customers; intermodal transit must have consistent on-time performance. Railroad companies such as UP, says economist Jack Kyser, "have been under criticism for their quality of service. Trains do not always reach intermodal facilities within an acceptable time frame."[2]

The problem is compounded by the continued proliferation of intermodal centers that depend on trucks, railroads, truck drivers, and rail crews. Adds Kyser, "The long-haul trucking industry has an ongoing shortage of qualified drivers, and the rail industry, after three decades of downsizing, has a shortage of rail workers, leading to fatigue and staffing issues." Both industries are actively seeking additional workers and are instituting fast-track training programs.

NIMBYism

Even with city and state support, building or expanding an intermodal center is not guaranteed final approval. Residential neighbors near a rail yard, for example, can delay building or expanding an intermodal center or even curtail project plans. A proposed $100 million, 500-acre (202-hectare) UP intermodal center for West Chicago, an independent municipality outside Chicago, was blocked by residents who believed the facility would bring unacceptable levels of noise, pollution, and heavy truck traffic to local roads.

Complicated Brownfield Remediation

Many inner-city sites appropriate for intermodal centers and ancillary development suffer from land and even water contamination. Often such sites have been abandoned by previous owners that have since gone out of business. The question then arises of what party is responsible for cleaning up the sites in order to attract development. Without state and federal protection from future liability, few railroads, industrial developers, and commercial firms are willing to purchase and remediate a brownfield site. As a result, cities must take cleanup initiatives if they are going to attract intermodal centers and spin-off industrial redevelopment.

Costly Infrastructure Improvements

Intermodal centers often require major infrastructure improvements in the surrounding area, and generally the city or state must pay for these improvements, primarily through taxes and bonds that always can be defeated at the voting booth. For example, intermodal traffic needs to be routed to avoid residential neighborhoods and that often means constructing a connector road from the nearest highway to the intermodal center. In addition, telecommunications often have to be improved. Cities must proactively resolve these kinds of infrastructure challenges if they are to capture intermodal centers and ancillary industrial redevelopment.

The Chicago Area Transportation Study (CATS), the transportation agency for greater Chicago and northeast Illinois, is studying present and future roadway requirements in its six-county region. "Using seed money from the U.S. Federal Highway Administration, we are reviewing infrastructure challenges," explains F. Gerald Rawling, director of operations analysis. "We are to look at the physical condition of roadways, load-bearing capacity, signage, and the capacity of connectors. Then we will look at a theoretical ideal," he says. "We will identify the difference between real and ideal, so we can plan future improvements most effectively."[3]

Land Assembly

Intermodal centers generally require 100 to 500 acres (40 to 202 hectares) or more to provide the kinds of service customers need. This often requires the assembly of numerous parcels, which means complex and often-lengthy negotiations with multiple land owners.

New Directions

How will the emerging trend of recentralization affect inner-city industrial real estate markets, and what kind of opportunities will it offer for industrial developers? While it is difficult at this point to accurately predict the full impact, supporters believe the potential could be enormous. Just as the interstate highway system shaped industrial location decisions in the past, intermodal centers, brownfield cleanup programs, and logistics companies' growing demand for warehouse/

distribution space with easy rail and highway access could reshape long-derelict industrial areas. New warehouse/distribution operations, for example, could generate tremendous ancillary development, such as the off-site logistics company centers that Ford Motor, Goodyear Tire, and Toyota have recently opened in Chicago.

Public policies are increasingly focusing on intermodal development as an economic development policy. Developers are also recognizing the synergies between intermodal centers and regional industrial and distribution opportunities. And finally, the business community, which is constantly seeking new efficiencies in production and distribution systems, is beginning to see the presence of intermodal centers as critical in choosing where to locate new facilities. Certainly, both public sector and corporate planners need to pay greater attention to these changing freight transportation dynamics in implementing their land use and location policies.

"Thanks to the new industrial paradigm, where the completed item is not actually produced in one site but uses large components made all around the world, we should start to see actual factories, as well as warehouse and distribution centers, that will bring back good-quality, well-paying jobs to the inner-city areas that need them the most," says Kyser. In addition, the creation of new suburban intermodal centers will bring major transportation efficiencies to a wide range of companies that will choose to locate near them. This dynamic will change the shape of suburban business park development to larger intermodal anchored centers, with good interstate access and a wide range of on-site support logistics services.

Notes

1. Interview with Jack Kyser, Los Angeles County Economic Development Corporation, June 1999.

2. Ibid.

3. Interview with F. Gerald Rawling, Chicago Area Transportation Study, July 1999.

Chapter 7

DEVELOPMENT OPPORTUNITIES
AROUND SEAPORTS

Peter V. Hall

All transportation and freight terminals and nodes face a land development dilemma. In order to fulfill their function in the flow of goods, the terminals must be accessible. Precisely because they are accessible, however, they attract a variety and high density of users. This development tension is particularly sharp around seaports, since waterfront land is scarce, desirable, and highly regulated. Despite considerable recent attention directed toward relieving congestion on the roads and railroads that connect ports to their hinterlands, the competition for land in and around seaports remains intense. Public agencies, particularly the nation's many port authorities, aim to ensure sufficient land for cargo-handling operations. Opportunities for warehouse and industrial development do exist, but often they are in the area surrounding ports and not necessarily directly on the waterfront.

To understand the land dynamics around seaports and to identify opportunities for development, it is necessary to understand:

- current trends in the port business;
- the role of port authorities and other public agencies in regulating and influencing land markets in and around ports;
- how seaports influence economic development and real estate opportunities; and
- the likely development trajectories for U.S. seaports.

The Port Business

Over the last 50 years, waterfronts have been fundamentally transformed by the advent of containers and intermodal distribution of goods. With containerization and the reorganization of the shipping industry have come larger ships that require deeper channels, longer berths, bigger cranes, more and reconfigured terminal space, and improved surface transportation connections.[1] Some seaports have been more willing and able to respond to these demands more effectively than others.

Surface transport deregulation and changes to shipping law that allow service contracts and all-inclusive pricing have stimulated the growth of intermodal transportation.[2] Carriers have a choice about which markets to serve directly from a local seaport, and which to serve from a remote seaport coupled with overland transport. Hence, ports can no longer assume that they will serve a given "captured" hinterland.[3] Instead, seaports compete for the discretionary cargo that constitutes an ever-larger proportion of all ocean-borne cargo.

These two forces have led to increasing differentiation among seaports. A few ports have been able to attract the lion's share of containerized cargo and intermodal movements, while others have virtually ceased operating as cargo ports.[4] The number of foreign-loaded containers handled by U.S. seaports

Courtesy Port of Los Angeles

Commercial real estate development around seaports is complicated owing to land scarcity, strict regulations, and competition with water-dependent uses. Shown here is the Port of Los Angeles.

while only 12 percent by weight of foreign ocean-borne cargo travels in containers, 66 percent by value travels in containers. Virtually all manufactured and consumer products, with the exception of large items such as automobiles, now ship in containers.

Only a few ports, however, are likely to secure container hub port status. It is important to remember that many other ports handle cargo, and the U.S. marine transportation system moves more than 2 billion tons (2,032,093,817 metric tons) of freight annually. The entire system consists of over 1,000 harbor channels; 25,000 miles (40,234 kilometers) of inland, intracoastal, and coastal waterways; 300 ports; and 3,700 terminals. These ports and related facilities represent important economic development engines for local economies and can offer many niche development opportunities.

There is considerable uncertainty about the likely future course and impact of changes in the shipping industry. The newest containerships on order are still getting bigger, suggesting a continuation of the hub effect. However, given the limitations on waterborne transport between U.S. ports, it is unlikely that any U.S. ports will become transshipment megaports like Singapore and Hong Kong. Similarly, proposals for smaller, high-speed ships may provide alternatives for handling time-sensitive cargoes in nonhub ports. The most likely scenario thus resembles the current pattern of a small number of dominant container ports in the major metropolitan regions, combined with considerable differentiation across the entire U.S. marine transportation system.

grew by about 6 percent per year over the 1990s. Over the last decade, the top three U.S. seaports captured just over half of this growth, and by 1999 they accounted for nearly 46 percent of foreign-loaded (imported and exported) containers (see the accompanying table).

Not only are containers concentrated in just a few seaports, but containers also carry the most valuable cargoes. Maritime Administration statistics show that

Figure 7.1 **Top U.S. Container Ports for Foreign-Loaded TEUs**

Port	1999	1990
Long Beach, Calif.	3,050,019	1,214,312
Los Angeles	2,538,596	1,454,621
New York	2,027,582	1,210,173
Charleston, S.C.	1,168,224	558,853
Seattle	59,352	767,303
Hampton Roads, Va.	908,918	497,719
Oakland	912,255	578,892
Houston	713,456	370,069
Savannah	623,941	313,208
Miami	618,183	296,188
Tacoma	577,097	483,319
Remaining ports	2,520,210	1,657,730
Total	15,717,833	9,402,387
Top 3 share	45.8%	41.3%

TEU = 20-foot (6-meter) equivalent unit, a standard measure of container throughput.

Source: PIERS, www.piers.com.

The Role of Port Authorities

Public regulation plays an important role in the allocation of waterfront land. The reasons for government involvement include the need to protect scarce and sensitive waterfront and tidal lands, and the large and risky nature of port infrastructure investments. Public trust doctrine is often invoked to protect and promote water-dependent land uses over others.

Although numerous federal, state, and local agencies influence land use decisions along the waterfront, the most important player in any port land market is the port authority. In the United States, almost all seaports are administered by public authorities controlled at the state or local level. In addition to maritime functions, port activities may also include jurisdiction over airports, bridges, tunnels, commuter rail systems, inland river or shallow draft barge terminals, industrial parks, foreign-trade zones, world trade centers, terminal or shortline railroads, shipyards, marinas, and other public recreational facilities. Ports may also undertake community or regional economic development activities beyond those of direct benefit to the port itself.[5]

Port authorities are generally compelled by law, by financial and political pressures, and by good planning sense to reserve land in and around ports for water-dependent land uses. This preference for water-dependent land use often brings them into conflict with real estate developers. Most often, these conflicts concern non–cargo-related land uses, such as commercial and recreational waterfront development and environmental remediation. These land uses increase the competition for and costs of land on the waterfront, the potential for safety hazards, conflicts among land uses, and environmental impacts.[6]

Many port authorities are increasingly resistant even to cargo-related land uses that do not need to be near the waterfront. This is because port authorities do more than regulate land use in and around the waterfront; they also actively use land to pursue their own goals. Although most port infrastructure is partially subsidized with public money, all U.S. port authorities have a mixed public/private nature. They have to deliver jobs and other economic benefits to the cities and regions that play host to them, and they also must deliver some financial return on the land they hold in public trust and on the investments they make.

Both these goals are fulfilled when a cargo port attracts ships to visit its terminals and when cargo moves across its wharves. Some port authorities operate terminals themselves, others are simply landlords leasing terminals to steamship lines or terminal operating firms, and some combine elements of both approach. Regardless of the leasing and pricing policy, the more cargo handled, the more port jobs are created and the healthier the authority's revenue base. So cargo ports all share one goal: to attract as much cargo as possible. This does not necessarily mean that they want that cargo to stay in the area near the port.

The Influence of Ports on Economic Development and Real Estate Opportunities

It is useful to distinguish between two ways of thinking about the role of a port in a city and regional economy. A port can be thought of as a center of economic activity in its own right, or as a set of facilities and services that reduces the costs of doing business or consuming. These different economic development implications of cargo ports create an ambiguous relationship between port authorities and real estate development.

Ports and Economic Activity

As cargo moves through a port, it stimulates a range of economic activities (see Figure 7.2). Each ship that visits a port requires various vessel-related ser-

All goods that pass through a port require handling. At the Port of Houston, jobs generated by companies providing cargo-handling and vessel-related services total nearly 90,000.

Courtesy Port of Houston Authority

vices. Each container, each automobile, and each ton of grain that moves through a port requires handling. Some cargoes need to be processed at or near the waterfront. Once the cargo is off-loaded, it has to be stored or transported somewhere. All this transportation and distribution activity generates jobs and other economic activity, and of course it all requires space.

The activities stimulated by cargo movement vary in how close to the waterfront they need to be or what might be called their degree of "water dependency." Just because an activity is water dependent, however, does not mean that it can command waterfront rents, nor does low water dependency imply that waterfront locations are not desirable. With containerization, many of these cargo-throughput activities have become much more efficient, thus requiring less space, while information technologies have allowed some of these activities to be more widely dispersed. However, both the growth in cargo handled by ports and the attractiveness of waterfront land to alternative users have ensured that the pressure to find land for water-dependent uses has not abated.

Port-related activities also vary in terms of the real estate opportunities they represent. In general, the most highly water-dependent land uses associated with shipping often represent the least interesting and valuable real estate opportunities for developers. Terminal construction is a highly specialized field, while land transportation services demand only low-grade industrial sites.

Manufacturing and warehouse facilities are often located at or near waterfront sites to take advantage of low-cost inbound transportation of raw materials for production and outbound shipments of finished products. Foreign-trade zones on port property also encourage value-added manufacturing and services

to locate in port areas. Warehouses, one of the more attractive real estate opportunities, do not necessarily have to be near a waterfront, though. With containerization has come the practice of transloading, which involves unloading a full container and reloading the contents into one or more different containers or trucks for distribution. Transloading at or near ports does provide enormous competitive advantages to distributors serving a local or regional market. Hence, flexible distribution centers with good access to large container ports are highly attractive property developments. For the largest national distribution operations, however, other factors generally not present near seaports—such as access to cheap land and good interstate highway access—may be more important.

Ports and Throughput Efficiency

Ports deliver more than jobs and economic activity for the transportation and distribution sector. They also offer cost and time advantages to different industries, provide trade connections for regional economies, and reduce the cost of imported goods. Shippers using just-in-time production technologies and postponement in distribution systems are demanding greater efficiencies from their logistics systems. Some of the largest shippers have complained about the speed with which containers are handled in the nation's two largest ports, Long Beach and Los Angeles, especially during the pre-holiday peak import periods.

A central concern for port users, therefore, is the efficiency of port throughput. Throughput depends on a variety of factors, including land use configurations and land-side access. For example, port managers tend to discourage non–cargo-related development on and near port land. A series of research reports has high-

Figure 7.2 Real Estate Opportunities Resulting from Cargo Activities at Seaports

Activity	Examples	Water Dependency	Real Estate Opportunities
Vessel-related services	Tugs, ship repairs, and supplies	High	Limited to port
Cargo handling	Stevedoring, terminal operations	High	Limited to port
Container services	Repair, storage, and drayage	High	Limited to low-grade industrial space
Cargo services	Forwarding, legal, and financial	Low	Office space
Processing	Automobile accessorizing	Moderate–high	Industrial and warehouse space
Warehousing	Transloading, consolidation	Moderate	Accessible warehouse space
Land-side transportation	Intermodal yards, trucking services	High	Limited to low-grade industrial space

What Is a Foreign-Trade Zone?

A foreign-trade zone (FTZ) is a site in the United States in or near a U.S. customs port of entry where foreign and domestic merchandise is generally considered to be in international commerce. Foreign or domestic merchandise may enter this enclave without a formal customs entry or the payment of customs duties or government excise taxes. Merchandise entering a zone may be stored, tested, sampled, relabeled, repackaged, displayed, repaired, manipulated, mixed, cleaned, assembled, manufactured, salvaged, destroyed, or processed.

If the final product is exported from the United States, no U.S. customs duty or excise tax is levied. If, however, the final product is imported into the United States, customs duty and excise taxes are due only at the time of transfer from the FTZ and formal entry into the United States. The duty paid is the lower of that applicable to the product itself or to its component parts. Zones thus provide opportunities to realize customs duty savings.

This popular policy tool is used by port authorities to secure cargo and import processing activities. Each U.S. port of entry is entitled to a zone project, provided it can demonstrate significant public economic development benefits. Users can avoid duties on re-exports, defer duties and excise taxes on imports, and take advantage of lower duties on finished products.

Source: National Association of Foreign-Trade Zones, www.naftz.org.

---

lighted how crowded highways and at-grade crossings impede access to ocean terminals.[7] Many port authorities are investing considerable effort toward in resolving surface transport congestion issues (see the Alameda Corridor example in chapter 8).

With the trade associated with U.S. ports expected to triple in the next 30 years, the infrastructure serving ports will continue to be challenged by growing congestion. Problems as simple as a lack of left-hand traffic signals and turn lanes for trucks serving marine terminals, or at-grade rail crossings on local streets, can create significant transportation bottlenecks.

Different ports place different emphases on the two aspects of the port-economy relationship. Ports that serve customers in remote locations tend to emphasize throughput efficiency, while those particularly concerned about local job benefits may try to get cargo to "stick" in the local economy for as long as possible. One policy tool for making cargo remain in a region is the foreign-trade zone, which has important implications for land use and development opportunities around a port.

Likely Development Trajectories for U.S. Seaports

Cargo ports can be classified according to the number of containers and tons of "roll-on, roll-off" (such as automobiles) and bulk cargo (such as grains or ores) they move, as well as the overall degree to which they specialize in particular commodities. In looking ahead to the likely development trajectories for U.S. seaports, four types of cargo ports can be distin-

guished: hub ports, container ports, diversified ports, and niche cargo ports.

Dominant Ports

There are three dominant ports in the United States today: Los Angeles, Long Beach, and New York–New Jersey. These ports rank among the world's largest container ports, but they have also maintained a strong presence in other commodity groupings. Thus, they handle the most diversified set of commodities. It is no accident that these ports are located within the nation's two largest metropolitan areas; the huge markets they serve make them attractive to a variety of shippers. As a result, they each have experienced intense land use, surface transportation, and other pressures resulting from the sheer scale of cargo movement.

Dominant ports such as the San Pedro Bay ports at Los Angeles and Long Beach (shown here) handle a variety of commodities and serve a nationwide market.

Figure 7.3 Cargo-Based Classification of U.S. Seaports

Class	Port Examples	Cargo Characteristics	Land Development Issues
Hub	Los Angeles, Long Beach, New York/New Jersey	More than 2M TEU Ro-ro and bulk Low specialization	Core metropolitan location Intense land pressures Inland distribution systems
Container	Oakland, Miami, Charleston, Seattle, Tacoma, Savannah	Average 1M TEU Moderate specialization	Large metropolitan location Intermodal focus
Diversified	Baltimore, Norfolk, Jacksonville, Houston, Portland, Ore.	Average 0.5M TEU Ro-ro and bulk Moderate specialization	Metropolitan location Intraport land use conflict Water-dependent processing
Niche	Boston, Philadelphia, San Diego, Wilmington, Brunswick, Ga., Hueneme, Calif.	Less than 0.2M TEU High specialization	Small metropolitan location Dedicated facilities Water-dependent processing

M = million

TEU = 20-foot (6-meter) equivalent unit, a standard measure of container throughput

Ro-ro = roll-on, roll-off cargo

The pressures in the San Pedro Bay differ from those in the New York region in one important respect—namely, the size and shape of the hinterland served. (The term *hinterland* refers to the location of shippers using a port.)

Most of the cargo that moves through the Port of New York and New Jersey has a U.S. inland destination or origin within 280 miles (450 kilometers) of the Statue of Liberty. This ten-state market area accounts for one-fifth of the U.S. population: a relatively small but intense hinterland that generates considerable congestion on the region's roads and rail network. The port has proposed a port inland distribution network (PIDN) as a means of relieving traffic overload in and around the seaport; it would use a combination of dedicated rail, barge, or truck services to move containers between the ocean terminals and inland container depots.[8]

By contrast, the hinterland of the Long Beach and Los Angeles ports extends across the continent. Through the 1980s and 1990s, these ports were able to ride two powerful growth trends: the rise in transpacific trade and the expansion of cross-continental intermodal traffic. By 1996, half of all foreign containers handled by the San Pedro ports had a U.S. origin or destination outside California or Nevada.[9] Although the number of containers circulating in the greater Los Angeles region is enormous, the port authorities emphasize their throughput efficiency. Their growth pressures have contributed to the nation's largest urban infrastructure project, the Alameda Corridor, which is designed to expedite the movement of containers

from the waterfront to rail yards 20 miles (32.2 kilometers) inland (see chapter 8).

Container Ports

Unlike hub ports, container ports do not handle significant volumes of the noncontainerized commodities that require specialized handling technology. These ports are often found in metropolitan locations and hence face competition from tourist, commercial, and residential land uses; the Oakland, Miami, and Seattle ports all face these pressures. Their future growth depends on capturing discretionary cargo destined for or originating in remote locations. The resulting intermodal focus will place a premium on throughput efficiency.

For example, the Port of Oakland is currently implementing an ambitious expansion plan entailing dredging, new terminals and cranes, and an on-site rail yard. While the conversion of the Oakland Naval Supply Station has added land for development, port-related land uses are facing increasing development pressures from commercial, residential, and amenity users along the waterfront. At the same time, the port is seeking to reduce the congestion and community resistance resulting from truck traffic on area roads. (See "Real Estate Opportunities at the Ports of Seattle, Tacoma, Portland, and Oakland.")

Diversified Ports

Diversified ports do handle significant numbers of containers, and some aggressively pursue intermodal discretionary cargoes. However, ports such as Baltimore, Houston, and Portland, Oregon, have been negatively affected by the intermodal revolution, while others such as Norfolk, Virginia, and Jacksonville, Florida, lack large local markets.

Ironically, these ports can often offer attractive real estate development opportunities near the waterfront precisely because land development pressures are less intense. For example, the Port of Portland's 2,800-acre (1,133-hectare) Rivergate Industrial District has attracted distribution centers for various domestic and international firms. The district is located adjacent to the Port of Portland's marine terminals and is served by two major railroads.[10] (See "Real Estate Opportunities at the Ports of Seattle, Tacoma, Portland, and Oakland.")

Diversified ports also handle a range of noncontainerized commodities, which often require specific handling technologies, thus resulting in specialized or dedicated terminal facilities. Noncontainerized commodities also often require water-side processing and storage activities.

The Port of Baltimore offers an example of a successful diversified port. While the number of foreign containers handled by the port has declined over the last two decades, it has become one of the nation's largest handlers of automobiles and other wheeled ("ro-ro") cargoes. Imported automobiles require large parking lots and facilities to make repairs, add accessories, and prepare vehicles for distribution to dealerships. The Maryland Port Administration recently indicated its willingness to purchase a parcel of land adjacent to the Seagirt Marine Terminal to help accommodate such land uses.[11]

Similarly, steel, forest products, and bulk commodities—grains, ores, coal, and petroleum—have specialized storage and handling requirements. These processing activities often generate considerable employment and real estate development opportunities, although such facilities are generally custom-designed and built with the direct involvement of the cargo shipper.

Certainly, such development opportunities are easier to find when the port authority incorporates such land uses in its long-range planning, as in Baltimore. In a 1996 strategic plan, the Maryland Port Administration recognized its strengths in attracting a range of noncontainerized cargoes. Port officials have also been active in a port land use planning process

Courtesy Jaxport

that seeks to identify vacant and underused properties within 3,000 feet (914 meters) of the waterfront in Anne Arundel and Baltimore counties and within the city itself.[12] Although the impetus for this planning effort came from the Maryland Smart Growth initiative and from a desire to extend the Inner Harbor development, it did prompt port officials to consider which properties should be preserved for port-related activities.

Niche Ports

Niche ports form a fourth category. They specialize in a small number of commodities such as automobiles, fruit, lumber, grains, and other cargoes with particular handling requirements.[13] Unlike diversified ports, they typically move small numbers of containers and may not even have specialized equipment for handling containers. For example, the Georgia Ports Authority has designated Brunswick as a niche port for noncontainerized cargoes, Savannah being the state's main container port.

Most but not all niche ports are located in small metropolitan regions, and such ports may be vulnerable to market shifts in the particular commodities they handle. These ports do, however, offer many of the processing-related development opportunities that are also found in and around diversified cargo ports.

A good example is the relatively small Port Hueneme, located to the north of Los Angeles. It was originally established to promote agricultural exports from California's Central Valley. Recently, the port has expanded its niche focus by attracting various automobile importers. Both Mazda and BMW have established

Diversified ports such as Jaxport in Jacksonville, Florida, often provide more real estate development opportunities than larger container and hub ports that have more stringent requirements for types of uses that can be located on or near the waterfront.

Real Estate Opportunities at the Ports of Seattle, Tacoma, Portland, and Oakland

The port authorities in Seattle, Tacoma, Oakland, and Portland, Oregon, have recognized that, in addition to planning for their operational facilities, they must also provide opportunities for developing industrial, warehousing, and distribution facilities to service their ports and the surrounding regions. Current activities at these four Pacific Coast ports illustrate the real estate development opportunities that may be available to developers.

Seattle

The Port of Seattle is one of the busiest ports in the nation. Besides handling cargo traffic, it manages Sea-Tac Airport, provides both commercial and recreational moorage, and serves as a main terminal point for many Alaskan cruise ships.

The port is investing more than $1 billion over ten years in capital improvements aimed at upgrading and expanding waterfront facilities. Bigger terminals, better technology, and improved freight mobility are just a few of the enhancements already completed, underway, or planned for the future.

An excellent example of such infrastructure investment is the recent expansion of Terminal 18. The $300 million expansion of the terminal included the addition of 90 acres (36 hectares), doubled intermodal container and rail capacity, and improved ground and rail transportation access. At 196 acres (79 hectares), Terminal 18 now ranks as the second largest container terminal in North America.

The port's substantial marine-related investments like the Terminal 18 expansion, coupled with technological and other marketplace changes, have created greater flexibility in how the port manages its properties while maintaining traditional marine uses. For example, high-capacity container Terminals 5 and 18 are handling high volumes of seaborne containerized cargo, freeing up acreage at other terminals.

Over the past 15 years, the port's extensive real estate portfolio has been managed to maximize broad economic benefits to Seattle and the region. One of the port's earliest projects was its central waterfront revitalization project, which, beginning in the early 1990s and finishing in 2003, converted derelict fishing and cargo piers into a vibrant mixed-use development that melds traditional maritime activities with commercial, hotel, retail, entertainment, office, and open space. Currently, the port is working with the city of Seattle and other stakeholders on a number of exciting redevelopment efforts, one of which is the North Bay Uplands redevelopment project.

The North Bay Uplands redevelopment is a 198-acre (80-hectare) revitalization project encompassing Piers 90 and 91 plus 100 acres (40 hectares) of nearby upland property. This effort marks the port's first endeavor to convert a site devoted largely to traditional maritime uses to a new mix of uses. Mark Griffin, the port's real estate development manager, states that "at North Bay, we have an enormous opportunity to revitalize the area, much in the same way that our Pier 66 project and the surrounding uses helped bring new life to the central waterfront." The pre–master planning work at North Bay involved a preliminary analysis of a mix of commercial uses such as offices, research and development (R&D) labs, and light industrial space. "The burgeoning vision for the site is one of a vibrant blend of commercial uses that will provide quality jobs in growing and emerging employment sectors to help sustain the city's and the region's long-term economic vitality, while generating new revenue for the port and the region," says Griffin. These commercial uses would likely be complemented by open space and other uses to create a lively new community that is well integrated with the surrounding neighborhoods and the marine uses that will continue on the piers.[1]

Tacoma

Seattle's southern neighbor, Tacoma, is home to another large northwestern port. At 2,400 acres (971 hectares), the port holds about 40 percent of the land available on the U.S. west coast for container development.

Over the next 20 years, the port plans on spending $250 million in capital improvements to accommodate larger ships, stimulate business growth, and secure its position as one of the world's foremost container ports. Its real estate program reflects the industrial focus of this vision. The port plays an important role in the region's industrial development, provid-

A capital improvements plan at the Port of Seattle is revitalizing its waterfront and encouraging a mix of uses.

ing sites and facilities for manufacturing, fabrication, assembly, maintenance, and repair, in addition to warehousing and distribution.

The port has four primary industrial areas: the Commencement Bay Industrial Development District, the Early Business Center, the Frederickson Industrial Area, and the Port Commerce Center. The Frederickson Industrial Area, located 13 miles (21 kilometers) south of port terminals in unincorporated Pierce County, is the largest single site in the Puget Sound area that is zoned for heavy manufacturing and has industrial capacity utilities and infrastructure already in place. The port currently has 270 acres (109 hectares) available for sale at Frederickson in tracts ranging in size from six acres (2.4 hectares) to more than 100 acres (40 hectares). Rail lines run through the site.

The port is also home to Foreign-Trade Zone (FTZ) 86, which encompasses 833 acres (337 hectares) of port-owned land in 19 sites. Some sites are adjacent or very near port terminals; others are on port-owned property zoned for manufacturing and heavy industry and are served by industrial-capacity utilities. More than 1,300 acres (520 hectares) of privately owned and managed properties in Pierce County are also part of FTZ 86.

Portland

Located at the intersection of two interstate highways, two mainline railroads, and the Columbia/Snake/Willamette river system, the Port of Portland is well positioned for access to Pacific Rim markets. It maintains vibrant commerce in both container and bulk cargo, shipping more than 31 million tons (31.4 metric tons) in total cargo in 2001. It offers the largest auto port on the West Coast, handling Honda, Toyota, and Hyundai automobiles. It is also the world's second largest grain export port. Portland has more weekly domestic intermodal train departures to the east than any of the Puget Sound ports.

The port, which holds 10,000 acres (4,047 hectares) of property, owns and maintains four marine terminals, the Portland International Airport, three regional airports, and seven industrial parks that support marine, aviation, and other industrial activities. At 2,800 acres (1,133 hectares), the Rivergate Industrial District is the largest port-owned industrial park. The site is designed for warehousing, distribution, manufacturing, and processing facilities linked to the port's marine terminal facilities. The property takes excellent advantage of Portland's transportation strengths; its well-developed network of rail, highway, air, and marine connections link the metropolitan area with the region, as well as with major domestic markets. Both Union Pacific and Burlington Northern and Santa Fe railroads service the property, which offers sites available for development up to 100 acres (40 hectares).

The Portland International Center, which lies adjacent to the Portland International Airport (PDX), is the state's largest mixed-use, master-planned business park. The 458-acre (185-hectares) office and light industrial commerce center is positioned between the PDX terminal entrance and Interstate 205. The site is developable for Class A office space, flex-space warehousing, and light manufacturing.

The port also has sites available at its 22-acre (9-hectare) Brookwood Corporate Park. This facility, in the center of the region's high-tech area, lies adjacent to one of the regional airports and near a new west-side light rail line.

Oakland

The Port of Oakland owns, manages, and markets seaport facilities on San Francisco Bay and the Oakland estuary. It ranks fourth in the nation and twentieth in the world for container traffic. It also owns and manages the growing Oakland International Airport as well as more than 400 acres (162 hectares) of developable land. Much

of this property is currently being redeveloped into housing, commercial, retail, and mixed-use developments as part of the city of Oakland's aggressive redevelopment program.

Once largely industrial, the port is undergoing the most dramatic changes in its 75-year history. Much of the 1,040 acres (421 hectares) of commercial land that has been put to industrial use in the past is being transformed through $1.2 billion worth of redevelopment projects. Two of these projects are the Estuary Plan and the Oakland Airport Business Park project.

The Estuary Plan calls for the transformation of a 5.5-mile (8.8-kilometer) corridor of waterfront into a diverse mixed-use corridor that will link the city with its waterfront. Realizing this goal will involve the removal of barriers, the creation of a necklace of parks and open space, the enhancement of the area's transportation system to improve both local and regional access, the preservation of existing productive industrial areas, and a large-scale mix of new residential, retail, cultural, and commercial uses that will complement the planned open spaces and parks.

The Oakland Airport Business Park is currently under development. Metroport, the cornerstone of the $451 million development, is a transit-oriented business campus development that will become the new gateway to the Oakland International Airport. Scheduled to open in 2003 and developed by SIMEON Commercial Properties, Metroport is situated prominently at the intersection of Interstate 880 and Hegenberger Road. It will provide 1.3 million square feet (120,770 square meters) of offices for tenants seeking Class A space, served by both a 300-room full-service hotel and by BART (the Bay Area Rapid Transit system).

Note

1. Interview with Mark Griffin, Port of Seattle, May 22, 2003.

processing operations in the town, as has a subsidiary of Wallenius-Wilhelmsen, a steamship line specializing in shipping automobiles.

Development Opportunities around Seaports

Real estate development opportunities around the nation's seaports are constrained by a variety of factors. Private developers often have great difficulty securing scarce waterfront parcels, and port authorities tend to be protective of land for water-dependent uses. These activities are vital to the core business of ports, which is to move cargo from ocean-based to land-based transportation modes.

Development opportunities near the waterfront do, however, exist. Their scope depends upon the type and scale of port activities present, the amount of land available, and the degree of cooperation between ports and city governments in the planning process.

SUCCESSFUL PORT-CITY PLANNING MODELS AROUND THE WORLD

Laurel Rafferty

Experience at port cities around the world demonstrates the difficulties in achieving a compatible co-existence between industrial ports and nonindustrial waterfront areas. An emphasis on planning has been shown to be a primary ingredient for success; in particular, participatory planning, with its emphasis on consensus building, can facilitate agreement on plans that will be both feasible and acceptable to a broad constituency. Other significant elements include:

- coordinated planning by the city, port, and region on land use and economic development;
- decision making shared by port and city, as well as by port users, civic groups, and conservationists;
- decision making informed by an understanding of the issues critical to both port and city, sustaining the port's competitiveness port and the urban area's quality of life;
- promotion of reciprocal contributions between the port and the city; and

- cooperation between the ports of a region to promote opportunities for fully exploiting existing port area capacity—for example, through sharing information and facilities or such programs as feeder port distribution networks.

Rotterdam: Integrating Port and City Uses

The port authority and city of Rotterdam, the Netherlands, in partnership with port operators, civic groups, and conservationists, has undertaken a comprehensive regional planning process to resolve conflicts between these parties. Recognizing that their land use problems were linked and that solutions to these problems therefore would need to be linked, the port is now emphasizing the integration of port and city uses.

Waterfront space is at a premium in Rotterdam, and the pressures are intense for competing uses of this space. With a port that contributes 10 percent to the national gross domestic product and is in need of expansion space to remain competitive, and a city with critical land needs, conflict resolution became a matter of national, regional, and local importance. A regionwide participatory planning process proved fundamental to resolving critical land uses.

In 1993 the port proposed a highly controversial Maasvlakte 2 project, leading in 1997 to the Port Mainport Development Project, to meet the need for more space through major land reclamation. To evaluate the necessity of this project, the Dutch national cabinet entered into a lengthy consultative process that led to a comprehensive regional planning initiative undertaken jointly with industry, interest groups, the state, provincial authorities, Rotterdam, and surrounding communities. Principal stakeholders committed themselves to the dual objectives of improving the port's competitive position by expansion and of improving the quality of life in the Rotterdam region. They also committed themselves to the terms of an integrated solution. The pivotal result of this approach was the determination that 2,500 acres (1,011 hectares) of new waterfront land to be created through reclamation would be used both for a new port and port-related industrial activities and for recreation space and a wildlife reserve. Planning is still in progress, with the specific layout of the new land, the so-called Second Maasvlakte, under development.

A portion of the new port land is to be used for port-related industrial development in the form of "distriparks," a concept developed by the Rotterdam Port Authority in response to trends in international trade and distribution. These logistics parks feature the latest information technology and facilities required for efficient storage and just-in-time distribution, as well as the custom tailoring of goods to meet consumer and country destination requirements, such as repacking, labeling, weighing, assembling, quality control, and customs clearance. The port now has three distriparks: Maasvlakte on 309 acres (1,250 hectares) closest to the seacoast on the most recent land reclamation; Eemhavem on 35 acres (14 hectares) along the Rhine River, closest to the inner city; and Botlek on 125 acres (50.5 hectares) midway between the two.

Two of the critical lessons learned from Rotterdam's experience were:

- the importance of shared decision making— between port and city and other groups, including port operators, civic groups, and conservationists —to gain a consensus; and
- the need for a governmental organization to carry out an integrated solution to port and city issues.

Sydney: Satellite Inland Ports

Sydney has taken a different approach than Rotterdam in its proposed solution to its space and conges-

tion needs. After extensive consultation with the city and other stakeholders, the Sydney Ports Corporation (SPC) made the decision to meet these needs by developing an inland port terminal in combination with land reclamation. With expansion needs met either off the waterfront or on new waterfront land, the project has allowed existing waterfront space to remain available for commercial, recreational, and tourist uses desired by the city. The site of the inland terminal is an existing manufacturing and distribution center that was selected to avoid land use conflicts. It is linked to seaport facilities by a dedicated freight rail shuttle, providing for increased rail freight transport opportunities and thereby reducing urban truck traffic and related air and noise pollution. The project furthers the port's long-term strategic plans to enhance logistics services by redeveloping a network of inland ports within 19 to 25 miles (30.5 to 40 kilometers) of the port; locating distribution facilities with respect to consumer markets; and placing greater reliance on rail.

Satellite inland ports and land reclamation are physical solutions. The port also recognizes that its approach must include management solutions to address ongoing pressures for the expansion of non-port activities on the waterfront. Toward this end, the port has developed a good neighbor policy to foster harmonious coexistence with the city. The policy has encouraged a number of small yet effective measures such as providing access to places where the public may fish or view the waterfront and port activities;

East Asia Ports: Integrating Port and City Uses

The East Asian port cities of Shanghai, China; Kobe, Japan; Incheon, South Korea; and Ho Chi Minh City, Vietnam; each illustrate the successful integration of port and city uses.

Shanghai: A New Port City

The depth constraints of the Yangtze River, the imperatives of logistics accessibility, and the need for new development that will relieve pressure on the densely developed historic city center have led Shanghai to build the new deepwater Yangshan port on offshore islands. The new megaport has three principal elements: offshore terminal facilities, a 26-mile (42-kilometer)-long vehicular bridge, and a logistics park on the mainland. The logistics park is included within a new port city at Luchao, in which uses such as housing, businesses, educational, cultural and recreational facilities, parks, and other landscape amenities including a newly constructed lake will be integrated with port-related uses. The urban master plan for Luchao Port City was based on an international design competition, and the winning team consisted of an architectural firm and a port planning firm committed to integrated port-city solutions.

Kobe: Port Island

Kobe has an established record in combining everyday city activities with port uses within the same area. The land use plan for Port Island offers an example of this integration. Created in two stages through reclamation, Port Island and Port Island Stage II host cargo terminals, warehousing, manufacturing, logistics services, housing, green space, office, hotel, and conference and exhibition centers.

Recently, Kobe has taken this mixing of uses one step further in housing the di-verse activities of warehousing, assembly, manufacturing, R&D, and office space under one roof to promote the integration of production, distribution, and administration. Its International Business Center, in which this concept is being implemented, is located on Port Island Stage II and contains 215,258 square feet (20,000 square meters) of floor space on 10,000 square feet (929 square meters) of land. The space is available for lease. Owned by the Kobe City Urban Development Corporation and approved under the Private Industry Promotion Law, the project receives subsidies form the national, regional, and city governments. The city offers various incentives, including facilities for startup enterprises.

Port Island, Port Island Stage II, and other port areas fall within special zones of a Foreign-Access Zone designated to promote imports. These zones include import "promotion facilities" such as the Kobe International Distribution Center, which provides sorting, storage, exhibition, distribution, and processing operations.

Incheon: A Tri-Port Plan

In Incheon, the port serving Seoul, planning and development is underway for a project that will encompass expansion of the port, a new Incheon International Airport, and development of the Songdo Media Valley. The city reports that a comprehensive logistics complex will be constructed within the new port development area of South Harbor that has been created through extensive land reclamation. The complex is to serve as a logistics hub for northeast Asia, including a distribution and production center for international trade and a counterpart domestic com-ponent that will provide such services as the distribution and processing of fishery products. The port and surrounding area, encompassing Incheon International Airport, are to be established as a free-trade zone.

Ho Chi Minh City: A Port City Industrial Triangle

In Ho Chi Minh City, the integrated development of a deeper-water port and industrial park is planned for the new Hiep Phuoc Industrial Zone (HPIZ). HPIZ is located along the Soai Rap River outside the inner city, in close proximity to the major new urban development of Saigon South. It is conceived as an element of the Industrial Triangle defined by the HPIZ, the Tan Thuan Export Processing Zone, and Saigon South. General planning is completed for both the 4,942-acre (2,000-hectare) industrial park and the port area. The industrial park is intended for large-scale, heavy industries, particularly those dependent on water-borne transport. It will also provide assistance with investment proposals, factory design and construction, labor recruitment and training, and logistics. The Tan Thuan Export Processing Zone, Vietnam's first export-processing zone, covers an entire 741-acre (300-hectare) peninsula adjacent to the inner city's existing port area. As of the end of 2000, more than 100 companies were operating in the zone with industries ranging from food processing to semiconductors. Four additional facilities were under construction, and a total of 343 acres (139 hectares) were under lease. Development opportunities and investment incentives are available at both the Hiep Phuoc Industrial Park and Tan Thuan Export Processing Zone.

sponsoring guided tours of the port; and creating buffer areas to give visual relief and noise protection to its neighbors.

Boston: Coordinated Planning

Boston offers an example of ongoing coordinated planning between the city, state, and port authority to preserve opportunities for primary port and port-related uses, both water-dependent and non–water-dependent. The scope of coordination encompasses land use as well as economic development planning.

Boston's municipally developed waterfront land use plan, covering port and nonport uses and supplemented over a decade to include expanded geographic areas, is legally binding on the state in its granting of licenses for waterfront activities. Its seaport economic development plan, jointly developed by the city and the Massachusetts Port Authority, complements these land use planning efforts.

Municipalities must obtain state approval for their waterfront zoning plans and adapt state waterfront land use and development standards to meet their local objectives. Plan approval also serves to streamline the state process for licensing uses complying with the plan. This city-state partnership ensures consistency between state-based Designated Port Areas (DPAs) and city-based Maritime Economy Reserve and Waterfront Manufacturing Zones, which support maritime and industrial uses. Through the same state plan approval process, the city can also tailor the requirements of the state DPAs by taking advantage of provisions that allow for greater flexibility in these port areas. The city can achieve this fine-tuning by developing a master plan for specific DPAs and manufacturing zones, also subject to state approval. State approval of city waterfront plans requires evidence of consultation between port and city, ensuring that every reasonable effort is made to maximize the compatibility between their respective land use plans. The city is pursuing further coordination with the state and state port authority on issues concerning the boundaries of DPAs and changes in use plans when boundaries are altered.

Because Boston's seaport economy is composed of a range of businesses large and small that contribute significantly to the local and regional economy, a Port of Boston Economic Development Plan (also known as the Seaport Master Plan) was devel-

oped in 1996 to target opportunities for this economic sector. In addition to cargo handling and the cruise industry, the plan identified the seafood, ship repair, and marine service and support industries as those with further growth potential and recommended the expansion of space for these industries. To support cargo terminal operations, the plan recommended that the port become a full-service port. It identified substantial amounts of industrial space surrounding its main terminal facilities that could be used for transload facilities, climate-controlled warehousing, and fumigation facilities. Further recommendations included the development of on- or near-dock infrastructure improvements to support distribution centers and the creation of additional foreign-trade subzones to encompass and promote warehousing, container stripping and stuffing operations, and repackaging, assembling, and manufacturing of products. Many of these recommendations have now been implemented.

New York/New Jersey: A Feeder Port Distribution Network

At the prompting of the U.S. Environmental Protection Agency and the U.S. Army Corps of Engineers, the Port of New York and New Jersey is taking the unusual step of developing a major port improvement plan in tandem with an environment impact statement. The objective is to address the port's capacity problems in an environmentally sound manner. In the meantime, to provide more immediate relief for its chronic congestion, the port is implementing a feeder port distribution network.

As at many of the top container ports of the United States, the twin issues of port congestion and waterfront space scarcity have made terminal facilities the development priority for available land at the Port of New York and New Jersey, leaving virtually no room within the port district for the expansion of supporting uses such as warehousing or distribution/logistics centers. Currently, there are 3.4 million square feet (315,870 square meters) of warehouse space and 20 acres (8 hectares) devoted to trucking firms.

While waterfront land is available in neighboring communities, it is environmentally encumbered. Large distribution centers are being built 40 miles (64 kilometers) away where land is available, less expensive, and without the environmental constraints. Based on

Competition between maritime industrial and commercial uses is a key issue at ports.

containers to a network of feeder ports throughout the region. In addition to relieving congestion and improving throughput, the system will expand value-added logistics and warehouse opportunities at the participating ports. The PIDN would reduce the time that containers occupy valuable waterfront space, and shift short-haul trucking pressures from the port's immediate vicinity to various remote locations. If successful, it could lead to a decentralization of various port services, creating real estate opportunities in locations as far inland as Buffalo and north and south along the coast at disused port facilities in Connecticut and New Jersey.[14] Five ports have been identified as feeder candidates: Albany, New York; Bridgeport, Connecticut; Camden, New Jersey; Providence, Rhode Island; and Wilmington, Delaware. As of this writing, Albany and Bridgeport have agreed to participate in the system, with barge operations already underway in Albany.

To prepare for its participation in the PIDN, the Port of Albany has launched plans for expanding its existing warehousing, distribution, and processing operations and associated uses. It believes that the barge feeder service has the potential to benefit these operations and attract future development.

Bridgeport also sees the potential of a feeder operation to attract port-related development. A study conducted by Greater Bridgeport Regional Planning Agency to assess its feasibility as a feeder port identified a 50-acre (20.2-hectare) site within a half mile (.8 kilometers) of the waterfront that holds the potential to become a distribution or regional maritime center.

San Pedro Bay/Long Beach: A Port Facilities Master Plan

In the late 1980s, the Port of Long Beach (POLB) adopted the San Pedro Bay Ports 2020 Plan as its master plan and shortly after developed a supporting Facilities Master Plan (FMP). The FMP has recently been updated to provide for the expansion of facilities necessitated by the latest forecasts of cargo volume. The FMP update is complemented by a comprehensive odd parcels plan, which outlines additional port-related uses supportive of terminal operations, such as warehousing and distribution. These updates reaffirm that warehousing and distribution should continue to be important to the port.

recent studies showing that port-generated truck traffic represents 5 percent of regional truck traffic, the port estimates that its existing warehouse space is small in comparison to regionwide warehousing and distribution capacity serving oceangoing cargo. While comparatively limited, the warehousing located within the port area is considered to make a meaningful contribution to region's economy. Its role is seen as parallel to that of the port area as a whole, which at 2,200 acres (890 hectares) is also small relative to the total regional land area but contributes 3 percent of the gross regional product.

To address the capacity problem for both terminal facilities and other port-related and industrial uses, the port has undertaken a new Port Inland Distribution Network (PIDN) initiative that aims to barge

The port thus has given priority to terminal facilities—what it defines as "primary port uses"—in identifying land for development. Opportunities for other port-related uses include cargo storage and transfer, materials processing, rail yard uses, and similar uses interdependent with terminal facilities. Port plans support the location of port-related uses within the port area, with the proviso that they support primary port uses and are sited to minimize their impact on water-dependent uses.

Because new terminal development creates conflicts with existing port-related uses, the FMP addresses the requirements of existing port-related uses and identifies new locations for these uses on odd parcels, should new terminal development preempt their continued presence at their current locations. Currently, within the POLB's 60 acres (24.2 hectares) of land are located 34 facilities that are either port-related or ancillary uses, 27 of which are water-dependent. To provide for future port-related uses, the port is buying privately held land as sellers appear and assembling land to create parcels large enough to serve as host sites. It now owns 80 percent of a 100-acre (40.4-hectare) parcel it has targeted for port-related uses; in a reversal of its usual practice, it is soliciting large transload operators for their interest in developing facilities at this location.

Philadelphia: A Niche Port Strategy

Recognizing that it could not succeed in a head-to-head competition with the nearby Port of New York and New Jersey, the Port of Philadelphia developed a strategic plan advocating that its competitiveness lay in becoming a niche port. Succeeding remarkably in its strategy to develop a niche market, the port is now a national, if not world, leader in handling perishable cargoes.

Unlike many urban ports, Philadelphia has enjoyed ample room for expansion, but competition between maritime industrial and commercial uses is becoming a key issue. A legislatively defined port district on the waterfront, where the port holds zoning supersession powers, serves to protect that area for industrial development. The port area also lies within the jurisdiction of a foreign-trade zone, although the zone has not yet been activated.

As a leader in temperature-sensitive cargo, the Port of Philadelphia has 1.2 million square feet (111,484

square meters) of on-terminal temperature-controlled storage. Existing storage and distribution facilities of all types hold a capacity of 3.7 million square feet (343,741 square meters). Most of these facilities are on-dock, with 2.5 million square feet (232,258 square meters) dedicated to forest products, 400,000 square feet (37,161 square meters) to cocoa beans, and 800,000 square feet (74,322 square meters) at two of its major terminals, which combined handle steel, meat, fruit, heavy-lift, and project cargo, in addition to containers and automobiles.

With no developable space remaining, the port must acquire new acreage to meet future storage and distribution needs. The zoning powers it has make land acquisition an easier approach than for many other ports; waterfront land it acquires within the legislatively defined port district can only be developed for port, port-related, or industrial uses, regardless of its prior zoning. The port can also prevent changes from industrial to commercial use, though it has yet to exercise this power. Now in the process of acquiring 70 acres (28.3 hectares), the port is gaining this land in exchange for permitting the owner to sell another of its properties, an intermodal site, for commercial use.

Notes

1. Paul Chilcote, "The Containerization Story: Meeting the Competition in Trade," in *Urban Ports and Harbor Management: Responding to Change along the U.S. Waterfront.*, ed. M.J. Hershman (New York: Taylor and Francis, 1988).

2. N. Shashikumar and G.L. Schatz, "The Impact of U.S. Regulatory Changes on International Intermodal Movements," *Transportation Journal,* Fall 2000: 5–14.

3. Brian Slack, "Pawns in the Game: Ports in a Global Transportation System," *Growth and Change* 24 (1993): 379–388.

4. Some ports, such as the Port of San Francisco, have successfully converted most of their terminals to tourism and commercial uses. We do not deal with this development option in this publication.

5. "AAPA Online," American Association of Port Authorities, www.aapa-ports.org (November 1, 2002).

6. *An Assessment of the U.S. Marine Transportation System: A Report to Congress* (Washington, D.C.: Maritime Administration and Coast Guard, U.S. Department of Transportation, 1999).

7. Ibid. See also *Landside Access to U.S. Ports* (Washington, D.C.: Transportation Research Board, National Research Council, 1992).

8. *Building a 21st Century Port* (New York: Port Authority of New York and New Jersey, 2000).

9. Mercer Management Consulting, Inc., and Standard & Poor's DRI, "San Pedro Bay Ports Long-Term Forecast," report prepared for the Ports of Long Beach and Los Angeles, 1998.

10. J. Lamb, "Not Your Father's Storage Facility," *Plants, Sites, and Parks,* June/July 2001, pp. 68–72.

11. S. Graham, "Baltimore Trying to Anchor More Land to Region's Port," *Washington Business Journal,* September 14–20, 2001, p. 10.

12. See LRD International, "Port Land Use Development Zone Master Plan," prepared for Maryland Department of Transportation, 2000.

13. Bulk ports—none of which were included in this analysis—constitute another type of niche port. These ports handle petroleum, ores, coal, fertilizer, and similar commodities, and are often linked to specific mineral extraction or processing activities.

14. Similar proposals for distribution by barge along inland waterways could lend added attractiveness to distribution facilities sited at inland port locations in the Midwest.

Chapter 8

FREIGHT TRANSPORTATION CHALLENGES AND SOLUTIONS

Millions of tons of freight move through and between the world's cities every day. The process of transporting raw materials and finished goods affects us all, and the impacts to our communities will continue to grow as economies become more global and as consumer and business expectations for the delivery of goods rise. Advances in transportation and logistics have made the supply chain process faster and more efficient, but there are still many on-the-ground issues. Freight traffic adds congestion to highways and areas around ports, airports, and other transportation terminals. Smaller trucks and vans providing home deliveries add stress to local streets. And pollution resulting from the added traffic and congestion permeates neighborhoods and cities.

Many different land use issues are created by freight transportation. The lack of available land around ports and airports has pitted port authorities, local governments, shippers, and industrial real estate developers against one another. In urban fringe areas, the construction of large-scale warehouse and distribution centers on greenfield sites has created a pattern of industrial sprawl with disconnected land uses and wide distances between developed areas.

Solutions to these freight-related challenges range from simple, commonsense measures such as traffic-light synchronization on heavily traveled freight corridors to major infrastructure improvements and even land reclamation. In southern California, for example, the Alameda Rail Corridor project was implemented to ease traffic congestion and facilitate the flow of freight between the ports of Los Angeles and Long Beach and major rail yards 20 miles (32 kilometers) away. This ambitious infrastructure project includes new bridges, street improvements, and a below-grade section of rail track that separates freight trains from automobiles and trucks. Similarly, the Puget Sound Region Fast Action Strategy uses a system of rail and road improvements to facilitate the movement of goods in Washington State's Seattle/Tacoma/Everett corridor. (See the Alameda Rail Corridor and Puget Sound Region Fast Action case studies in this chapter.)

The reuse of former industrial and brownfield sites offers another solution to land availability and freight access issues. The North Jersey Transportation Planning Authority, in conjunction with the New Jersey Institute of Technology, has undertaken an innovative approach to promote freight-related redevelopment at abandoned industrial sites in and around the port of north New Jersey. (See the New Jersey Brownfield Economic Redevelopment case study in this chapter.) In cities such as Chicago, the redevelopment of old rail yards as new intermodal facilities has helped revitalize inner-city industrial areas. The conversion of decommissioned military bases into cargo airports such as Rickenbacker International Airport in Ohio is another example of brownfield reuse.

Public Sector Responsibilities

Joseph H. Boardman

The public sector created much of the American transportation network. The federal highway system, established by President Dwight D. Eisenhower in the 1950s, set the framework for the interstate highways that remain the primary routes for moving goods throughout the country. The nation's busiest ports—including the Port of New York and New Jersey, and the Ports of Los Angeles and Long Beach—airports, and rail terminals are also publicly owned and funded.

Today, despite the privatization of some port and rail facilities, the U.S. public sector remains primarily responsible for the maintenance and development of this transportation network. Public policy—in the form of federal laws, plus state and local regulations— shapes the direction that this development will take. When laws such as the massive transportation act known as TEA-21 come up for reauthorization, debates rage over funding levels and allocations. Should funds be set aside to support an inland barge system? Should gas tax monies remain in a trust fund, or should they be used to build new highways? Should trucks be required to meet more stringent emissions standards?

The stakes are high. These decisions impact the direction of the nation's entire transportation network. Yet public policy appears to lag well behind what is actually happening today. As discussed in other chapters of this book, three massive changes have permanently altered the transportation landscape: the globalization of trade, the technology revolution, and the resulting massive increases in traffic flows, particularly of truck traffic.

While trade agreements have spurred an increased flow of goods across borders, the associated transportation infrastructure in most countries has not expanded to meet the need. Consider that in 1984, when New York State officials conducted a roadway congestion study, some few areas in and around Manhattan and Long Island, near the Port of New York, showed evidence of moderate congestion. By the year 2021, if no new highways are built, much of the New York City metropolitan area will suffer from severe congestion on a routine basis, while moderate and severe congestion will extend north, well into upstate New York.

In fact, the situation in the northeastern United States is indicative of the types of challenges that developed nations' roads, rail, and ports will continue to face. The Northeast states, Quebec, and the Maritime Provinces of Canada in aggregate constitute the third largest economy in the world (behind Japan and the United States). One-quarter of the goods used in this area come from other parts of the world, and approximately one-quarter of the goods produced in this bloc are sent to other parts of the world. Half of all this trade—an estimated $920 billion in 2002—is thus interregional. Since the passage of the North American Free Trade Act (NAFTA), truck traffic into Canada and back across western and northern New York bridges, such as the Lewiston-Queenston Bridge and the Thousand Island Bridge, has grown by as much as 40 percent in the past five years. The increases in Hudson River truck crossings—at bridges such as the George Washington and the Tappan Zee and at tunnels such as the Holland and Lincoln—have congested roads to the point that New York City metro traffic is now notorious.

Such growth is only going to continue, probably at an even more rapid pace. The Federal Highway Administration predicts a 70 percent increase in the amount of freight being moved across the country by the year 2020. With an estimated 70 percent of the population living to the east of the Mississippi, much of this traffic will flow eastward, exacerbating the congestion in the Northeast.

The Northeast is experiencing an upturn in shipping traffic from Asia as well. While many ships opt to dock at West Coast ports and send goods by rail or truck across the country, ships with goods bound for the northeastern United States are increasingly coming through the Suez Canal across the Atlantic to dock on the East Coast. With close to 90 percent of this cargo offloaded onto trucks, the reason for the clogged roads becomes clear.

While some of these congestion problems are unique to the Northeast, other parts of the country, particularly around those large urban centers such as Los Angeles and Chicago with major ports and rail terminals, face similar situations. Certain corridors—Interstate 95 in the East, Interstate 5 in the West, and Interstate 10 in the Southeast—face daily challenges brought on by too many vehicles on highways that cannot accommodate them.

Increasing the density of development provides another method for dealing with high prices and limited land availability in strategic freight distribution locations. As described in "Global Variations in Distribution Facility Design: The Toys"R"Us Example" in chapter 4, some of the more densely developed and expensive real estate markets in Europe and Asia are already experiencing the construction of land-efficient "vertical" distribution facilities. A new multistory high-throughput distribution building developed by AMB Property Corporation and Boustead Projects Pte., Ltd., in Singapore illustrates this phenomenon (see chapter 4).

An integrated approach to planning large-scale distribution facilities is also crucial. In Europe, the

If these issues are not addressed in a forward-looking manner, the situation will only deteriorate, eroding the ability of many businesses to remain competitive in their current locations. According to the Port Authority of New York and New Jersey, road congestion near the Port of New York costs the regional economy $10 billion per year in 2001. Residents of local communities, too, will become exasperated as their quality of life suffers. There is no choice but to change the way our nation thinks about, operates, and manages its freight transportation system.

In the past, the public response to overcrowded transportation facilities was to build. But today nations are running out of land opportunities, and the patience of communities is running out as well, particularly when the available land is not being used efficiently. In the United States, local and federal transportation officials are beginning to talk about developing an overarching transportation management system that would address both current and future bottlenecks, with an understanding that the nature of freight transport has changed permanently. Logistics today more often than not involves transporting goods via a combination of modes, and a comprehensive system designed to enhance the smooth flow of goods should reflect this reality.

One aspect of meeting the challenge involves operating the entire national transportation network more reliably. This is difficult because local authorities understandably see the issues through the local lens, while federal authorities may not fully comprehend the impact on a community. For example, in Rochester, New York, the inability to efficiently operate trains through Chicago means that more trucks will be on the roads in upstate New York.

Specific operational changes can help ensure the viability of a region's transportation system as well. Current efforts in New York State target three traditional bottlenecks: payment of tolls, permitting, and traffic tie-ups owing to accidents or other incidents. The state—as well as other areas such as the Washington, D.C., metropolitan region—is working to implement a single payment system: a regionwide "smart card" type of payment that would allow a faster flow of traffic through tollways, regardless of transportation mode. The second project would institute a one-stop permitting process, so that a trucker bringing goods from Canada would be able to complete all the administrative paperwork at one time, creating a more seamless process. The third goal is to make use of technology to disseminate real-time information about traffic accidents or closures, so that truckers and rail operators can redirect their freight and avoid jams.

An efficient freight transportation network is also inextricably linked to intelligent long-range land use planning. Certainly, this process will differ in each community, reflecting the particular features of the local economy. But since all communities are tied to the global economy in some way, they must work together to understand how the parts of the puzzle fit together.

In the United States, those involved with the public sector aspects of transportation are beginning to consider establishing a broad-based national strategy that will take into account the realities of the transportation environment today and into the future. The strategy would be based on a comprehensive study that will provide a full review of the changes that have transpired since the last U.S. transportation study was conducted 30 years ago, so that future economic growth will not be impeded by a transportation infrastructure that cannot support it. The strategy would also take into account the importance of high-quality communities as a part of long-range economic development planning. In order for stakeholders to produce high-quality communities, we must use all of our transportation assets to deliver results that the public can understand and hold us accountable for: improved mobility and reliability, improved safety and environmental conditions, added economic stability, and enhanced travel security.

A partnership that includes all stakeholders, including local and nationwide authorities as well as transportation, real estate, and industry experts, will ensure that freight distribution and supply chain systems receive the attention they deserve while peacefully coexisting with local communities and contributing to a positive quality of life.

This text is an edited version of remarks made by Joseph H. Boardman, Commissioner, New York State Department of Transportation. The comments are his own and not those of the Department of Transportation or any other organization or entity.

construction of the rail tunnel between Britain and France created the need for large-scale distribution facilities with rail connections. The Daventry International Rail Freight Terminal (DIRFT) in Birmingham, England, is a major rail-served intermodal facility that was planned with regional considerations for freight traffic and environmental impacts. (See the Daventry International Rail Freight Terminal case study in this chapter.)

Some large-scale developments combine transportation, distribution, commercial, recreational, and residential uses in one location. The CenterPoint Intermodal Center in Joliet, Illinois, integrates direct rail, truck, transload, and intermodal services with distribution and warehousing in a single location. It also serves as a model for the reuse of a brownfield site (see chapter 6). Another example is Alliance, Texas, an international trade and logistics center that includes an industrial airport as well as office, retail, residential, and recreational uses (see chapter 5).

THE ALAMEDA RAIL CORRIDOR

Background

The ports of Los Angeles and Long Beach, collectively known as the San Pedro Bay ports, are the two busiest container ports in the United States and, together, the third busiest port complex in the world after Hong Kong and Singapore. Clearly, the San Pedro Bay ports are vital to the Los Angeles region but also to the nation as well; however, their long-term vitality and competitiveness depend on maintaining an efficient transportation system.

Los Angeles's development was spurred by the growth of its ports, but in recent decades the city's growth has stifled port operations. Urban development between the ports and inland rail yards created slowdowns and inefficiencies in transporting goods; freight bound for or leaving the port of Los Angeles was forced to weave its way slowly through 20 miles (32 kilometers) of heavily populated municipalities in Los Angeles County. The route through these areas—known as the Alameda Corridor—not only backed up freight but also continually stopped local traffic at more than 200 street/rail crossings and added to Los Angeles's already woeful air pollution problems.

In 1981, a Port Advisory Committee (PAC) was created by the Southern California Association of Governments (SCAG) in response to growing concerns about the ground transportation system's ability to accommodate increasing levels of traffic. The first phase of the PAC's study, completed in 1982, dealt with the problems of highway access around ports. The second phase, a study of rail access and the impact on local communities north of the ports, was completed in 1984. It recommended the consolidation of train routes along an upgraded Southern Pacific San Pedro branch right-of-way. To pursue this objective, the Alameda Corridor Task Force (ACTF) was created by the SCAG. The ACTF concluded that a joint powers authority should be created to exercise design and construction responsibility for the Alameda Corridor, and the Alameda Corridor Transportation Authority (ACTA) was created in 1989.

The ACTA provides the overall management of the corridor improvement project. Its seven-member governing board includes two representatives each from the ports of Long Beach and Los Angeles, one representative each from the cities of Los Angeles and Long Beach, and one representative from the Los Angeles County Metropolitan Transportation Authority (LACMTA). ACTA also provides outreach and coordinates with the various stakeholders involved with the project, including numerous funding and governmental agencies such as the California Department of Transportation, railroad companies, the eight municipalities that the corridor transects or borders, and multiple community groups.

Project Description

The completed Alameda Rail Corridor is a 20-mile (32-kilometer) rail cargo expressway linking the ports of Long Beach and Los Angeles to the transcontinental rail yards near downtown Los Angeles. Its series of bridges, underpasses, overpasses, and street improvements separates freight trains from street traffic and passenger trains, facilitating a more efficient transportation network.

Prior to the construction of the corridor, trains made 20 to 35 daily trips on the branch lines serving the ports, with trains averaging ten to 20 miles per hour (16 to 32 kilometers per hour). The corridor is designed to accommodate the 100 daily trips to and from the ports projected for 2020, with trains averaging 30 to 40 miles per hour (48 to 64 kilometers per hour).

Construction began in 1997 and was completed in 2002. Running parallel to Alameda Street along much of its route, the project was divided into three primary construction zones: south, mid-corridor, and north.

The south section stretches about seven miles (11 kilometers) from the end of the ports' rail lines north to California Route 91 in Compton. The key projects in this area included construction of new bridges that allow trains to travel at greater speeds over waterways; street improvements; and building street bridges over existing rail lines.

The corridor's impressive middle section is a ten-mile (16-kilometer) -long, 33-foot (10-meter) -deep trench north of Route 91, where trains are separated from automobile traffic and able to travel at accelerated speeds. It includes 30 bridges. Improvements included 150 million pounds (68 million kilograms) of rebar; 1 million cubic yards (763,358 cubic meters) of concrete; the relocation of 1,700 lines for sewers, gas, electricity, and fiber-optic service; and the treatment and removal of several million gallons of sludge tainted with heavy metals and other pollutants.

The north section connects the mid-corridor trench with the rail yards just east of downtown Los Angeles. Its key project component was the Los Angeles River Bridge: the existing single-track bridge was replaced with a modern, 300-foot (91-meter), three-track bridge. Another key project involved separating passenger rail from freight rail by elevating the corridor's Amtrak and commuter rail lines.

Financing

An innovative financing plan was used for the $2.4 million project. Using its broad powers, the ACTA was able to sell $1.165 billion in revenue bonds, which were backed by the Burlington Northern and Santa Fe Railway and the Union Pacific Railroad. The bonds will be paid off by the railroads and shipping companies that use the corridor through a $15 fee for every loaded container that uses the corridor and lesser fees for other types of rail cars and empty containers. (Bonds often fund public construction projects, but they have rarely if ever been used to fund railroad construction.) Other funding included a $400 million loan from the U.S. Department of Transportation, which will also be paid off through user fees; $394 million in grants from the ports of Los Angeles and Long Beach; $347 million administered by LACMTA; and $154 million from other state and federal sources and interest income. The end result of this diversified funding is that the project did not have to rely heavily on funding from a single federal, state, or local source. All the stakeholders were willing to pay something to gain the advantages of the dedicated rail corridor.

Economic Impacts

The economic significance of the Alameda Rail Corridor is huge, not only regionally but nationally. It has

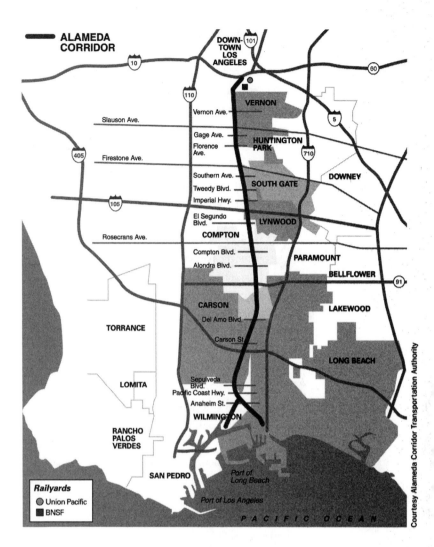

solidified the San Pedro Bay ports as the primary conduits for Pacific Rim trade. The ports now have both the terminal capacity and the efficient transportation access to keep pace with projected trade increases.

Over one-third of shipping containers entering or leaving the United States pass through the San Pedro Bay ports. These containers are not being shipped to only the West Coast—an estimated 60 percent of all imports bound for the Chicago area enter through the San Pedro Bay ports. Of the $97.3 billion a year in trade generated by the ports, about $14.9 billion comes from or goes to the Atlantic Coast states. ACTA estimates that 2.5 million jobs nationwide are linked to trade that enters or leaves through the San Pedro Bay ports.

The local benefits of the rail corridor are clear. The Los Angeles County Economic Development Corporation estimates that one in 15 jobs in southern California is directly linked to the international trade passing through the ports. The corridor will ensure that these hundreds of thousands of jobs will stay in the region and the billions in state and local taxes generated from the ports will continue to flow. ACTA estimates that 700,000 local jobs will be added, as well as $5.2 billion in state and local taxes annually, by the year 2020. The corridor will open up new business opportunities for the region and better opportunities for economic development in the communities lying along its route.

Port activities consume considerable space, but the provision of a more efficient transportation network to move goods in and out provides some opportunities for potential real estate development near the ports, particularly development associated with distribution facilities. At the same time, secondary distribution centers at inland locations such as San Bernardino and Ontario are now more attractive for development.

Community Impacts

The Alameda Rail Corridor will bring about positive environmental change thanks to a significant reduction of noxious emissions from idling vehicles. Prior to its construction, 15,000 hours of vehicle delay were logged per day along the old rail lines. Assisted by state-of-the art technology, the new double-track corridor reduces the number of times trains have to stop and wait for other trains to pass. This factor is estimated to reduce railroad emissions by 28 percent and train operations by 30 percent. The placement of new base material under the tracks in the trench, and the use of continuous welded track, will promote quieter operations. Noise walls have been constructed where the corridor cuts through residential neighborhoods and other sensitive areas.

ACTA has worked closely with the eight municipalities the corridor transects to ensure that community concerns are dealt with effectively. These communities are benefiting from less congestion and better emergency-vehicle response times. They also have enjoyed numerous street and aesthetic improvements that have made the area more attractive for investment.

ACTA manages three community programs aimed directly to provide benefits to area residents. The Alameda Corridor Business Outreach Program is designed to improve the ability of disadvantaged business enterprises to compete for contract work related to the corridor. The Alameda Corridor Job Training and Development Program, established as part of the Mid-

Corridor Trench contract, required that the contractor provide job training and placement services to 1,000 residents of communities along the project route. Finally, the Alameda Corridor Transportation Authority Conservation Corps recruits and trains young adults for conservation work along the corridor; this work earns them high school credits.

Source: James C. Hankla, chief executive officer, Alameda Corridor Transportation Authority, Carson, California.

THE PUGET SOUND REGION FREIGHT ACTION STRATEGY (FAST)

Background

Seattle, Tacoma, and Everett, Washington, make up the third largest marine container terminal complex in North America. The central Puget Sound region's tremendous port capacity and role as a shipping center linking Asia to the United States offer both opportunities and challenges.

In response to legislation such as the Intermodal Surface Transportation Efficiency Act (1991) and its successor, the Transportation Equity Act (TEA-21), public and private leaders formed a roundtable in 1994 to address the growing amount of freight transported within and through the Puget Sound region. The most prominent early action package to emerge was the Freight Action Strategy Corridor (FAST Corridor) Phase I, a plan for rail grade separations and port access projects to serve the ports and other important freight distribution centers along major rail and truck corridors.

The FAST Corridor's partners are concerned first and foremost with the big picture: Seattle's pivotal position in the large top-down logistic chain that stretches from the Pacific Rim to Chicago. Acutely aware of the likely doubling of West Coast container trade by 2020 and the stiff competition from nearby Vancouver, central Puget Sound region partners want to ensure that they do not miss out on what is sure to be an increasingly important role in international trade. It is estimated that by the year 2015, Asian countries will constitute 45 percent of the world population. This population growth, combined with growing economies and the consequent increase in wealth and standard of living, means that an increasing volume of goods will flow to the region from the United States and vice versa. Seattle occupies an ideal position to capture a substantial portion of this market because it is a full sailing day closer to Asia than the other large West Coast ports. Despite this advantage, however, its market share has been in steady decline since 1990, largely because competing ports in California serve much larger local market areas and have mounted aggressive campaigns to improve access, economies of scale, and mobility in their ports.

The FAST Corridor's response has been to take a bottom-up approach to solving the Puget Sound region's congestion problems. While railroads, transit agencies, and ports have made commitments to improving capacity, extending rail lines, and improving truck mobility on local and state roads, FAST is concentrating on the connecting points between these modes of transportation, where it is unclear whose responsibility it is for improving the transportation gap. The long-term FAST Corridor plan includes action steps for highways, rail, port, air, and rail grade separations.

Project Description

The biggest challenge facing the group was filling in the gaps in the system that were not the responsibility of any one party or agency. To accomplish this, the Puget Sound Regional Council, an organization composed of a broad base of public and private entities, and the Washington State Department of Transportation collaborated with affected cities, counties, ports, and trucking and rail carriers to pinpoint freight access improvements in the Everett-Seattle-Tacoma metropolitan area. The cost-sharing partnership relies on shared funding and linked actions at all levels. The Regional Council also partnered with the Economic Development Council of Seattle and King County to sponsor the public-private Regional Freight Mobility Roundtable. The roundtable serves as a communication hub, helping to create an environment within which the freight story can be told and translated into further partnerships for action.

Phase I

FAST Corridor Phase I's primary purpose has been to advance a system of railway/rail projects related to on-dock intermodal (marine-rail) facilities at the ports

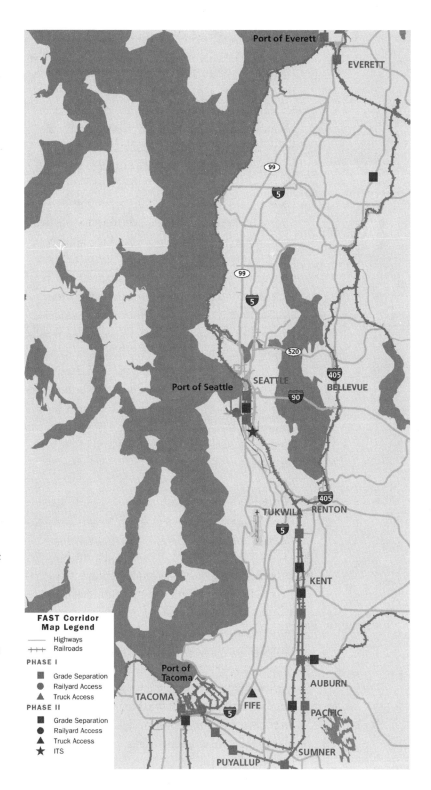

and to the rail movement of double-stack container trains through the densely developed region. The focus is on the points where goods are transferred between transportation modes and where bottlenecks can occur in the land-side freight system.

The 15 projects identified by FAST partners as the highest priority received a $470 million physical upgrade package. Funding is particular to each product, even though they are mutually supportive and share some common funding sources split among the lead agency, federal, TEA-21 earmarked funds, state, ports, railroads, and a mix of other sources. As of January 2003, ten of the 15 Phase I projects were complete or nearly complete, and the rest were scheduled for implementation in 2003–2006. An additional ten projects—FAST Phase II—were identified and prioritized in May 2002 for construction over the next three to five years, depending upon funding.

Several Phase I projects have entailed construction of grade separations at railroad crossings, building either overpasses or underpasses so that the road and rail tracks are at separate grades, reducing traffic bottlenecks and facilitating the movement of freight by road and rail. The second type of projects in Phase I were port access upgrades. As with railroad crossings, no single entity is entirely responsible for facilitating travel between port facilities and the land transportation systems for trucks and railroads. For better railyard access, the Phase I projects have improved grade separations to allow more space for trains to be assembled and held until they are ready to be pulled onto the mainline tracks.

Phase II

Phase II encompasses additional rail grade separations, two road projects, and two intelligent transportation system (ITS) projects. It will include nonstructural reforms that can be implemented to improve transportation efficiency—in particular, freight truck mobility. The FAST corridor partners have explored less costly management measures that could be taken, aside from physical upgrades, to improve freight movement. Anticipated nonstructural changes include streetlight synchronization in a large industrial area to improve truck movement along busy urban streets. Port managers have also discussed the merits and difficulties of twenty-four-hour labor rotations in order for goods to be moved at times of less congestion; shared use of private and public facilities as truck mobility staging areas; exclusive truck lanes and truck climbing lanes at selected locations; and wider implementation of 7-day/24-hour trucking operations schedules.

Project Benefits

The FAST Corridor offers a model for regional transportation planning and implementation. Its successful

roundtable has brought together disjointed investments and operations involving overlapping systems with different time horizons and boundaries, convincing participants of the importance of aligning and partnering on decentralized actions for the system as a whole. The key to facilitating this process was to create an atmosphere of cooperation based on regular discussions among willing parties representative of the disparate groups.

Regional freight partnerships in the United States have been spurred by federal initiatives, but federally created regional organizations are only a beginning. These regional organizations must connect with states, private agencies, transportation industry, cities, and others in order to create successful freight mobility strategies.

Implications for the Puget Sound Regional Economy

Nearly one in four jobs in the Seattle–Tacoma region is related to international trade. Direct export sales in 1995 were estimated at $24.8 billion, which was double the amount in 1987. The central Puget Sound region, by virtue of its being an important freight center, also benefits in ways that cannot be measured. Freight passing through the region is generally high-value goods from Asia and elsewhere, on the way to other continental U.S. destinations and to Europe. For return trips, rather than arriving empty, carriers prefer to carry Washington State exports back even if they are lower-value goods. This factor allows Washington businesses lower-cost access to markets than would otherwise be the case.

The FAST Corridor will increase these benefits by making it easier for the freight industry to move goods around the region. By improving regional freight mobility, the FAST Corridor will help the region maintain and possibly improve upon its status as an international gateway, and will enable it to attract corporations in need of better facilities and more efficient transportation routes. It also provides a solid foundation of public/private partnerships to build upon when meeting new challenges.

Sources: Peter Beaulieu, Puget Sound Regional Council; and Michael Cummings, Washington State Department of Transportation. Web site: www.wsdot.wa.gov/mobility/fast.

NEW JERSEY BROWNFIELD ECONOMIC REDEVELOPMENT

Background

The North Jersey Transportation Planning Authority (NJTPA) and the New Jersey Institute of Technology (NJIT) have undertaken an innovative approach to exploit opportunities for freight-related redevelopment of abandoned industrial brownfield sites in and around the port of northern New Jersey.

Northern New Jersey has the largest port on the Atlantic Coast and is located in one of the world's largest consumer markets. Excellent highway and rail connections to inland markets serve the port district, which also boasts a major air cargo facility at New Liberty International Airport. The public and private sectors in northern New Jersey are currently investing billions of dollars in dredging marine channels, upgrading terminal facilities, rehabilitating roads and rail links, and undertaking a variety of other freight-related projects.

It is estimated that containers moving through the region's marine port will double by 2010 and increase six-fold by 2040. By 2010, Newark International Airport will become the Northeast's largest cargo center, and railborne freight will increase steadily. The result is likely to be a large increase in the number of ships, airplanes, trucks, and trains moving many millions of tons of freight to, from, and through the northern New Jersey region.

The increase in freight activity will have a positive impact on economic development, leading to thousands of new jobs, not only in freight businesses themselves, but in spin-off businesses engaged in warehousing, packaging, assembly, and other support services. But there are also potential threats. Over the past two decades, much of the goods distribution for the region has been accomplished through using large warehouses of 250,000 to more than a million square feet (23,225 to 92,900 square meters) established on greenfield sites at the fringes of the metropolitan area, where land costs are lowest. This trend threatens to compound roadway congestion, consume precious open space, worsen the region's air quality, and disrupt life in the region's communities. Ultimately, these problems could imperil future economic growth.

Project Description

To tap the hidden assets of the region and to counter the potentially negative aspects of increased freight growth, the NJTPA and NJIT have undertaken a broad-based, coordinated planning effort to encourage freight businesses to locate in the region's brownfield sites near the port and airport. The NJTPA is the metropolitan planning organization (MPO) for 13 northern New Jersey counties. Under federal legislation, an MPO provides a forum through which local officials, public transportation providers, and state agency representatives can cooperatively plan to meet a region's current and future transportation needs. It establishes the region's eligibility to receive federal tax dollars for transportation projects.

Developing northern New Jersey's transportation assets requires government at all levels to join with the private sector in implementing a plan to create large-scale distribution centers and industrial parks served by upgraded transportation infrastructure in the port district. One element of the plan, for instance, will involve the development of warehouses and distribution centers on hundreds of acres of brownfields immediately north of the port. Freight containers too heavy for regional highways could move quickly and efficiently to these sites via the semidedicated truck route called the Portway, initial elements of which are already being assembled. Major freight service companies have shown a willingness to invest private capital in and around the port to create advanced freight distribution facilities.

The three-year project was funded under the federal Transportation and Community and System Preservation (TCSP) pilot program, administered by the Federal Highway Administration, U.S. Department of Transportation. A steering committee composed of representatives from the New Jersey Department of Environmental Protection, the New Jersey Department of Transportation, the New Jersey Office of State Planning, the Port Authority of New York and New Jersey, and the New Jersey Commerce and Economic Growth Commission provided guidance on project activities.

Phase I of the project took place in 2001 and included a market analysis that confirmed the opportunities for reclaiming brownfield sites through freight-related redevelopment. It also included an environmental scan that identified a large number of brownfield sites close to the port. The Phase I final report identified the need for a comprehensive plan to redevelop brownfields in the port district and for implementing the Portway project to speed the movement of goods between the port, airport, rail terminals, and regional highway.

The focus of the Phase II effort in 2001 was a detailed investigation of several case study sites. This process included obtaining estimates of remediation costs, conducting community outreach, developing an analysis of transportation issues relating to improved freight and workforce access to the sites, evaluating potential redevelopment at each site, and suggesting appropriate marketing strategies.

In January 2002, NJTPA and NJIT presented the findings of their Brownfield Economic Redevelopment (BRER) study. The report focused on the issues and policy options involved in accomplishing this redevelopment and considered several case studies of brownfield sites in the port district. It concluded that tremendous potential value exists in the thousands of acres of brownfields adjacent to the port, airport, and rail terminals. These sites can be used for warehouses and distribution centers that will employ hundreds of workers in final assembly, packaging, order fulfillment, and other tasks. These services are required as part of international shippers' logistics pipeline, and their availability strongly influences shippers' port preferences.

Key recommendations of the study included:

- using regulations or fees to reduce or eliminate container storage on sites that can be redeveloped;
- creating a new body or designation of an existing agency responsible for comprehensive planning in the port district; and
- supplementing public funding for freight infrastructure with a modest fee on container movements or other port activities.

Brownfield Case Studies

The BRER study identified at least 2,500 acres (1,011 hectares) of brownfield sites suitable for freight-related redevelopment within ten miles (16 kilometers) of the port. Thousands of additional acres are estimated to be available in the larger port district, stretching out 25 miles (40 kilometers). These sites are generally removed from residential areas, have access to highways, and range from 12 to 100 or more acres (5 to 40 hectares), with opportunities to assemble neighboring small sites into larger parcels.

While redevelopment of such sites often poses environmental hurdles and other challenges, the improving prospects for brownfield redevelopment in northern New Jersey have prompted a number of successful reclamation projects, with more on the drawing boards. Yet these projects account for only a small portion of the brownfield acreage in and around the port district. To explore the opportunities and constraints involved in redeveloping brownfields for freight purposes, case studies of five representative sites in the port district were undertaken.

An overall finding of the case studies was that a complex interplay among factors particular to each site—including the extent of environmental contamination, access to the highway network, the availability of rail service, surrounding land uses, and concerns of local officials and residents—determines its viability for value-added warehouse and distribution use. The case studies also suggested that the policies and procedures of state and local governments often create additional barriers for property owners and developers. Effectively addressing these barriers at the state level would require the establishment of a center to offer multidisciplinary brownfield technical assistance to aid property owners, developers, and municipalities in realizing freight-related redevelopment. The BRER study also suggested that the state must improve financial and other incentives to make brownfields more competitive with greenfields in attracting freight-related development.

Since the completion of the case studies in mid-2002, several initiatives by the New Jersey governor's office have addressed some of these issues. A new office of Brownfield Reuse was created, aiming to facilitate expanded use of financial and market incentives for redevelopment, a certification program for consultants, and zero tolerance for "mothballing" abandoned sites.

Project Benefits

For northern New Jersey, the successful reclamation of brownfields by freight businesses would not only make most efficient use of its land and transportation resources, but it would help reverse the loss of jobs and economic activity in the region's blighted urban areas. Freight-related businesses are a potentially good fit for the region's brownfields. A large number of brownfields lie within several miles of the Newark/

Elizabeth transportation hub that includes the marine port, airport, and major rail terminals. Even brownfields located at greater distances from this hub tend to have good highway or rail connections—though these often would need to be rehabilitated and upgraded.

Attracting freight businesses to brownfield sites would help reduce the need for long-distance trucking of goods, increase rail use, and create new unskilled and semiskilled jobs in proximity to urban populations with significant unemployment. It would also provide new warehouse and distribution center development opportunities.

Sources: John Hummer, principal investigator, North Jersey Transportation Planning Authority, Inc., and "Final Report, Brownfield Economic Redevelopment: Preparing Modern Intermodal Freight Infrastructure to Support Brownfield Economic Redevelopment" (Newark: North Jersey Transportation Planning Authority, Inc., and the New Jersey Institute of Technology, January 2003). Available at www.njtpa.org.

DAVENTRY INTERNATIONAL RAIL FREIGHT TERMINAL

The second half of the twentieth century saw a dramatic decline in the volume and market share of freight transported by rail in the U.K. In the early 1950s, rail had a 42 percent market share. By 1994, when the privatization process for Britain's railways began, its share had fallen to 6 percent.

Despite significant investment, British Railway's freight business was increasingly unable to compete with the trucking industry. As a result of policies advocated in *The Reshaping of British Railways* (published by the British Railways Board in 1963), which sought to cut back rail infrastructure toward a profitable core, much of the wagonload business was abandoned, with wholesale closures of freight yards and private sidings. The overall rail network was cut by about a third, and many branch lines and some duplicate trunk routes were closed. Some of the reasons why rail freight has failed to compete with trucking are fairly common, but one factor is relatively unique to Britain: it is an island, and the longest distance between major population centers is from London to Glasgow, which is about 400 miles (644 kilometers).

British rail freight thus contracted considerably toward its "natural" core of heavy goods such as coal, minerals, steel, and oil products, although considerable investment continued to be made in locomotives, wagons, and infrastructure for this business. British Rail also introduced its "Freightliner" service to move trains of containers between road-rail intermodal terminals.

An important outcome of the decline of rail freight was that British town-planning policy makers came to assume that, except for specific activities such as mineral extraction, new industrial and distribution facilities required road access only. Planning authorities zoned land for these facilities adjacent to highway junctions with no rail connections and no potential for them. Two of the most striking examples were in the planned new towns of Milton Keynes and Warrington, both designated in the 1960s, which subsequently developed major distribution clusters but with no access from the West Coast Main Line, the primary London-to-Glasgow rail freight and passenger route running through both towns.

As a result of the construction of a rail tunnel link between Britain and France (the Channel Tunnel), the need was recognized for a new generation of strategic, rail-served intermodal freight terminals and distribution hubs. The typical site requirements were large land areas at points where the railway network conjoined with the road network, near major urban centers. British Rail took the lead in proposing such projects, but private developers and local authorities were involved as well.

This is the context within which the Daventry International Rail Freight Terminal (DIRFT) project was conceived; it received planning permission from the local authority in 1994 and opened in 1997. The site lies adjacent to the West Coast Main Line and the M1 highway near its junction with the M6 highway, some 80 miles (129 kilometers) northwest of London in an area known in the distribution industry as the "golden triangle." This location between London and Birmingham, next to these major roads, is highly accessible to a huge market. In addition to its modern rail and road attributes, it is bisected by the line of Watling Street (a Roman road), and the Grand Union Canal, built in the eighteenth century but now just a leisure facility, runs nearby.

DIRFT is located on what was open countryside, just beyond the southeastern boundary of the greater

Birmingham metropolitan area, but fortunately not within a statutory greenbelt, as some of its more controversial contemporaries were. In a greenbelt there is a presumption against development such as warehousing, so such a proposal would only be permitted if it could be shown to offer major strategic benefits.

The developers wished to build just over 4 million square feet (370,000 square meters) of warehousing in association with, but quite separate from, an intermodal terminal, the capital costs of which would be subsumed within the overall project. They lobbied vigorously to promote the project's environmental benefits, arising from the potential to shift freight traffic from road to rail. They also highlighted the high aesthetic quality of the overall development's design.

Community leaders' recognition of the site's strategic potential for distribution could be traced back through supportive regional planning guidance and a 1993 amendment to the statutory local plan permitting the area to incorporate a terminal and freight village. This preparation meant that when the DIRFT planning application was submitted, it enjoyed a relatively smooth ride: local council members were supportive of the economic benefits and overruled objectors. Following the granting of planning permission, the developers and the local planning authority jointly produced a design guide in 1996 to ensure that implementation would be coordinated and of high quality.

The rail freight terminal comprises a 30-acre (12-hectare) complex with five reception sidings, each of which is long enough to accommodate an international train (2,460 feet or 750 meters); the latter are operated by Britain's largest rail freight company, English Welsh and Scottish Railway. Tibbett and Britten, which became the terminal operator, wished to develop rail freight beyond the intermodal terminal, and the first of two rail-served warehouses was thus completed in 1999, with the second opening in summer 2003. A third warehouse managed by another operator opened between these dates. All three warehouses are served by a rail spur off the terminal complex.

The overall DIRFT project as originally envisioned will be built out by 2006. In late 2002, the developers submitted a preliminary planning application to the local council for a rail-served extension of 1.9 million square feet (180,741 square meters) of warehouse space on land to the west. In line with recent trends in Britain, these are projected to be high-bay structures up to 115 feet (35 meters) in height. The application proposed eight warehouses, with six of them having direct rail access provided by another spur off the existing rail terminal complex.

Following the completion in 1997 of railway privatization, rail freight's market share has increased. However, owing to serious problems with the network's management and reliability, including a series of controversial crashes, rail has had difficulty in moving beyond its traditional markets in bulk goods. In particular, the amount of rail freight using the Channel Tunnel has been well below expectations, owing largely to high costs and poor reliability. The business nearly collapsed totally as a result of the asylum seeker crisis in 2001–2002, which led to a significant loss of business by the DIRFT rail terminal; before the crisis, it had been operating 800 lifts of containers or other freight units a week.

Moving into new markets partly requires on developing more rail-served distribution hubs on the DIRFT model, particularly around London itself, where there are none at present. But finding suitable sites around London is extremely difficult; where there is an existing rail freight terminal, as at Willesden in north London, there is usually insufficient space for warehousing. Facilities abandoned during the years of retrenchment have generally been redeveloped for other purposes, owing to the huge demand for land. Typically, promising locations can only be found outside the existing urban area, and these may well be subject to greenbelt or other planning restrictions.

A recent abortive proposal highlights the difficulties. A London International Freight Exchange was proposed by Argent developers for greenbelt land near Heathrow Airport. It was rejected by the local planning authority, Slough District Council, in 1999. Argent took the case to appeal, but after the expense of several million pounds and a delay of several years, the appeal was rejected by the secretary of state for the environment in mid-2002.

Notwithstanding all the problems facing rail freight in Britain, and particularly in securing permission for the development of distribution facilities large enough to generate sufficient volume for rail, there are grounds for optimism. Owing to globalization and the increasing integration of European economies, importation of goods through the Channel Tunnel and the container ports are likely to increase. Developers are increasingly interested in building large warehouses in excess of 400,000 square feet (37,160 square meters), and some are so convinced of the long-term benefits of rail access that they are prepared to take the time to prepare their proposals on the DIRFT model before submitting planning applications. The opportunities are there to be grasped, and DIRFT has played a significant role in demonstrating how such projects should be handled.

Source: Russ Hayward, Faculty of Development and Society, Sheffield Hallam University.